JOSÉ ANTONIO PÁEZ

GENERAL JOSÉ ANTONIO PÁEZ
Gloria de Acarigua, Jefe incomparable de los inclitos Llaneros de
Venezuela a quienes llevó siempre a la victoria en todas sus batallas.
The Glory of Acarigua, incomparable Chief of the famous Llaneros
of Venezuela, whom he led to victory in all his battles.

JOSÉ ANTONIO PÁEZ

BY

R. B. CUNNINGHAME GRAHAM

" De los generales, cual es el valiente?
Mi General Páez con toda su gente."
—*Llanero Soldier's Song.*

LONDON
WILLIAM HEINEMANN LTD

First published 1929

Printed in Great Britain at
The Windmill Press, Kingswood, Surrey

TO

JUAN EATON KENT

OF

SAN FERNANDO DE APURE

ILLUSTRATIONS

PREFACE

A HUNDRED years ago, the name of Páez was a household word in Europe. Kings sent him swords of honour, queens corresponded with him upon equal terms. Later in life he sat beside the Empress Eugenie at a banquet at the Tuileries.

To-day who knows his name in Europe except a few mole-eyed historians or biographers, who inhale into their lungs the dust of libraries and whose brains are sicklied over with the shadows of the past? A dreadful occupation that of the historian or biographer, more dreadful than the samphire gatherer's trade, for if he miss his footing on a cliff, he does not live to see his fall!

Still, the historian (or biographer)—the two are as near akin as is the poacher to the tramp—persists, just as men go to the north pole, and ladies swim the channel.

Certainly his reward is scant, for he does not obtain even that notoriety that golfers or pugilists enjoy, in their own right, as heiresses succeed to peerages.

Páez without a doubt, of all the heroes of the epic struggle for independence against Spain, was the most sympathetic character. Bolivar, the greatest man the Americas have yet produced, was superior to him in genius. San Martin, the hero of the amazing march with his Gaucho cavalry across the Andes, was a better and a more experienced soldier, but Páez had what is called in Spanish " el don de gentes," that is a personal magnetism, that none of them possessed.

Born in a little straw-thatched house, on a lost little river of the Llanos, educated at a hedge school by an old woman almost as illiterate as her pupils, he rose to

be the first man in the land. Twice president, in both
his terms of office, he showed a liberality of ideas surprising in a man who had passed his life on horseback
with lance and lazo always in his hand.

He was the first to advocate the freedom of the negro
race in the Americas, urged to it as he says in his
Memoirs, not by any theories of the rights of man,
for at the time he first advocated emancipation he had
never heard of them, but by his native breadth of mind
and generosity. He had himself passed several years in
a state nearly approaching slavery, apprenticed to a
brutal negro, one Manuelote, who, after a long day of
hard work on the plains, mounted on a half wild horse,
forced him to wash his feet. This, however, could have
weighed with him but little, for generous natures are
not influenced by personal suffering, and bitterness in
any shape or form was alien to him.

Venezuela that cast him out with ignominy, after his
second term of presidency, owed more to him even than
she owed to the Liberator, Simon Bolivar. Had he not
risen to the occasion and championed the national desire
for autonomy a disastrous war with New Granada* was
certain to have ensued.

Had Venezuela been defeated, she would have been
to-day a mere dependency of the more powerful state.

These were his exploits in the field of statesmanship.
He shone most as a guerrilla leader, for military tactics
were unknown to him. To see the enemy and charge
home with the lance, himself two or three horses'
lengths before his men, if unsuccessful to retire " en
barajuste," as the Llaneros called the Parthian manœuvre, and then to form and launch his charge gained
him success, time and again, against the heavy armed
dragoons which the Spaniards led against him. Only
such tactics could have succeeded with his followers,

* Now Colombia.

wild horsemen of the plains, undisciplined, half-naked and ill fed. Their one superiority was in their horse-manship. Páez himself a horseman, before the Lord, if there have ever been such, was their born general.

Opposed to him was General Pablo de Morillo, an officer selected by the Duke of Wellington himself to lead Spain's army to subdue her colonies. He too had risen from the ranks, was brave and skilful, disposed of money and unlimited resources, and was in every way a leader to be feared.

Yet Páez, after a duel that lasted sixteen months, first drove him from the plains, and then, in junction with Bolivar, vanquished him utterly.

His victories at Mucuritas, La Mata de la Miel, Queseras del Medio and Carabobo are in the mouths of everyone in Venezuela even to-day, for he appeals especially to youth, who see in him youth *in excelsis* and personified.

His reddish hair and fair complexion gained him the nickname of " El Catire Páez," Catire meaning " fair " in the Llanero dialect. White on all four sides, as runs the Spanish saying, with no admixture either of Indian or of negro blood, that alone marked him out amongst his fellows on the plains.

His prowess with the lance, his skill in horsemanship, his courtesy and openhandedness made him their idol. Of middle height and very strongly built, he endured hardships like an Indian and kept his strength and his activity to the end of a long life. Of simple habits, luxury made no appeal to him, and there was something boyish in his nature that appealed strongly to his fellow children and to animals. No man can have a better testimonial to his character, and if he occasionally made mistakes in the difficult position fate imposed upon him, even his enemies allow his honesty and disinterestedness.

Although, after the way of many married men,

he had a mistress to help him bear the yoke of matrimony, women seem to have influenced him but little, all through his career.

His mistress Barbara Niéves is described as being fond of gaiety and a great dancer. His wife, a lady of good family, was serious and reserved.

When Páez was confined in the insanitary and stifling prison in the Castillo de San Antonio at Cumaná his wife whom he had deserted, poured coals of fire upon his head, by doing all she could to alleviate the sufferings of her erring husband. Perhaps the lightfooted Barbara was learning some new dance, asleep, pursuing, absent upon a journey, or otherwise employed, for she did not appear in Cumaná. All that is as it may be, but what is certain is that Páez took neither his wife nor mistress with him in his long exile, and in his bulky memoirs hardly mentions them.

As he was fond of dancing and of music, it may be that he found other consolations, but certainly no woman influenced his life, as did the fascinating Manuela Sáenz, that of the Liberator.

Such men as Páez are rare in any country. Only heroic periods bring them forth; but when they do appear, they carve a niche out for themselves in history.

Páez has cut his own niche deep in the chronicles of Venezuela, but deeper in the Venezuelan heart.

Out of the vast and sun-scorched Llanos that saw his birth, fate called him to be one of the Liberators of his country. No title, in the power of man to grant, can equal Liberator.

King, emperor, president, even protector (unless it be, Protector of the Poor, as say the Arabs), fall into nothingness beside it.

Páez indeed was a true Liberator. He broke the chains that bowed his country under the yoke of Spain. He struck the shackles from the slaves in latter years.

Lastly he gave the greatest proof of virtue a public man has in his power to give, for he died poor.

It is not meet that such a man should fall into oblivion in the land where Canning called a new world into existence, to redress the balance of the old.

Hence this poor tribute from his last biographer, imperfect, halting, and with how many sins, both of commission and omission only the writer knows.

R. B. CUNNINGHAME GRAHAM.

PÁEZ

CHAPTER I

JOSE ANTONIO PAEZ was born on the 13th of June, 1790, in a farm upon the banks of the river Curpa, near the town of Acarigua, in the district of Araure. This district is part of the province of Barinas, in what is now the republic of Venezuela. At the time of the birth of José Antonio, destined to be a hero of the Wars of Independence, it was still a viceroyalty of Spain.

He was the seventh son of Juan Victorio Páez, and Maria Violante Herrera. The little village church of Acarigua. where he was baptized, still exists. His parents were very far from rich, his father being employed in a government tobacco store in the town of Guanare. For one reason or another his mother lived apart from him, and as Páez himself says, she and her sons never had a fixed abode.*

* " Nuestra fortuna era escasisima "—Memorias del General José Antonio Páez, Biblioteca Ayacucho, Madrid, 1916. For all that the family must have been in a good position, although poor. In 1776 Don Juan Victorio Páez, the father of General Páez, brought a complaint before Governor Aquero that the Alcalde of San Felipe had forbidden him to carry pistols on his saddle, alleging that he was not " white " (un blanco). Páez sustained that he was " white " on all four sides (de los cuatro costados). It was found on enquiry that he was of pure blood, without admixture of Jewish or Moorish, still less of Negro or of Indian blood.

Therefore Governor Aquero declared that Don Juan Victorio Páez had the right to carry pistols on his saddle-bow, as well as other lawful arms (y demas armas licitas). The privilege, or right, no doubt was of more use to him on occasion, than arms emblazoned on a motor car are to a profiteer.

The above information is from " Estudios sobre Personajes y Hechos de la Historia Venezolana" por El Doctor, Pedro M. Arcaya, page 53.

Caracas, 1911.

I

At eight years of age his mother sent him to what we should have called in former days in England, a hedge school, kept by one Gregoria Diaz, in the township of Guanare.

Páez says in his autobiography: " As a general rule in Venezuela there were no schools under the government of Spain, except in the chief towns, because it was their policy not to allow the spread of education in the colonies."

Possibly this is a mistake on his part, for as he says, " Except in the chief towns," it does not seem reasonable that any government that desired to keep the people ignorant, should deliberately neglect to do so in the countryside, rather than in the towns.

The real reasons must have been the well known slackness of the Spanish government, and the want of communications in Venezuela at the time.

Doña Gregoria taught the rudiments of Christian doctrine badly,* making her pupils learn them by heart, by force of whipping. Her school must have been exactly like those schools in Morocco where the children learn the Koran by heart, all gabbling it together, as loud as they can shout. Koran or Christian doctrine acquired in such style seems to imbue the scholars with a faith impervious to reason, and as the chief object of a creed is to hold it pertinaciously, perhaps the method is the best.

Writing, the future liberator learned after the method of Professor Palomares,† no doubt a paleograph of those days, of whom it is a pity that we do not know more.

From this Pierian spring he was delivered by his brother-in-law, Bernardo Fernández, who took him to

---

* Enseñaba á leer mal la doctrina cristiana, que a fuerza de azotes se es hacia aprender de memoria, a los muchachos.

† El metodo del Profesor Palomares.

his shop and instructed him in selling across the counter, occupying his leisure hours by making him plant cacao in the farm.

It appears that the Páez family originally came from the Canary Islands, for an uncle Domingo Páez, a native of the Canaries,* took him and his brother José de los Santos to the town of San Felipe, where he had large interests.

Páez, who was then just seventeen, soon had the first of his many adventures by flood and field. His mother summoned him to Guanare, where she lived, upon an important family affair. In the month of June in 1807 she sent him off with certain documents and a sum of money to a lawyer who lived in Patio Grande, near Cabudare, in the neighbouring province of Barquisimeto.

His equipment reminds one of that of D'Artagnan in the *Three Musketeers*, although instead of being mounted on a sorry jade, young Páez was furnished with a good mule. For his expenses on the road he had two hundred dollars, and for his defence an old sword and two brass pistols, only one of which was charged. A peon accompanied him, most likely trotting on foot beside his mule. His outward journey he accomplished without novelty.† On his return home, highly satisfied with himself, seated comfortably on his pacing mule, most likely crooning one of those interminable songs that the Llaneros of Venezuela call Galerones, he stopped for breakfast at the hamlet of Yaritagua.

Wishing to show himself a person of importance, and proud of his armament, his fine mule and the considerable sum of money that he carried, he went into a store

---

* Natural de Canarias.

† Sin novedad. Novedad, literally means novelty, but as any novelty on the road, in those days, either in Spain or in her colonies, was almost certain to be of a disagreeable character, gradually the word, came to be used in the sense of adventure, or of accident.

and having bought some trifle, threw down a heavy
purse upon the counter. Then once more he mounted,
pleased with himself and with the world. He had some
reason to be pleased, for when can the world look
brighter and more fit for a young man to live in, to
stick his toes in the stirrups, hollow his back, and let his
Pelo de Guamo* hat be blown back on his head, than
when well mounted and well armed, his mule devours
the leagues?

In all the country stores of Venezuela, as in the
pulperias of the Pampas in the Argentine, there are
always a set of more or less barren spectators, loafing
about the counter, drinking and playing cards. Their
horses are tied outside to the palenque, that is the
hitching-post of Texas and Western America. They
themselves delight to drag their big spurs on the brick
floors just as the gallants of Elizabethan times delighted
to jingle theirs on the stone flags of the main aisle of
Powles.†

These gentry in the days of Páez were always well
armed. Some of them observed the young man and
his ostentatious exhibition of his purse, and instantly
determined to relieve him of it. Confident and as
pleased with the world as with himself, the young Páez
jogged along the road, following a narrow path overhung with trees, rising to the mountain of Mayurupi.
Nothing was more natural than that he should wish to
try his pistols, and seeing a parrot on a tree he was just
about to fire at it.

His good genius, the feeling that some one was walk-
ing on his grave, or perhaps mere prudence caused him

---

* Pelo de Guamo is the name the Llaneros give to the wide-brimmed,
long-napped hats they usually wear, either black or brown, and made in
Austria. They are kept in place by a band under the chin, called a barbiquejo.
 The name comes from the likeness of the napp of the hat to the inside of
the fruit of the Guamo tree—the Inga Lucida of botanists.

† S. Paul's.

to reflect that he had still to ride all night before he reached his home, and the thought that he had but one shot in the locker, made him lower his pistol without discharging it.

It was well for him he did so, for not long afterwards a tall ruffian, followed by three others, sprang into the path and seized the bridle of his mule.

Had he been riding on a horse he might have spurred it through them with a shout; but mules are made of other stuff, and to cram the spurs into them suddenly, often makes them stop. Young Páez bounded to the ground on the offside, his pistol in his hand. That he did so, shows that though young and inexperienced he had not lost his head. When a man seizes the bridle of an animal to stop him, it's ten to one he does it from the near side. Had Páez got off on that side he would have played into their hands. As it was he probably left them surprised, holding the bridle of the mule.

The headman of the robbers, the tall fellow who had first appeared, slowly advanced towards him, holding a machete* in one hand, and in the other hand a stick.

Twice did young Páez warn him not to advance, but the robber stealthily continued to gain ground on him. This went on for twenty yards, and then the ruffian suddenly bounded forward, aiming a desperate blow with his machete, at the young man's head. He avoided it, and aimed steadily, but as he says only to wound him in the leg.

The man jumped back violently and luckily for Páez received the bullet in the groin.

Although the ruffian fell, Páez stood motionless for a moment, then not thinking that the man was dead he drew his sword and bounded forward to give the *coup*

---

* A machete is a knife used for cutting sugar canes and brushwood. It is about three feet in length, has a broad blade and no hilt; the point is blunt, but the blade can be sharpened like a razor.

de grace. Finding him dead, he rushed upon the other rascals with his drawn sword. They turned and fled; then mounting his mule that had remained feeding close at hand, the young adventurer once more set out upon his way.

On passing by the body of his late assailant, he hurled the empty pistol at it, and then for the first time observed that it had burst, and hurt his hand.

This first adventure and baptism of blood* showed of what kind of stuff the future liberator was made.

However, he was still not out of the wood. A sudden storm with deafening peals of thunder and torrential rain caused all the mountain streams to rise. On every side he found himself cut off from the high road. Fording and swimming now and then and slithering in the mud, at last he got clear of the hills; but it was four o'clock in the morning before he reached his home.

Not a word did he say to anyone of what had happened to him, fearing apparently that he would be accused of murder, though he had acted only in self defence.

At last, tormented by his fears, he left the district, and set his face towards the Llanos, where then as now, a man may hide himself from the whole world. At a great cattle ranche† called La Calzada, belonging to one Leon Manuel Pulido, he engaged himself at a salary of three dollars monthly, as a cattle peon.

This determination of the young adventurer affected his whole life and all his subsequent career.

Born as he was of parents belonging to the poorer

---

* Commentators seem to be agreed that this sort of baptism is usually vicarious.

† These ranches are known as Hatos, in the Llanos of Venezuela. They correspond to the Estancias of the Argentine, and the Haciendas of Mexico. Hato in Spanish means a herd or flock. In Venezuela the word is applied to the ranche, on which the herd pastures.

commercial class, who evidently had come not very long before from the Canary Islands, he had nothing in common, either in upbringing or in blood, with the swarthy herdsmen of the plains.

The very nickname of El Catire Páez, that he received at the Hato of La Calzalda, where he had engaged himself to work, shows they saw that he was different from themselves. Catire in Venezuela is used to designate a fair-haired man, that is upon the Llanos, and we know from descriptions that have been left of Páez by British officers who served under Bolivar in the Independence wars that the nickname was properly applied. Nothing could well have been more different from the life Páez had led up to the age of seventeen, than that in which he was about to embark.

At that time (1807) the Capitania General of Venezuela contained some 800,000 inhabitants, according to the calculations made by Humboldt. It comprised about 500,000 square kilometres.

Few regions of the world speaking a European language, professing the Catholic faith, and whose inhabitants, in the main, had at least a tincture of Spanish blood, could have been wilder, or more remote from the life of Europe at that period. Spain with a short-sighted policy had never paid attention to any of her possessions in America, except they were endowed with mines.

Above all the rest, her attention had been fixed on Mexico, Bolivia and Peru. Thus the enormous territories of Venezuela and the Argentine had been practically abandoned to the descendants of the first conquerors, who by degrees were forced by the climate in some instances, and in others by the lack of communications, to adopt a slothful style of life. True in the capitals, intellectual pursuits had always flourished to some extent, but as all posts in the service of the govern-

ment were reserved for natives of the mother country,
there was little outlet for ambition, so stagnation was
the rule. The struggle that so soon was to begin showed
that the Creoles* were wanting, neither in spirit nor
intelligence.

On the great plains, that stretch along the Orinoco,
the Apure and Arauca, colonial life tended to revert to
a wild type of feudalism, though never to the same
extent as in Peru or Mexico. Although in Venezuela
rich men owned enormous stocks of cattle and of mares,
in all the Llanos none of those great old fashioned,
Spanish houses, with their flat roofs and watch-towers,
chapels, and stores, immense corrals, and huge buildings
for the dependents, of which so many still exist in
Mexico, were ever to be seen.

The owners almost invariably lived in what may be
called the Llano towns, such as Calabozo, Villa de Cura,
San Fernando de Apure, Arauca and the like.

Upon the ranches, with few exceptions, the houses
were slight erections, usually built of wattle, and daub,
called Pajareque, and thatched with palm leaves. In
many instances they had no sides, and then were called
Caneys, copied in fact from the houses of the original
dwellings of the Achagua Indians.

Admiral La Puebla, the first man to navigate the
Apure River, is said to have remarked, on seeing them,
that they were excellent for such a climate,† and that
his men had better copy them.

* Creole, from the Spanish word Criollo, signifies native. Thus a Creole
may be a white or a black Creole. Cattle and horses reared in Venezuela,
Mexico, Peru or the Argentine are always spoken of as "Criollo." The
term, however, is seldom used in speaking of animals of foreign blood born
in the country.

† If he really did give vent to such a saying, given the great heat of the
climate, it was not so foolish as it may appear. In San Fernando de Apure,
some put the mean temperature at 90 deg. Fahrenheit, others at 92 deg.
Thus, almost any kind of shelter would be adequate, so that the roof kept
out the sun or rain.
The Achagua Indians have left much of their blood amongst the

The Llanos stretching to the north, up to the Andes that separate them from Colombia, and to the south where they touch the mountains of Guayana and the Brazilian province of Amazonas, present the appearance of a great inland sea. A sea of grass, broken by islets of slender palms,* that spring up out of the waves of grass, as coral reefs rise from the depths of the Pacific Ocean.

Great rivers, such as the Apure and Arauca, flow through the plains before they fall into the Orinoco, and would form a means of communication with the West Indies, even with Europe at certain seasons of the year, if they were free to navigation. Those rivers also have their affluents such as the Portugesa, the Urinaute and the Tarare, streams that in Europe would be the site of cities, but which actually have but a few scattered, semi-Indian townships on their banks. For half the

---

Llaneros. Little has been written of them, although Padre Juan Rivera, an Andalusian Jesuit, composed a grammar of their language.

It is entitled " El Arte Gramatical de la Lengua Achagua y Vocabulario Achagua—Español."

Father Rivera founded the mission of San Francisco de Regis on the Alto Orinoco. He is described as " Hombre incomparable en la educacion de aquellos Indios." Although he suffered " innumerables Trabajos," one's sympathy is with " aquellos Indigenas." It is not known where he died . . . " se ignora donde acabó sus dias," 1700 ?—" Los Idiomas de la America Latina," Felix y Soloron, Madrid, 1872.

* These are generally of the variety known as Moriches, the Mauritia flexuosa of botanists. Father Gumilla, in his " Orinoco Ilustrado," Madrid, 1741, page 84, says : " Del tronco desfrutado de las dichas palmas, sacan tablas para el suelo de sus casas, calles y plazas y las paredes de sus casas . . . los delantales, que usan las mujeres y los guayucos que usan los hombres para alguna, aunque poca, decencia, sacan de unas entretelas que hay . . . las redes ó chinchorros en que duermen, todo el material es de cañamo que dixe sacan de las hojas tiernas de la dicha Palma."

The full title of the book is " El Orinoco Ilustrado, Historia Natural, Civil y Geographica, de este Gran Rio y de sus caudalosos verticales, Govierno usos y costumbres de los Indios, sus habitadores, con nuevas y utiles noticias de animales, arboles, frutos, aceytes, resinas, yervas y raices medicinales y sobre todo se hallarán conversiones muy singulares á nuestra Santa Fé, y casos de mucha edificacion."

year, the Llanos become inundated forming a huge lake. The inhabitants, centaurs during the six dry months, then navigate their plains in their canoes, just as expert with paddle as with the lazo, and just as much at home in a dugout, as on the back of a wild horse. Nothing is left above the flood, which averages six feet in depth, but islets of palm trees and the banks of sand, known locally as "Mesas" and as "Medanos." These curious formations in places run for leagues. On them the cattle and the herds of mares congregate to escape the waters. When the floods subside there comes a period of six months with hardly any rain, except an occasional cloudburst, then gradually the plains dry up, leaving at first a luxuriant growth of pasture, which soon becomes parched and burned up in the sun.

All kinds of grasses clothe the Llanos, such as the high growing Gamalote* with leaves like little sword blades. Cattle and horses find it too coarse to feed upon; but the Chiguires, those curious amphibious rodents, known in the Argentine as Carpinchos,† eat it greedily.

The Granadilla,‡ a grass that grows nearly four feet in height, the Carretera and the Lambedora, afford a never ending pasturage for the herds of horses and of cattle that roam upon the plains.

Few portions of the world can have changed less to the outward eye than have the Llanos. A paradise for birds, only the garden by the Tigris, or the great lagunas about Chascomus in the Argentine, can be compared to them. Sportsmen from Buenos Aires, no doubt, by this time have devastated that marshy paradise. The garden on the Tigris we can

---

* Panicum maximum.

† Hydrochærus capybara.

‡ Chætochloa palmifolia.

only take on hearsay, or by poring on the book of Genesis.

As regards Venezuela and its plains, especially those on the banks of the Apure and the Arauca, imagination fails to take in the multitude of birds. All species that frequent the rivers, marshes, lakes and lagoons, rise from the water or the sedges, in countless myriads. Parrots scream in the thick woods along the river banks, and great macaws, blue, red and yellow, soar, looking like variegated hawks, above the trees. Humming birds flit about and hang poised, masses of brilliant jewellery, above the flowers, their tiny wings vibrating beyond the power of any human eye to mark their movements. Great solitary cranes stand fishing in the marshes. Down all the rivers sweep in disciplined battalions, company after company, black aquatic birds, known as Cotuas on the Llanos, so vast their numbers that they throw a shade upon the stream over which they pass. Ducks of a hundred species, from the huge Pato Real to the swift flying Guiriri, haunt the lagunas.

They would form a sportsman's paradise, for doubtless every kind of bird was created but to teach men to shoot them on the wing. Luckily guns are scarce upon the plains, and the true sporting instinct, to kill for pleasure, only begins when life is sheltered and secure. Certainly on the Llanos, life is not sheltered, nor even easy, in those vast solitudes where man has to contend with the wild animals, thirst, hunger, malaria, and a climate in which the thermometer seldom falls much below ninety or ninety-two.*

Hawks, eagles, buzzards and swarms of vultures abound and prey upon the other birds. Their numbers are so great that all the ravages of the predatory pirates of the air make scant impression on them. Adam

* Fahrenheit.

himself, unless he had worked ten times as long, in Eden, as we may suppose, could not have given names to more than a small fraction of the birds.

The Rey Zamuro, ruler of the vultures, with his whitish plumage, his bare neck tinted blue, red and orange, rears his high crest, as he descends amongst his subjects, who even when feeding on a dead horse or bullock at once make way for him and recognise him as their king. The other vultures take up an attitude towards their king, not servile, but as if they felt that some great power had ordered it from the beginning of the world. The king adopts the air as of a Czar of Russia, or a Trade Union leader, aloof and quite oblivious of the wishes of his subjects, even if they should chance to have a wish. Pigeons and doves and quails, with orioles and mocking birds, called arrendajos in Venezuela, are commoner than sparrows in the north. Turpials,* house-haunting Gonzales, Uripopos,† Gaviluchos,‡ Caricaris,§ Guris, Gallinetas, Goatsuckers—their name is legion!

An ornithologist (word of fear to feathered things!) might spend a lifetime in the Llanos, collecting specimens, and then omit a dozen of them, no matter how he toiled.

Meanwhile a providence less careless of the conservation of the beauty that he has created than is usual, has kept them all away. Thus the great tiger owl, the Titiriji of the Llaneros, still sounds its melancholy hoot at eventide. The Alcaravan, a kind of long-legged plover, still calls every hour at night, a self created watchman, and in captivity when it becomes tame and companionable, is better than a watch dog in the house.

* Turpialis guianensis.
† Turkey Buzzard.
‡ Vultur barbatus.
§ Polyborus brasiliensis—the Carancho of the Argentine.

Yet there are more to mark as one rides out upon the plains: Arrucos with their heavily spurred wings; the Carretero goose, the whirring of whose wings sounds just as if a heavy cart were being driven through the air; and Scissor Birds, cutting the air in patterns with the long feathers of their tails as they whisk about the tufts of grass.

The crested Curassow, known by an infinity of names in the various Republics, sits nobly on the trees, sticking his breast out like a pouter pigeon, apparently to let the sun fall on his blue metallic-looking feathers, that make him such an easy mark, either for the Christian's trade guns or Indian's blowpipe with its tiny darts whose slightest touch is death. Jacú, Paujil, Pauji, give him whatever name you choose, according to the Republic in which he is an involuntary citizen, he does not merit the harsh label of " Crax Alector," given by scientists.

In such an Eden as the Llanos, the man of science should go hand in hand with an observer as was Hudson,* that inspired field naturalist.

He alone could have given an adequate description of the flocks of egrets dazzlingly white, as they alight at sunset on the branches of the trees that stretch out, forming peninsulas and capes into the mighty rivers of the plains. At first, as the sun begins to sink, a few thin lines of birds appear. These are soon reinforced by thicker columns. By degrees, masses of birds float through the air; then descending on the trees cover them thickly with a white pall, just as a heavy fall of snow blankets the branches in the North.

The peninsula of forest that but a quarter of an hour before was ink, reflected in the waters of the stream like a vast bed of blackest coral, now

---

* W. H. Hudson, the author of "El Ombrí," "Idle Days in Patagonia," and "The Naturalist in La Plata," besides many works on birds in the southern counties of England.

glints like some cape in the New Hebrides or Kerguelen's Land.

The screaming of the birds is stilled as the sun sets. When its last rays fall upon the myriads of egrets settled on the branches, they for a moment turn rosepink, and as the darkness gathers in the sky, the birds, trees and the jutting tongue of land for a brief moment, once again are mirrored black as a northern pine wood, in the slow flowing stream. This teeming feathered life is but one facet of the magic that the Llanos hold.

A wealth of tall, rank growing grass, a lurking place of tigers, forms the first outwork between the grassy, bushless plains, and the thick vegetation on the banks of all the rivers and streams. These grasses, nearly four feet in height, whose edges cut like razors, are reinforced by a barrier of almost impenetrable thorny bush. Further back tower the trees, the last defence against the all devouring plains.

Wide spreading Samaans* and many another of the mimosa family, as Caro, Mora,† and Sanguiro, ranging from the gigantic Samaan itself, to the sweet smelling bushes, with their little yellow balls of flower, known in the Argentine as Espinillo de olor, a wealth of every kind of wood, destined one day to be a source of riches to the country, grows in the forest that clothes the river banks.

Tacamahaca‡ and Guayacán, trees that are known to commerce, both in Brazil and the Guayanas, but that in Venezuela, live and die just as they have lived and died since the beginning of the world with Angelinos,§ and Acapro,¶ that furnish a light wood, the Indians use for

---

* Inga Samaan.
† Mora excelsa.
‡ Elaphrum tormentosus.
§ Homalium pedicellatum famidacea.
¶ Tecoma spectabilis, Bignomacœ.

rafts, and Algarrobo, out of whose bark the dwellers on the Orinoco make their canoes, are but a few of the best known varieties. The Matapalo, a sort of wild fig tree, and the Cañafistula* with its yellow flowers and pods a foot in length, the Lignum Vitæ and a hundred more, some larger than the greatest of our oaks and sycamores. Huge bulbous trunked Ceibas,† the silk cotton of the West Indian Islands, with their long bunches of violet flowers, stand on the edges of the marshes, antediluvian in their monstrosity and size. They tower up and dwarf even the gigantic, tropic vegetation. Nor are there wanting orchids that spring out of the crevices in the trunks, or hang down from the branches of the trees.

Lianas, known as Bejucos in most parts of South America, bind the giants of the woods and crush their life out, just as a boa-constrictor crushes the life out of an ox. The flowers of the liana crown the top of a dead tree that it has killed, so that the bald, sere trunk appears a mass of bloom.

The Guaco,‡ that in Venezuela, Colombia, Mexico and Texas is held to be a specific against snake bites, although snakebitten people die maliciously, in spite of it, just as they do despite the incantations, and the injections of the medicine men, climbs up the trees and hides them with its dark green leaves. This plant, and the liana, called in Venezuela, El Chaparro, and an Aristolochia,§ sovereign for snake bites, but seldom thoroughly enough to save the sufferer, hang from the trees in coils, giving them the appearance of a sailing ship suddenly taken all aback, with broken halyards dangling in the breeze.

Behind the screen of wood, the rivers flow, yellow

* Cassia fistula.
† Bomba Ceiba.
‡ Mikania Guaco.
§ Aristolochia Apurensis.

and turbid, the home of alligators and crocodiles. Few
rivers have such multitudes of fish. From the Caribe*
with its blue black and reddish fins, more dangerous
from its ferocity and numbers than the alligator, to the
huge fresh water porpoise, known as the Tonina, and
the striped catfish five feet in length, the Coporo that
emits a sound as if some water sprite was blowing in a
conch, and the sword shaped Payara with its razor teeth,
their name is legion, and includes the Curito,† that in
the dry season buries itself in the dried-up mud, leaving
but a little breathing hole.

Jaguars and tiger cats, peccaries and anteaters roam
in their monstrosity and size. They tower up and dwarf
red howler known as the Araguato,‡ with his stentorian
voice, that sounds as if a lion were roaring in the woods,
and the small black Machango,§ with his prehensile tail,
and air as of a frustrated humanity.   Hundreds of deer
browse on the plains and edges of the woods.

Sloths, in Venezuela called La Pereza,¶ cling to the
topmost branches of the great Ceibas and Samaans, so
closely, that to the inexperienced eye, they seem excres-
cences upon the boughs.   Tortoises, the Morocoy and
Terecay, Lapas** and Armadilloes,†† seem to have
survived from bygone ages when the world was young.

Mosquitoes, sandflies, and every insect plague known
to the entomologist, make life a battle to animals and to
mankind, in the thick woods and swamps. Vampire-
bats suck the blood of the incautious sleeper, fanning
him so gently with their wings, that he sleeps on uncon-

* One of the genus Serrasalmonæ.   In Brazil it is called Piranha.

† Silurus ; this curious fish is also found in the Gran Chaco.

‡ Mycotes teniculus.

§ Simia Sajous.

¶ In Colombia they are known by the ironic name of Perico Ligero, that
is, Lively Peter.

** Myopotamus Coypú.

†† The Llaneros call them Cachicamas.

scious and in the morning wakes in a pool of blood. They fasten on the necks of horses underneath their manes, leaving them spiritless and weak.

Nor are there wanting snakes in this terrestrial paradise, from the great boa-constrictor thirty feet in length, thick as a palm tree's trunk, able to kill an ox if he entangles him within his deadly folds,* to the small eel-like Matacaballo, dangerous to horses, as its name implies, and countless rattlesnakes.

The Sabanera ten feet in length, is harmless, and as it lies basking on the paths, it illustrates the Spanish proverb, " A snake that comes out on the road, comes out in order to be killed." Lithe water serpents swim in the stream writhing their way along with heads held high and menacing, and green tree snakes hang from the trees in narrow forest trails, to startle travellers.

The climate of the Llanos with its temperature of ninety-two, the snakes, the boas, the crocodiles, the electric eels, the stinging rays, caribes, the tigers in the woods, the inundations and the droughts, the ever present insect plague, make life in the great plains a constant battle to the inhabitants.

Those that survive it grow up hardy; fit to face perils, both by flood and field; careless of heat, cold, and hunger, braving the dangers of their daily lives, from their youth upwards, with equanimity. The western cowboy, the Gaucho, Cossack, Butero, the Australian stockman, the Arab and the Mexican vaquero all are men of iron constitutions, inured to hardships, but the Llanero vies with the best of them, in his endurance and sobriety.

The mirage haunted plains, trackless as uncharted oceans, where roam troops of wild horses, and of asses,

---

* The Boa is known locally as El Tragavenado, that is the Deer Swallower, for he often swallows the carcase of a small deer whole.

wild as their remote progenitors of the Steppes of Asia, are a fine school for the production of a hardy race of horsemen.

Beef is the staple,* almost the only food, of the Llanero; his ordinary drink the muddy water of the neighbouring stream or the lagoon. His luxuries, coffee, and the rough brown sugar full of lye, known as Panela; his bed a hammock, that he carries rolled up, behind his saddle; his pride, his horse, the companion of his dangers and his toil, sober and hardy as himself.

These wild surroundings, the constant struggle against nature, the isolation, the lack of most of what makes life worth living to the inhabitants of other countries, have produced a race of men that retains habits and customs of an older world. Unlike the Gaucho and the Mexicans, or the Indian of the western plains of North America, the Llanero is neither taciturn or melancholy.

His sayings, sometimes sententious, as are the sayings of all those who boast of Spanish blood, are usually gay and malicious, and on the rare occasion of a feast the songs he sings, called Trovas and Galerones, to the accompaniment of his small four-stringed guitar, are never tragic as are the Tristes of the Gauchos of the south, and rarely amorous.

The national dance, called El Joropo, is as quick as a Scotch reel and just as violent. Harps, Cuatro,† and a strange instrument La Maraca, a gourd filled with hard seeds form the accompaniment. The players on the harp and the guitar are seated, but the performer on La Maraca is bound to stand, either from old world etiquette, or because only in that position can he get full effect out of his instrument. A proverb says that the

---

* Arepa, maize bread and Queso de Mano, the white curdy cheese used by nearly all pastoral nations, only appear on great occasions.

† El Cuatro, named from its four strings.

CURPA

Pequeño monumento en el sitio que ocupaba La Casa donde Nació el General Páez. La inscripcion dice : Gral José A. Páez, nacio aqui. Juno 12 de 1790.

A small tablet erected on the site of the house in which General Páez was born. The inscription runs : " General José A. Páez, born here, June 12th, 1790."

office of a Maraquero is accursed, for though the rest of the musicians all play sitting, he is condemned to stand.

Churches are few and far asunder, distances are great, and journeys to the towns are rare as pilgrimages to Mecca amongst poor Mohammedans. Thus marriage, generally, is but a counsel of perfection, as far as mother church has anything to do with it. It seems to matter little to the Llaneros for they live happily enough without the ceremony, and are as faithful, or unfaithful to the partners of their lives, as if they had been duly married in Latin as the Spanish saying has it, or had been born in the best quarters of New York or London.

Into this wild, hard-riding world, just at the time the leaven of independence was stirring in the blood of South Americans, making them remember they were descendants of the Conquistadores, Páez was thrown, at the ripe age of seventeen.

CHAPTER II

EL HATO DE LA CALZADA where the young Páez found himself about the year 1807 or 1808, must indeed have been a wild and savage place.

The straw roofed hut, open on all four sides, stood upon an island in the vast pampa, a sea of grass, whose waves flowed up almost to the door. A line of bones of animals that had been slaughtered as near as possible to the house, to save the trouble of carrying home the meat, lay amongst thistles and filth of every kind. This was known as Los Escoberos and corresponded to the midden that in old days adorned the entrance to Scottish cottages. Inside the house, there was no furniture; the skulls of horses or of oxen formed the seats, on which the owners squatted, with their knees up to their eyes. In the same way Artigas, the Protector of the Republic of Uruguay in the year 1811 is described as seated on a bullock's skull, engaged in dictating to two secretaries* at the same time.

The picture of Artigas would have done equally for that of Páez about the year 1816, with the exception, that in his case there would have been probably no deal table and no rush-bottom chairs. As to the gin that Artigas drank out of a cow's horn, no such luxury was procurable in the Llanos at that date.

* " What do you think I saw, the most excellent Protector of half the New World, seated on a bullock's skull at a fire kindled on the mud floor of his hut, eating beef off a spit and drinking gin out of a cow's horn. . . . The Protector was dictating to two secretaries who occupied at one deal table the only two dilapidated rush-bottom chairs in the hovel."—Francia's "Reign of Terror," J. P. & W. Robertson. London, John Murray, 1839. pages 101—102.

Páez himself in his autobiography says that the greatest pleasure in the Llanero's life was to drink cool water out of a gourd.*

Páez does not mention Cocuy, the spirit made from the root of aloes, or the wild pineapple and called in Mexico, mescal. No doubt it existed in his time, as probably the Llaneros inherited the secret of its manufacture from the Achagua Indians, in the same way the Mexicans inherited mescal from their wild Indian tribes. Gin never made its way to the Llanos in those days. Therefore in this respect, the Pampas of the Argentine Republic were in advance of those of Venezuela, as they had more communication with Europe or at least with Spain.

Meat was the Llaneros' diet, and river water his chief beverage. He who had a hammock, Páez says, thought himself fortunate. This hammock most likely was made of cords of the wild pineapple, or else cut out of a raw hide. The bed most used was a dried horse's hide. The Llanero, like the Gaucho of those days, had but one regular repast. The hour was sunset, and throughout the day he probably chewed a piece of jerked beef steeped in water. The Gaucho was more fortunate for he had Mate, the Paraguayan Tea of commerce, a most sustaining beverage.

Both in the Argentine and Venezuela of those days, watches were practically unknown outside the towns. Gaucho and Llanero alike were wakened by the crowing of the cock. In both their ranches was a pack of cross-bred dogs, usually of a yellow colour, hungry and fierce as wolves. Woe to the stranger who got off

* El mas deleitoso regalo consistia en empinar la tapara, especie de calabaza donde se conservaba el agua fresca.

He quotes a distich, with which his countrymen were wont to console themselves on their hard life.

" El pobre con agua justa
y el rico con lo que gusta."

his horse before being welcomed by the owner of the house.

The pack attacked him, as wolves used to attack an ailing buffalo on the northern plains. If the unlucky stranger happened to be riding a half tamed horse, by intuition the dogs seemed to know it, and one of them was sure to seize him by the tail, giving the rider ample opportunity to prove his horsemanship. When the owner of the hut appeared, brandishing a whip and cursing strenuously, the dogs by magic disappeared and slunk into their lairs. Neither the Gaucho nor the Llanero ever fed his pack of devils, who lived upon the country, almost as thoroughly as if they had been jackals, though when an animal was killed, they were allowed the offal as a treat.

The plainsman's dress in these days was a variation of the peasant's dress of Spain, adopted to the needs of a much hotter country. Upon his head he wore a handkerchief with two tails hanging down upon his shoulders, such as may be seen to-day amongst the older peasants of the provinces of Toledo and Estremadura. This may have been an atavism of the turban left by the Moors. Over the handkerchief, that generally was of a gay coloured silk, unlike the almost universal black of the Castilian countrymen, the Llanero wore the wide brimmed Pelo de Guama hat, so called from being made of a tawny coloured plush, resembling the inside of the fruit called Guama,* both in the districts of the Apure and of Guárico. This hat was kept in place by what sailors call a chinstay, and by the Gauchos and Llaneros, a barboquejo, made of black silk with two tassels underneath the chin.

A white linen shirt much pleated in the front, and a

---

* " Guamo es un arbol tropical que produce un fruto muy dulce, carnoso, en el interior de unos estuches peludos, que parecen terciopelo."   Page 25 ' El Llanero," Daniel Mendoza, Caracas, 1922.

loose turnover collar, fastened by two small silver coins joined by a little chain. The shirt was worn hanging outside the trousers, perhaps for euphony.

Their trousers also were a relic of the " charro " dress of Salamanca, that made in buckskin instead of velveteen has become the national costume of Mexico. The Llanero trouser, tight in the thigh and wide over the instep finished in two points, and was called either " peacock's* toes " or more usually was known as Garraci.

Their clothes were as it were a counsel of perfection, for the British officers who served under Bolivar and Páez in the Independence wars, describe the Llanero cavalry as being often nearly naked, with but a rag or two bound round the waist by a thin strip of hide.

The saddle most in use was what is called " La Silla Vaquera," a sort of compromise between the Argentine " recao " and the high peaked, high cantled saddle of the Mexicans. That is to say it has a horn, usually made of brass, but more for ornament than use. The cantle is almost as high as is the cantle of the Western cowboys' saddle. The stirrups are small, and made to be used either barefooted, or with the alpargatas, that the Llaneros all affect. Underneath the stirrup is a wedge-shaped prolongation to make it hang more steadily, and easier to catch.

The seat is soft, and the saddle, like the Argentine " recao," has rugs or sheepskins piled upon it. The Llaneros almost invariably girth loosely, as they never fix the lazo to the saddle, but tie it to the horses' tails, after the ancient Spanish fashion, that Pepe Hillo sets forth in his " Tauromaquia."† Hillo, more prudent than

*Uña de pavo.

† " Tauromaquia ó arte de torear á caballo y a pie : por el celebre Profesor Josef Delgado (Vulgo) Hillo," Madrid, 1804.
Pepe Hillo was the most celebrated bull fighter of his day, if we except his great rival El " Zeño " Romero. Their rival schools, divided Andalucia

the Llaneros, insists that in broken or bushy ground, the lazo shall be fastened to the head of the saddle for fear of entanglements.

At the door of the Llanero's ranche in the time of Páez, as at that of the Gaucho even to-day in the less sophisticated provinces of the Argentine Republic, a horse, caught up overnight, stood all day saddled, waiting for whatever might occur. Still centaur as he was, and is, the Llanero is not so dependent on his horse as his fellow centaur of the southern plains. For one thing horses were never so plentiful on the Llanos as on the Pampas, and never can be, owing to the climate and the myriad plagues to which they are exposed.

The Pampa of Buenos Aires, temperate in climate, with perennial grass and water, was apparently designed by nature for the great breeding ground of the horse. There is no snowy winter, as in the Asian Steppes. No clouds of stinging insects, as on the Llanos, few snakes and hardly any beasts of prey. Upon the Llanos, snakes abound. The buzzing of an infinity of insects is always in the air. Alligators haunt the rivers. These and electric eels make all the waters dangerous. Tigers* abound in all the woods, taking a continual toll of foals and of the weaker full grown animals.

The poisonous vampire-bat sucks the blood of the horses when they venture into the woods. For half the year the plains are under water. For the other half calcined and dry under the fierce rays of the tropic sun. Thus horses all their lives fight with conditions unpropitious to them. That they survive in such considerable numbers speaks volumes for the resisting powers of the old Spanish breed.

---

into two parties, that perhaps, in real essentials, had as little to separate them as the Whigs and Tories, of a bygone age, or the more modern Conservative and Labour Parties, each so insistent that they can regenerate humanity if they receive long enough terms of office, and sufficient salaries.

* Jaguars, always known as " Tigers" throughout Spanish America.

Still, the Llanero is a horseman born. Mounted upon his wiry little steed, ambling along at its artificial pace, he covers sixty miles a day with ease. He swims rivers full of crocodiles and electric eels, lassoes, and breaks an untamed colt, with any horseman in the world. One feat that he performs is never practised by the Gauchos. He calls it " tailing."* Spurring up to a bullock, he grasps it firmly by the tail, bears off a little to the near side and with a jerk throws down the wildest animal with ease. The feat requires but little strength. Lads of sixteen perform it easily. This feat, the lazo, the high cantled saddle, and the powerful bit, originally all came from Spain.

In the " Tauromaquia " Pepe Hillo sets it forth in terms any Llanero would understand. "There is another way," he says, " though little used of throwing cattle, taking the animal selected by the tail and at the same time spurring the horse up to its side, it can be thrown with incredible facility." He adds, apparently for gentlemen adventurers:

" Although† this way of throwing (an animal) is very simple and showy, there are but few who venture on it." Of a truth it is but a poor sport for an indifferent horseman.

Páez was soon to learn its mystics and to become an accomplished Llanero in the hardiest of all schools. El Hato de la Calzada, the university in which young Páez graduated in all those arts, was at the time managed by a negro slave of General Pulido, the owner of the place.

This man's name was Manuel, but everybody called

---

* Colear un Toro.

† " Otro modo, aunque poco usado, de derribar las reses, es cogiendo la que se pretende por la cola y arreando al mismo tiempo al caballo emparejado con la res, esta se derriba con facilidad incréible, aunque este modo de derribar es sumamente facil y lucido, son muy pocos los que se determinan á exercitarle."—"Tauromaquia," page 49.

him Manuelote,* on account of his size, his strength and his brutality. Manuelote held the office of major-domo, that is overseer. It may seem curious that as a slave and as a negro he should have been in a position to exercise authority over free men, and even white men, such as Páez, who had no tincture of Indian blood.

Slavery in the Spanish colonies was never quite of the same character as in the colonies held by the English, Hollanders or French. The democratic nature of the Spaniard rendered slavery amongst them more of a patriarchal than a commercial affair, much as it is amongst Mohammedans. No doubt Manuel was brought up about General Pulido's house, almost on equality with his sons. They rode and fought together, and if one of the young Pulidos got a fall from his horse, Manuel would laugh at him, without fear of consequences. The lady of the house possibly taught him his catechism, and he would occupy a position midway between a favourite monkey and a Christian.† As years went on and Manuelote got too big to be a plaything he would be sent out into the country to one of his master's cattle ranches.

There, if he showed an aptitude for the life of the Llanos, he would become trusted and advanced, and as no colour line exists, or ever really can have existed, in despite of slavery, in Spanish colonies, he would be appointed manager. Being a slave himself, he would naturally treat all those under him as nearly as possible like slaves. The dwelling house upon the property having been burned down, General Pulido in the haphazard fashion of colonial days in Spanish colonies, had never built it up and hence years had gone by without his visiting the place. Therefore his manager must

---

* Manuelote—Big Manuel. The termination in Spanish, often carries with it the sense of brutality, as well as size.

† Christian, designates a man baptized into the faith, and of course equals Catholic.

have been looked at, by the other men, almost as the owner of the estate.

Suspicious as are all men in such a position as he was, he seems to have looked on Páez as a man sent to spy upon him. Suspicion, or the not unnatural desire to exercise authority over a white man, caused him to treat young Páez with such rigour as to verge on cruelty. His tyrant always called him El Catire* Páez. Páez merited the nickname, for though not fair for a European, his fresh colour, dark brown hair, and pale cheeks made him appear fair amongst the swarthy Llaneros, with their frequent dash of Indian blood.

Certainly Páez had not been brought up delicately, but little luxury, out of Caracas, was to be found in the Venezuela of those days, and none at all in such surroundings as those in which he first saw the light. Still he had not been born in a hut upon the Llanos. He himself tells all he had to undergo. Life as he says was a perpetual struggle with wild beasts. The horses and the cattle, brought by the Spaniards† at the conquest had become feral, and roamed the plains at their sweet will. Even to-day troops of wild horses and of asses are to be found, both on the Llanos del Apure and in the State of Guarico. Upon some Hatos (ranches) the bulls are so savage, that in the round-ups and the brandings that periodically take place, it is rare that several horses are not killed.

The life of the Llanero is of the rudest that it is possible to conceive. What must it have been a hundred years ago? Big Manuel, either in his zeal to make young Páez a perfect Llanero, from the suspicion that he was a spy, or simply because being a rough and brutal man, he had no compassion for his youth, never

* See Chapter I. Catire equals Rubio in Spain and the Argentine, and Huero in Mexico.

† A Spaniard, one Cristobal Rodriguez, first brought cattle to the Llanos in 1548.

allowed his pupil a tame horse. As the first duty of a peon in Venezuela is to get on his horse at daybreak to watch the cattle, guard them from the assaults of the wild animals, and endure the terrific heat out on the shadeless plains, it will be readily understood how much more arduous is the task, mounted on a half wild colt.

In addition to this work he had another duty which he says he hated more. It was, at night, to guard the horses, and see they did not stray. Those who have done this work know how slowly the long hours pass by, even in climates less severe than that of Venezuela. There, in addition there is the plague of insects, locally called " La Plaga," that is the plague. Mosquitoes, sandflies, and all the flying devilry of the whole insect world, waits for the nightfall to attack. The watcher must not strike a match to smoke, for fear of a stampede. He must not call to any comrade for the same reason, and all night long, watching the constellations as they shift their positions, he tries to guess the hour. Of course in the time of Páez, there were no matches, and probably he had no tobacco, and if your half wild horse doubles the rider's work by day, at night he quadruples it.

All this and more young Páez had to bear. Cutting wood to make corrals was only one of his occupations, and by no means the worst, and certainly the least dangerous of his work.

As all the Llanos are intersected with rivers and with streams, and cattle on the march often refuse to enter them, a man on horseback swims in front to give them confidence. He is in most cases an expert swimmer and accustomed to the work. If the stream is narrow he sits upon the horse's back, taking care not to touch his mouth with the bit, for that would almost certainly make him turn over on his side. The rider guides his horse by splashing water in his face, at the

side where he wishes him to turn, or if he has taken off
the bit as a precaution, so that the horse may have a
better chance to breathe he strikes him gently with the
halter that he holds in his hand.   In wider rivers he
slips off and grasps the horse's tail and is pulled over
easily enough, although he has to face the danger of
the alligators, the caribes, and the electric eels.

Should the man not be a swimmer, he holds
the horse's mane, and puts one arm across its withers
as a support.   One day, Páez with Manuel and
the other peons came to a river of tolerable width,
Manuel shouted to him to jump in and guide the cattle,
and when the miserable youngster said he could not
swim, answered " I did not ask you if you could swim,
what I said was jump in and guide the cattle to the
other side."   In such a school it is to be supposed that
swimming soon was one of the young man's accomplishments.

Páez, who in after life became so celebrated for his
amazing feats of horsemanship, wrote in his old age,
sitting as he says before a good fire in New York,
an account of how he acquired the skill that made
him remarkable even amongst the centaurs of the
plains.*

He gives a little picture of big Manuel the capataz.
" I had a capataz (he says), a tall negro, taciturn and
severe of aspect, a rough, thick beard made him look
more formidable."   One of the first orders that this
formidable negro gave the youth was, " in an imperious
voice," to mount an untamed colt.   Saddles were far
from plentiful in the Llanos in those days, so perhaps
to avoid losing a saddle (more valuable than a man) he
had to mount barebacked.   Páez says, without reins; by
this is to be understood most likely, without reins

---

* "Memorias del General José Antonio Páez," page 27, Madrid Edition.
The original edition appeared in New York, in two vols., 1867—9.

attached to a bit, and with but a halter round the nose.

It is a common feat, both in the Pampas and the Llanos, to get upon a wild horse barebacked and without a halter or anything at all to guide him.

The feat is generally performed by dropping from the cross bar of the gate of a corral on to the horse's back. It is usually done at cattle brandings, sheep shearings, or any other occasion, when men are gathered together and have drunk plentifully. Sometimes a man who has never seen it done, pays some one who fancies himself upon his prowess to perform it.

In any case it is but a trick done to show the rider's skill. In no case has it anything to do with breaking a young colt.

Therefore it seems that Páez means, he mounted, holding a halter in his hand with the end made fast over the horse's nose. But be that as it may, his description of the agonies of terror he endured is realistic in the extreme. As to the negro's orders there was no reply, the unlucky peon jumped on the wild colt, and seized his thick, rough mane with both hands. Hardly was he well seated, when the wild beast began to buck and try to catch the rider's legs between his teeth, in his efforts to get rid of the unaccustomed load. Then, with fire blazing from his eyes, he set off at a furious gallop after his companions in the plains, as if to ask their help to free him of his burden.

The wretched rider felt as if borne by a hurricane; the wind whistled in his ears; he hardly dared to breathe. If he kept his eyes open it was only to look for help, or to try and convince himself the peril was not so great as it appeared. The ground that to a man on foot looked level, to the frightened rider seemed full of precipices down which the wild colt must plunge.

There was no help except that which might come from heaven, and so, waiting for his last moment, he prayed fervently to Our Lady of Mount Carmel, whose scapular he wore round his neck.

At last the agony was over when, quite exhausted, the colt came to an involuntary halt. However as a smith only becomes a master by working at his trade, so the young Llanero, by degrees loses his terror, and at last he finds no pleasure greater than that of training a wild horse.

Apart from the doubtful pleasure of training wild and unbroken colts, the only solace to the lives of the Llaneros was listening in the evening to the melancholy galerones played on the four-stringed guitar* and plaiting horse-hair ropes. At least Páez himself so tells us in his memoirs. He laments that the sound of church bells never reached the Llaneros' ears, and that a visit to the nearest town, at rare intervals to attend Mass, was the only link that bound them to a more civilized life.

They lived and died as if they had no other destiny on earth than to struggle with the wild animals that occupied the plains.

In that rough school he graduated, and so his constitution gradually hardened, his strength increased, his body became as hard as iron, and the whole man emerged from the rude trial able to endure the hardships of the years of war in which he was called upon to take so great a part, and to preserve his vigour quite unimpaired, till eighty years of age. Besides these hardships there were not wanting humiliations he was called upon to endure. After a day of hard work in the saddle or with the axe, Big Manuel, lying down in his hammock used to call out " Catire Páez, bring a bowl of water and wash my feet." Then he had to swing the

* El Cuatro.

hammock till the negro fell asleep.   Years afterwards
when Páez had risen to fame and was a leader of importance in the Independence war, he chanced, after
an action at a place called La Mata de la Miel, to
take Big Manuel prisoner.   Páez treated him well and
sat him down to dinner at his own table.   At first the
negro was sulky and to all offers Páez made him to
remain with him, only answered, all he wanted was a
free pass to return to his home.

At length vanquished by the kind treatment he received, Manuelote entered the patriot ranks.   The
soldiers who had heard the story used to say, so that he
should hear, " Catire Páez, bring me a bowl of water
and wash my feet."   Manuel at last became annoyed
and said, " I hear you, but to me you owe having a real
man to lead you, and the country owes to me its best
lance, for it was I who made him."

So did the negro salve his conscience, as adroitly as if
he had been a white man on all four sides.   Out of this
servitude and the hard life of a cattle peon, a lucky
accident delivered Páez, and gave him the first chance
to rise.

The negro Manuel was sent from La Calzada to a
place called El Paguéy, to brand some cattle and get
others ready to be sold.   There Páez met the owner of
the ranch—one Manuel Pulido, who took a fancy to
him and as he knew the young man's family, employed
him to sell cattle in the nearest town.   Finding that he
discharged his duties well and carefully, Pulido kept
the youth about him; and as he could read and write, a
rare accomplishment in those days upon the Llanos,
gradually taught him such business as there was to learn
upon a cattle ranche.

The severe apprenticeship that he had undergone
now stood him in good stead.   So well he prospered
that he was able shortly to buy cattle for himself

and get together the beginnings of a little fortune. Not long afterwards, he married a girl called Dominga Ortiz.*

* In 1809. Doña Dominga Ortiz was born in Canagua in 1792. Páez, who was not an exemplary husband, abandoned her in 1820, and lived with one Doña Barbarita Nieves, a celebrated beauty.

His wife retired to Barinas, where she was much respected for her exemplary life. Years afterwards, when Páez was a prisoner in the castle of San Antonio, in Cumaná, his wife heaped coals of fire upon his head, by voluntarily sharing his imprisonment.

CHAPTER III

THE Captain Generalcy* of Venezuela in the time of the Spanish domination, embraced a vast extent of Territory. It was separated from the Viceroyalty of New Granada, now the Republic of New Granada, by the Andes. The Atlantic formed its boundary to the north, and British Guiana to the east. To the south it touched Brazil in the mountains of Tapirapecú and Pacaraima. Although roads were unknown and therefore communication difficult, the wealth of rivers in a measure supplied the want. The Orinoco, the great artery is fed by streams that in any other country but South America would be considered of first class magnitude. The Apure, Arauca, Portugesa, Meta, and half a hundred more, are all navigable to a greater or a less extent, by country-built craft; Indian canoes have sailed upon them long before the conquest. Little enough the rivers served in those days, except for the above mentioned small craft that plied between the little towns upon their banks.

The policy of Spain was to exclude all strangers from her South American possessions. Not so much on account of trade or contraband, but to keep out ideas. No government since the world began, however stupid, and some surely have been stupid enough to satisfy the most orthodox, but has felt instinctively, that once their people were to begin to think their power would soon be at an end.

Monarchs and presidents, liberals, conservatives and socialists and communists alike, are all agreed to stifle

* Capitania General.

34

"CABALLERO"
given by General Páez to
Admiral Fleeming.
(from a miniature
in a bracelet)

thought when once they are in power. In spite of all the Spaniards' efforts it proved impossible to keep South America thoughtless and undefiled. The celebrated Don Antonio Nariño translated Rousseau's Contrat Social, and it soon ran like wildfire throughout the country. It is difficult to account for the extraordinary influence it exercised, for it contains nothing that had not been treated, and far better treated, both by Plato and by Aristotle. Still in the Venezuela of those days it was deemed such dangerous stuff that poor Nariño was first committed to the dungeons of Cartagena, and then sent off a prisoner to Spain for the translation of it.

That which undoubtedly hastened the revolution of the Spanish colonies, was the occupation of Madrid, and the imposition of a foreign sovereign, by Napoleon.

When the news arrived in Venezuela in the year 1810, the authorities showed their intention of recognising any government in Spain, in order to defeat the aspirations of the Creoles towards independence. Nothing more shortsighted could have been hit upon, for the one chance Spain had of maintaining her authority over her enormous colonies, was to appeal to them for a general crusade against the French. So far from doing that, they received the French captain who had brought the news of the establishment of a foreign king, in Spain, with acclamations.

The people of Caracas, justly indignant, and far more patriotic than their governors, rose in revolt, and would have killed the French captain, had not the government sent him by night under strong escort to rejoin his ship.

An English sailor, one Captain Beaver, quoted by Páez in his memoirs, gives a curious account of the situation. He too had been sent off to take dispatches to Caracas. England had then made peace with Spain and Wellington was about to initiate his campaign in the peninsula. Beaver's dispatch brought the account

D

of the treacherous imprisonment and sequestration of King Charles IV and the installation of Napoleon's brother Joseph in Madrid.

Naturally Beaver's dispatches put a different construction on events, to those that the French naval captain brought. Beaver says, " The city (Caracas), immediately flew to arms, 10,000 of its inhabitants surrounded the Captain General's palace entreating him at once to proclaim Ferdinand VII, king of Spain. This he agreed to do next morning."

The people of Caracas seemed to have doubted his good faith, for Beaver says, " not being satisfied they, by the voice of heralds proclaimed King Ferdinand, during the evening, all through the city, with the usual ceremonies, and hung his picture up in the balcony of the town hall with lights on either side." Hearing the French captain had left the city under guard, three hundred men pursued him, but he knowing that he rode for life, spurred through the winding trail that leads down the high mountains to La Guaira and got on board his ship. " Although the governor received me coldly," Beaver says, " all the chief citizens waited upon me and acclaimed their liberator, breaking out into cries of gratitude towards England.

" At five o'clock, when I returned to the palace of the governor, I asked him to surrender the French frigate to me, or at the least to let me take it in the bay. He refused both my requests and told me that he had ordered it to put to sea at once. I told him that I had made arrangements to take it, if it left the harbour, and if on my return to La Guaira,* it was not already in the power of the authorities, that I would capture it myself. He answered, if I attempted it, that he would order the

* In those days the British captain and his staff could easily have reached La Guaira on horseback in three or four hours, for by the old mule trace the distance is not much above twenty-five miles.

ports to open fire upon my ship. I told him that I would take the consequences, adding that the reception he had given me was more fitting to an enemy than to a friend, as I had brought him information that hostilities had ceased between our countries, and that Spain now was at war with France. He answered that he knew nothing about that.

" I then repeated what I ha dtold him, and added if the imprisonment of the King of Spain and the occupation of Madrid were not acts of hostility, what did he think constituted a state of war? Again he answered that his government had not informed him of this war, and that he could not take as official the dispatches I had brought."

Quite an official answer, and one that no one need be surprised at reading, for it appears, once make a man a government official, even if previously he has been intelligent, he is attacked by a sort of Lues Gubernatoria that obfuscates his mind.

In 1810 news was received in Caracas of the bad state of Spain and that the government was disposed to sanction anything to frustrate liberty in the colonies. The chief citizens deposed the Captain General, and set up a Junta to carry on the government till the Spanish throne was once more occupied by its native sovereigns.

Nothing could well have been more patriotic, or more moderate. There seems to have been, at least at that time no disposition to break away from Spain. All that was wanted was common sense, a rare commodity in any government.

Reading the account of the negotiations that went on before the revolution actually broke out, the case of Ireland rises to the mind. The same intolerance and the same blindness to events, the arrogance in dealing with the peoples' representatives, the pride of race and above all the insolence of office, were shown in Spain by the government of Cadiz, towards the Creoles, as England manifested in days gone by to the extremely moderate advocates of self government in Ireland.

In Venezuela and in Ireland alike, events took the same course, and Spain and England lost the last chance of holding territories that might have been easily pacified. Nothing, however, seems to teach governments, and the rule both of England and of Spain ended in ignominy.

After much petitioning the Spanish Cortes that then sat at Cadiz, the rest of Spain being in the hands of the French invaders, and after having received nothing but insults in return to their petitions, on the 5th July, 1811, the representatives of the various states of Venezuela* declared their independence from the mother country. The two provinces of Coro and Maracaibo alone remained faithful to Spanish rule.

Then when too late, the Spanish government offered the reforms that had been so long delayed. Ports were to be open to international commerce. Equal rights were decreed between Spaniards from Spain and Creoles of the colony. Monopolies were to be abolished. Lastly all offices whether civil, military or ecclesiastical were to be open to every citizen of Spain.

When these terms became public, Lord Liverpool, the Prime Minister of Great Britain, ordered the governor of the island of Curuzao to mediate with a view to the conciliation of the colonies. His terms were: Immediate cessation of hostilities. A general amnesty for all those who had engaged in the revolution against Spain. Representation of the Creoles in the Spanish parliament, and liberty of commerce, with a preference to Spain. Viceroys and governors were to be chosen indiscriminately, either from Spain or from the colony. Municipalities were to be set up in the towns. Lastly

* Mexico, and the River Plate soon followed this example.

the colony was to recognise the sovereignty of the Spanish Cortes, as representing Ferdinand VII, then a prisoner in France.

These wise and generous propositions, that might have pacified the colonists and reconciled them to the mother country, had they been offered soon enough, were at once rejected by the Spanish parliament.

On the 24th of July, 1800, the Cortes issued a manifesto setting forth its belief that to allow freedom of commerce to the colonies would be the worst calamity that could befall the mother country. They further gave it as their opinion that such a course would involve Spain* in bankruptcy, make her the laughing stock of foreign nations and upset all religious order and morality.

After prolonged negotiations the colonists seeing that nothing was to be gained by them, deposed the remaining Spanish authorities and instituted a legislative body in the capital. Others were formed in all the provinces with the exception of Maracaibo, whose governor Migares, seized the new legislators and shipped them to Puerto Rico as prisoners of state. As his reward he was made Captain General of Venezuela, and received orders to take the sternest measures with the revolutionists.

The brave, but unfortunate Miranda whose delivery into the hands of Monteverde the Spanish general, on a charge of treason (never proved), was an indelible stain upon the career of Bolivar, was the first patriot commander in chief. The Junta of Caracas also sent the Marquis del Toro, a rich and liberal gentleman, who enjoyed one of the few titles in the country, to operate against the town of Maracaibo. After some

---

* No government ever seems to learn by the mistakes of others, or to comprehend that rights when they have been gained by force. are never looked on, either as acts of grace or privileges.

preliminary successes, the Marquis finding his communications threatened, was obliged to retreat.

Páez now just twenty years of age had been called to the colours early in 1810. He was by this time an expert Llanero, able to throw the lazo, to break wild horses, and well accustomed to all the dangers of a life upon the plains. He enlisted as was natural, in the cavalry, and served at first in the province of Barinas under his old master Leon Manuel Pulido. He does not seem to have seen much service at his first venture, and shortly before the country was occupied by the royalists under Don Domingo Monteverde, he retired from the army in 1813 as a sergeant, with an indefinite leave.* He seems to have gone back to his little cattle farm, and was living quietly when he received an order from the Spanish general Don Antonio Tiscar, to go at once to the Hato of Carrao, some fifty leagues away, to collect all the tame horses and the cattle he could find, and take them to the general's headquarters in the town of Barinas. Though he was not a Spanish soldier, but on the contrary a sergeant in the revolutionary ranks, he thought it prudent to obey. Had he not done so, it is probable he would have paid for his disobedience with his life. He went unwillingly as may be supposed, and from the great herds of El Carrao only took two hundred horses and a thousand head of cattle to General Tiscar's headquarters. The general took a fancy to him and invited him to dinner at his house. There were assembled several Spanish officers, men against whom Páez had been fighting recently. Most probably they were Venezuelan royalists, for at the time Spain had not many real Spanish soldiers in the country. They were to come later under General Morillo. As General Tiscar was raising money to carry on the campaign by a system of forced loans, Páez asked

* Licencia indefenida.

him how much he was expected to contribute as his
share.   Tiscar said " nothing for I am going to send
you into the cavalry with the rank of captain." Nothing
could well have been more disagreeable to the young
patriot.   Bolivar was already in the field, and though
his first attempts turned out disastrous to him, the eyes
of all the revolutionary party were fixed on the young
chief.   Simon Bolivar came from the same class of
society as the Marquis del Toro, was rich, had travelled
in Europe and had enjoyed all those advantages of
education that Páez entirely lacked.   As he was born
in 1783 he was just seven years older than Páez who
was so soon destined to be one of his most able officers.
Young, rich and enterprising, a daring horseman and
brave to a fault, Bolivar was the sort of general that
such a man as the young Llanero Páez was certain to
admire. For the time being he was detained by General
Tiscar, who no doubt was none too sure of his
fidelity.

After a month of inactivity at headquarters, Páez
received his commission as a captain and the command
of a troop of cavalry, sent by the hand of Lieutenant
Montero, with orders to be prepared to march. Tiscar
was anxious to attack Bolivar, who he was well aware
had at that time but scanty troops at his command.

Páez who had apparently by this time obtained the
confidence of General Tiscar, asked leave to return
home for a few days, to collect what he required for the
campaign.   This was his opportunity and he determined
at once to take advantage of it, and join the patriots.
Guided by one Acevedo, a smuggler, and accompanied
by a friend Don Antonio Maria Fernandez, he crossed
the mountains of Pedraza, and in a little town called
Santa Barbara, luckily fell in with a patriot officer,
Manuel Pulido, with a company of men.

Bolivar at that time had retired towards Caracas, with

the best part of the patriot forces, so that the local government of Barinas was obliged to rely on its own efforts to raise forces to oppose the royalists. General Tiscar from whom Páez had just escaped had been defeated and retired towards San Fernando de Apure, a town round which for several years much fighting was destined to take place. It is situated on the river Apure, about one hundred miles from where it joins the Orinoco, and is navigable for most part of the year, by the light-draught country sailing vessels. These boats, generally one masted and sloop rigged, carry a great square mainsail and a very large topsail, with but little headsail. They skim across the water at a considerable rate, and when they emerge from a long reach of the river heavily timbered and mysterious looking, into an open reach, appear to have sprung from another world.

At that time Venezuela was most sparsely populated. The extensive area of the Captain Generalcy was estimated to contain only 800,000 inhabitants. There was no considerable concentration of population outside the capital. Thus all the fighting that went on so long against the Spaniards, was largely of the nature of guerrilla warfare. The Llaneros were of all men the best fitted for that sort of war.

Patient of hardships, born horsemen, and broken from their youth upwards to all the perils of a frontier life, they wanted no commissariat, but lived upon the cattle that were so abundant on the plains. Horses were plentiful and these wild riders all seemed to understand how to use lance and sabre naturally, or at least wanted but little instruction in the art.

The temporary government offered Páez the rank of captain as compensation for the rank he had refused amongst the royalists.

In after years his enemies, and he was the kind of man

who made both enemies and friends with the same facility, used to throw in his teeth that he had served in the ranks of the enemies of his country. Nothing was more unjust, for it is difficult to see what possibility there was but to act as he did, in the circumstances.

In the month of October, 1813, he had his first success as a commander. Sent to attack a Spanish detachment about four hundred strong at a place called Canagua, Páez surprised them just as day was breaking, defeated them entirely, and set off back for Barinas with many prisoners.

His good luck was not destined to be permanent, and he was soon involved in an adventure out of which few but himself would have emerged with life. Upon the road home to Barinas he met a soldier who informed him Barinas had been taken by the Spaniards, and that the patriots had retreated to San Carlos, another little town. Thus cut off from his base Páez determined to seek refuge in Guasdualito, and from there if pressed to retire into the plains of Casanare, in what is now Colombia. These plains, a continuation of the Llanos of Apure were and still are, one of the wildest parts of South America. Inhabitants are few to-day, and at that time they must have been still fewer, but on the other hand there was plenty of wild cattle on which a party such as the men who followed Páez could easily maintain themselves. Páez had little faith in the fidelity of his followers, for they had followed him more from affection for himself than out of patriotism. So he adjured the soldier who had brought the letter to him to say nothing of the patriots' reverse. He promised faithfully not to breathe a word about it, but after the fashion of most promisers, instantly broke his word.

Early next morning Páez informed his men offially of the defeat, and asked them to accompany him if necessary to the wild plains of Casanare. All except twenty laid down their arms and left him in the lurch. At midday they halted at a cattle farm to eat. There all forsook him with the exception of José Fernandez, a lad of sixteen years of age. Four days they wandered in the wilds, suffering hunger, thirst, and the plague of insects that rendered life almost intolerable, not daring to approach a house though houses must have been few and far between. The wretched boy dying of hunger and of thirst, half maddened by the mosquitoes and soaked to the skin, for it was the season of the rain, in desperation hearing of a Spanish force several leagues off went and delivered himself up to them. They shot him after a day or two.

Páez left all alone, wandered about the country not daring to communicate with anybody, for in the province of Barinas all were royalists. What he endured can only be imagined by those who know the country and have felt the fury of the sun in these open plains, and have suffered the attacks of the fell insect plague by night.

He was well mounted and probably his horse suffered less than himself, as there was grass in plenty for him to eat. How Páez survived is wonderful. The arms of those days were not much fitted to kill game. Moreover he could not have dared to fire a shot for fear of bringing down on him some of the enemy. Possibly he now and then was able to lay hands on an iguana or an armadillo, and as a Llanero he would be sure to have flint and steel to make a fire. Day must have been a purgatory, lurking about the edges of the woods or hidden in the long grass by the river side, dodging the sun as well as he was able, under the scant shade of the moriche palms, always with one eye on the horizon and the other on his horse, for to lose him,

would have been to lose his life leaving him helpless
to escape if he should chance to be pursued. Night,
even in the most miserable Caney* would have been
some relief to him. Hidden in the woods or caves,
a prey to myriads of insects, it must have been intolerable to a man weakened by want of food and fevered
by the sun; he most probably, after having drunk as
much of the river water as he could swallow, would
build a fire.

To the leeward of it, well in the smoke, to keep
away, as far as possible the bats and the mosquitoes,
sandflies and all the other plagues, he and his
horse would cower waiting for daylight, as birds in
northern climates sit moping in the snow. At last,
after a week of misery the moment came when he must
either die of hunger and exposure, or give himself up
to the enemy, hoping to escape with life. Either
alternative was enough to appal the stoutest, for the
royalists usually shot their prisoners at sight.

After long cogitation and weighing well the chances
on both sides he chose the latter course. In his old
age, an exile in New York, after having twice been
president of Venezuela, he gives a full account of how
he fared.†

These reminiscences read as freshly as if they had
been written shortly after the event. Páez does not see
himself glorified by youth, after the foolish fashion of
so many writers in old age, but simply sets down what
happened to him, as in a diary.

As often is the case, during civil wars, fathers and
sons and friends fought on opposing sides. They still
were friends when any opportunity occurred to show
their friendship, but opportunities were scarce.

* A Caney is a hut, without sides. It has a roof generally thatched with
palm leaves or rushes.

† Memorias del General José Antonio Páez.

Páez does not say how he got into communication with Don Manuel Pacheco, the military commander of Canagua who was a friend of his. All that he tells us is, "One day, Pacheco sent a soldier with a message, asking me to come and speak to him." Most probably Páez had been seen, as he lurked in concealment, by several people who did not want to give him up. He says, "Pacheco though a friend had been pursuing me as if I was an enemy. Páez sent back a message by the soldier, asking Pacheco to come and meet him, but alone. Where they met he does not say, but Pacheco came to the tryst. He expressed his sorrow at seeing Páez in such a miserable state, and regretted that they were not on the same side. He said however that the royalist authorities were not enraged against him, and that as the governor of Barinas was Don José Maria Luzardo of Maracaibo, a friend of both of them, if Páez should present himself, he would be perfectly secure.

Páez conceived the plan of once more joining the patriots in San Carlos by taking out a passport from Pacheco to Barinas, and from that place another from Luzardo under the pretext of going to present himself to Colonel Yañez at his headquarters in Guanare. The risk was desperate, but at least armed with his passports he could travel openly, and trust to luck to join the patriots. Somewhat imprudently he went next day into the town of San Carlos where he had a house. The first thing that he saw was a detachment of some thirty cavalry, standing outside his house. When he got off his horse he took his loaded musket with him, then turning to the soldiers said "Gentlemen, here I am, I am the man you have been looking for, if you wish to take vengeance on me, now is your chance." "We want no vengeance" they rejoined, and then called out "Viva el voluntariro, José Antonio Páez," affecting to believe he had repented and would join the royalists.

Captain Pacheco then asked him for his sword. Páez immediately gave it to him, trusting to his good faith. No sooner had Pacheco obtained the sword, than he went into Páez's house and took away his gun. Páez then asked him for his passport, but Pacheco said that it was unnecessary for as he himself was going to Barinas next day, Páez could go with him, and in his company he would be safe. This seems to have made him suspicious, for he demanded back his arms and as Pacheco refused to give them up, Páez went to his house and took them. He says, " I then went out into the street and for half an hour challenged Pacheco and his men saying if you want my arms, come on and take them." Pacheco who seems to have acted in bad faith throughout, turned to the soldiers and said that they should take away his arms. An old royalist sergeant said, " Certainly it is our duty," and was about to try and take the arms by force. Páez sprang backwards and brandishing his sword said, " You can take them certainly, but it will cost a life or two, for I shall fight to the death." Seeing he was in earnest they refused to move, and Páez set out for Barinas with Pacheco and his company. At the pass of the river Paguay a friar one Simon Archila, a great friend of Páez, met him and drawing him aside, said he was sorry to see him and that he had done wrong to trust to promises, for without doubt the Spaniards would be glad to get possession of him. Páez informed him that his only object was to join the patriots, and that he would at once demand that Pacheco should dismiss his men, and if he refused he would not go with him. Friar Simon begged him not to do that, for having seen him talk with Páez, they would think that he was acting on his advice, and it would certainly go hard with him. Páez put his resolution into force two or three leagues further on upon the road, and after a long consultation Pacheco dismissed his men, and the two travelled on alone.

Upon arriving at the outskirts of the town, Páez said " now is the time, my friend, for you to show yourself a friend. Get me a passport from the governor Luzardo and I will wait here till you bring it to me." In a short time Pacheco came back with a letter from the governor saying he wished to speak to Páez, and that he could rely on being safe. The governor received him amicably, and told him that he thought his idea of going to see General Yañez was not a good one, and that he had better go and stay in his house. Relying on his word, Páez who seems to have been extraordinarily unsuspicious at that time, went to Luzardo's house. In an hour or two, a message came, that to save appearances he had better submit for form's sake to be arrested for three days. On the third day when he expected that he would be released, a Spanish major, Don Antonio Perez suddenly arrived with a strong force of cavalry. He having been proclaimed military governor of the province, immediately sent an officer to the prison, where Páez was under what he imagined was a hypothetical arrest, to put the prisoners into chains. The officer Captain Rafarte, when a lieutenant, one Garcia, asked that his fetters should be light, answered him " light fetters, eh, well we shall see." Páez who was young and on this occasion, rash, called out, he did not want light fetters and taking up a heavy pair, asked as a favour, they should put them on him. Captain Rafarte seems to have taken a fancy to Páez from the first, for instead of having him instantly executed as he might have done, he merely laughed at the bravado of the young Llanero. Páez heavily ironed, sat down upon his hammock, and began to sing in a low voice, possibly one of those interminable galerones, that the Llaneros* love. An officer, possibly touched by his youth and bravery, warned Páez not to sing, as it would indispose his captors against him, thinking he did it but in mockery.

In a short time Captain Rafarte entered the room, and telling Páez to follow him, said that he wanted the heavy fetters for an enormous prisoner, one Juancho Silva, a Mulatto and so strong, that he could take a wild bull by the horns and hold it, whilst he plunged a sword into its heart. From that time, Páez says, Rafarte showed much interest in him, and tried to save his life. He adds, that to be taken prisoner in those days, was the same thing as to be condemned to death. Unluckily in those days, and even almost up to the beginning of the present century, this has often been the case, in nearly all the republics, during their civil wars.

After an interval, Puy the new governor, who had arrived to replace Luzardo, appeared. Puy was a cruel barbarian who delighted to play cat and mouse with any wretched patriot who fell into his hands. He asked Páez his name, and after asking him what grade he had in the insurgent army, turned to the jailer, and said, " See that the irons of this captive gentleman are secure. If he escapes I will cut off your head," and as he spoke he touched his sword. After an hour Major Ignacio Correa came with a company of lancers to the prison. He then read out the list of those condemned

* Some of the galerones are interminable : but there are shorter songs in the form of " coplas " of four lines, that are called " corridos."

" Cuando monto en mi caballo
Y me fajo mi machete,
No envidio la suerte de nadie
Ni aun al mismo presidente."

It may have been something of this kind that Páez was singing. He had a good voice, and in after years was very fond of displaying it.

to die, or as the Spanish phrase runs to "Be put in chapel."* Páez was the fourth upon the list. As he was led off he asked to be allowed to take his hat, but the officer looked at him with a sneer, and said, "You will not find it necessary." The prisoners were taken to a little room and packed so closely that they could not sit down. In such a climate it is easy to imagine what sort of night they passed. In the morning Páez's wife Doña Dominga Ortiz arrived to seek for news of him, for she was unaware that he had been condemned. She brought a letter from Friar Simon Archila, in which he said, he hoped the Spaniards would not proceed to extremities with Páez, for he was young and bore the best of characters. As luck would have it, at the prison door she met the governor. When he knew who she was, he insulted her grossly and told her if she did not go away at once he would have her shot.

Puy read the letter, and all he said was, "This rogue of a friar must be a patriot." Luckily in an hour or two Páez was allowed to come up to the door to breathe and get a little water.

A Spanish merchant happened to see him, and expressed his sympathy at seeing the young man in such a sad position and condemned to death. Páez implored him to use his influence, for he was much respected in the town, to urge on Puy to accept a ransom. Helped by Captain Rafarte, who seems to have been much impressed with Páez, the Spaniard returned after an hour or two saying that for three hundred dollars, Puy would spare his life. Although the merchant, one Escutarol,

---

* "Poner en capilla," literally, to put into chapel. Spanish criminals in those days, when sentenced to death, were put into a little chapel or oratory, where they passed the night listening to the exhortations of a friar. By degrees the phrase came to be applied to any place where prisoners were put the night before their execution. In such a place as San Carlos, it was probably merely a room, in which the condemned man was separated from the other prisoners.

was afraid to be his surety, he got another man to stand for him.

Páez was then taken out from the prison and his irons knocked off. As he came up the prison stairs he met a gentleman Don Marcos Leon, who as Páez says was "of advanced age, and distinguished looking." Páez and he entered the governor's presence at the same time. After asking Leon some questions he ordered him to be taken off to prison. That night, the prisoners were all butchered by lance thrusts, including the unfortunate Leon. As he seems to have been charged with nothing, Páez thinks he was his substitute. Puy saw a chance to make a dishonest penny, and refused the ransom, saying he now demanded six hundred dollars, instead of the three agreed upon. There is no reasoning with a tiger when he has his paw upon you. So Páez had to pay. Why he did not at once get on his horse, when he was free, and hide himself even if it had been in the wilds of Casanare, he does not say. Possibly he was guarded all the time, and the pretended ransom was but a trick to extort money from him; from one cause or another he remained in the city of Barinas for a fortnight.

Then, on the 5th of December, a date that he was never likely to forget, a soldier came with a message from the governor, to speak to him. Hardly had he came into the room, than Puy asked a soldier, who had served with Páez, "with how many men had he attacked the detachment, that he had disarmed." The man said with a hundred and fifty. Then turning round to Páez he asked him, "where are their arms?"

Without waiting for a reply Puy turned to an officer and said "take me this gentleman back to the prison, fit him with fetters, and put him instantly into chapel." This time Páez thought his fate was sealed, and certainly it would have been had he not been saved, as by

E

a miracle. During the night a little band of patriots
made an attack upon the town. One of those panics
that now and then invade an army, making them
stampede, just as a troop of horses takes fright at
nothing and stampedes, ran through the royalists. In
haste they saddled up and with their governor riding at
their head, evacuated the town, too much alarmed to do
more than to send out a picket that was met by the
little band of patriots who to their challenge answered
" Free Soldiers of Death." As it was a bright moonlight night the little band of Soldiers of Death,
appeared more numerous than it was, and Puy fearing
that they were going to attack, gave orders to retreat.

He had not even time, as was his custom, to order
that the prisoners should be massacred, but fled at once
towards San Fernando de Apure, no one pursuing him.
So for the second time within a fortnight, Páez was
snatched from the jaws of death. The prison in Barinas had more than a hundred prisoners all waiting
death, and in another place, many of the wives and
daughters of the patriots were confined.

The first thing Páez did on finding himself free
was to go to his house to get his arms. Luckily his
horse had not been taken, and mounted on him, with
his drawn sword in his hand, he beat upon the prison
door. The guard fled, and Páez called for the jailer
and beat him with his sword, till he gave up the keys.
To open all the doors did not take long and when the
prisoners rushed out, most of them not even waiting
to have their manacles unlocked, Páez went to the
house in which the women were confined, and battered
down the door. So much enraged he was, that he
resolved to follow Puy and introducing himself into
his ranks, revenge himself upon him.

However Puy had got too good a start and in the
morning at the River Paguey, Páez encountered a

royalist lieutenant, Diego Ramirez, and rode along with him. At first, so furious he was that he intended to have murdered him. Better feelings luckily got the better of his rage, and the two men rode on an hour or two, Ramirez never knowing what an escape he had. When Páez got to Canaguá, where his house was, he found the town deserted, with the exception of a few families. His sister overjoyed to see him, was preparing breakfast for his brother and Ramirez when to his astonishment, the Spaniard Escutarol, and another Spaniard came to the door. When they saw Páez they were astonished at the sight of him, for they imagined he had been butchered with the other prisoners. All the four breakfasted amicably. As the two Spaniards were preparing to follow Puy in his retreat, and had no money, they asked Páez to assist them. All that he had was sixty dollars, fifty nine of them he gave to the two Spaniards, and when Ramirez told him that he had not a halfpenny, he gave him the last dollar, apologising for having nothing more upon him. The scene was typical of South America where in those far off days, money counted for so little, and though brutality was rife, a sort of comradeship as between man and man, was sure to manifest itself occasionally during the bloody strife. Páez once more found himself quite alone upon the Llanos. His horse was tired and the first thing was to provide himself with a fresh animal. Not far from Canaguá he had a rancho. There he changed horses; but his adventures were not finished, for on arriving at his house, five soldiers from the army General Yañez commanded, came out and seized his reins. They asked him several questions to which he answered as a man in his position answers, giving a false name and saying his intention was to join the royalists. The men were not deceived, and told him to give up his arms, as they intended to make a prisoner of him.

" I am resolved," said Páez, " not to give up my arms whilst I have breath in me." The soldiers who apparently had but little love of fighting, at once desisted, and asked him where they could get a meal. Probably none of them were Spaniards, but Venezuelan royalists. Their leader was a young man called Rafael Toro and as they talked, Páez and he struck up a friendship. Conviction, at that time, probably sat but lightly on the young leader, for upon Páez telling him he was a captain in the patriot army, and just outside the town had left his company, Toro called out " Long live the republic," so sturdily, that Páez had to caution him, and ask what his companions would think on hearing such a cry. " My men," said Toro, " will do just as I order them." So at once Páez found himself at the head of the little band of men, who but an hour ago had been his enemies. Next day, no soldiers having appeared Toro told Páez that he was sure that no such company existed, but as he had given him his word to join him and to serve the Patriots he would not break it, but on condition that they at once set out towards Barinas, to try and find recruits. Páez of course was willing, and as they rode along, in every hamlet a man or two came out and joined them, so that upon arrival at Barinas Páez had quite a company behind him. The citizens who seem to have passed from one side to the other without much difficulty, wished to name Páez governor. He told them that it was impossible to hold the town against the forces that would soon be sent against them, advised them to be quiet for the present and promised them his aid, in better circumstances.

As it turned out, Toro had had a good idea in coming to Barinas, for on the very night they had started out for Canaguá, Major Miguel Mendino with a strong troop of cavalry had passed by looking out for Páez, and swearing that he would kill him instantly if he could

come upon him. Horses in warfare on the Llanos are
the first element of war, and Páez and his little company were poorly mounted, so with seven of his men
he went to La Calzada, the Hato where he had served
his rude apprenticeship, to get fresh horses for his men.
Páez felt that it would not be safe to sleep at La
Calzada so with the horses that he had selected, he
went and camped upon the plain. It was well for him
that the idea had occurred to him, for just before the
dawn, Major Mendino and his men appeared before
the house. The bird had flown however, and a girl
who was washing clothes, of course knew nothing except
that Páez and his men had slept upon the plain. Toro
and his companions who did not know they were in
danger, wanted to drive the horses back to La Calzada,
where they could catch them in the corrals and begin
breaking them. At that time on the Llanos horses were
plentiful, but he who wanted one had first to break it in
and make it serviceable. Páez had chosen in his mind
some place or other, either beside a marsh or near the
river bank, against which the horses could be easily
held back for him to lasso them. Close to the place
there grew a solitary tree, into which Páez climbed,
and as his followers drove the horses underneath the
boughs he lassoed them with ease.

Those that he lassoed could not have been unbroken
animals, for his men saddled and mounted them, without difficulty. As they were getting ready for a start
one of his men observed a troop of cavalry, standing
already armed at the edge of a little wood known as
" La Mata* de Leon " ready to charge upon them.
As they were few in number, and had between them
only one musket and three lances, with which to face

* The knots of woods, generally composed of Moriche palms, that dot
the Llanos like islands, are known as Matas. Most of them have names,
such as La Mata del Leon, La Mata del Tigre, La Mata de Los Zamuros,
La Mata de San Juan, etc.

forty men, well armed and mounted, all they could do was ride. They rode for life, the cavalry firing occasionally, but without killing anyone. Arrived upon the banks of the Cajaro, they all plunged into it, in spite of alligators, electric eels and the caribes, that they dreaded more than either of them. Páez crossed last, and though the bullets whistled round his head, he gained the other bank in safety. The enemy not caring for so desperate* a swim did not pursue them, and Páez and his men, took the way towards Barinas, on their newly caught colts, that they had an opportunity to prove so thoroughly. One more adventure still was in store for him before he reached the town. His horse that up to that time had borne him gallantly, began to tremble violently, and only could advance at a slow walk dragging its feet behind him. Had it occurred upon the other side of the Cajaro, Páez would not have lived to write his Memoirs, but luckily it ended happily. Seeing a negro coming on the road towards him, riding a fine horse, he let him come up close to him. Then springing from his horse, his sword in his hand he seized the negro's bridle. The negro taken by surprise got off his horse without a word, and Páez mounted it. As they rode on towards Barinas laughing at their last adventures, they saw a group of men, pursuing them. At their head rode the negro on the horse Paéz had left behind him, for it had soon

---

* His escape is a parallel to the escape of Kinmount Willie, in the Border Ballads, from the Castle of Carlisle and his swimming the Eden on horseback with the exception that Willie the Kinmount was fettered.

> " Buccleugh has turned to Eden Water
> Even where it flowed frae bank to brim,
> And he has plunged in with all his band
> And safely swam them through the stream.
> All sore astonished stood Lord Scroope :
> He stood as still as rock of stane :
> He scarcely dared to turn his eyes
> Where through the water they had gane."

regained its strength and spirit, having apparently only been chilled, by swimming after a hard ride. The troop of horsemen turned out to be some neighbouring proprietors, who when they saw the incident of the negro and his horse, had taken Páez and his friends for bandits, and seeing they were few in number, wished to capture them. They welcomed Páez and his men, for they were friends of his, and took him and his followers back to their houses, where they entertained them royally.

Such was guerrilla warfare in those days. Republicans and Royalists alike butchering their prisoners conscientiously, salving their consciences by yelling " Liberty " or " Loyalty."

CHAPTER IV

WHILST Páez was perfecting himself in the Llanero guerrilla warfare, in which he rose to be so great a master, the struggle for independence under the leadership of the great Bolivar was gradually becoming more embittered every day. The Spanish government, though at the time but a mere rump in Cadiz, for the rest of the country was overrun by the French, and Joseph Bonaparte, whom the Spaniards called Pepe Botellas,* was enthroned in Madrid, was still as autocratic and as determined not to grant self government to the colonies, as in the days when Spain was really a great power.

The government of Cadiz not content with one great war against Napoleon for its own independence, determined to put out a supreme effort to stifle the revolt in Venezuela, an enterprise that needed greater resources than Spain possessed at that time, harassed as she was by war on her own territory.

The forces she disposed of were but small, but then the entire population of Venezuela at the time, according to Humboldt's calculations, was but 800,000. Although the forces on either side were small, for Spain never had more than 10,000 soldiers in the field, and the army of the patriots never could have much exceeded that number, the issues at stake were great. The massing of huge armies does not invariably mean that the prize for which they fight is in proportion to their

---

*Joe Bottles. A calumny was set about that he drank, hence the name. He was, however, a very sober man.

size. In Venezuela, the result of the struggle, meant the freeing, not only of 800,000 people, but the independence of enormous territories, so vast, that given the state of decadence into which Spain had fallen, they were left almost without government at all, at least, so far as the mother country was concerned.

During the year 1812, after the first successes of the patriots and the establishment of the first republic of Venezuela that only lasted from July 1811 to July 1812, a strong royalist reaction set in. A native of the Canary Islands one Don Juan Diaz Florez a rich merchant of Caracas instigated a royalist revolt. He and sixteen of his followers were taken prisoners and executed. The next revolt occurred in the city of Valencia. The Marques del Toro marched against the revolting royalists, but was defeated, and General Miranda, only reduced the city to obedience after a fierce battle in which he lost eight hundred killed and more than a thousand wounded.

The position was extremely perilous for the patriots at this juncture, for the whole country was passing through one of those moments of reaction, so frequent in all revolutionary wars. An Indian, Reyes Vargas raised the standard of revolt in Siquisiqui and the Governor of Coro, General Ceballos, detached Domingo Monteverde with a force to help him against the patriots. Domingo Monteverde, whose name is execrated as a blood-thirsty tyrant in Venezuela was a sailor, and had come out to Venezuela in command of a ship of war. Though not a man of education, he was both bold, able and ambitious, but without scruples of whatever nature. He at once joined up with Reyes Vargas, and without orders from his chief, Ceballos, attacked the town of Carora, took it and sacked it thoroughly.

Then, taking advantage of an earthquake that laid the

towns of Caracas, Barquisimeto, Merida and others, almost in ruins, he marched on Barquisimeto, from which most of the inhabitants had fled, and found sufficient arms and ammunition undestroyed by the earthquake, to equip a formidable force.

He then marched on, leaving a trail of blood and ruin and occupied Valencia, the second city of the country. The provinces of Merida and Trujillo then declared themselves in favour of the king. Only in the capital itself was the cause of the revolution flourishing. To save the republic the National Congress nominated General Miranda military dictator.

Francisco de Miranda was born in Caracas in 1750. Before the rise to fame of the illustrious Simon Bolivar, he was without doubt the most considerable man that Venezuela had produced. At the age of seventeen he was sent to Spain, where he entered the army, and served in the expedition to Algiers, and afterwards in the expeditions to New Orleans and Florida. When the war was over, he went to France, entered the army and took part with Lafayette in the war for independence of the United States. What he saw there and the ideas he imbibed, induced him to undertake the emancipation of his own country. With this ideal before him, he visited several of the courts of Europe and was received with sympathy.

In 1790, he was in London and presented Pitt with a plan for the formation of a South American Empire. Having by this time risen to the rank of General of Brigade in the French army, he served with much distinction under Dumouriez. His name was one of those placed on the Arc de l'Etoile, amongst those of the three hundred and eighty-five, judged worthy of the honour by the National Assembly. This was the man to whom the patriots of Venezuela turned in their extremity. At that time he was a national hero, tall, handsome and soldier-like in his appearance. He had passed his life in arms.

Of all the revolutionary chiefs, he alone had handled disciplined soldiers. This experience was to prove one of the causes of his failure. Accustomed as he was to the well equipped and well armed armies of both France and Spain, when he found himself at the head of an army, badly fed, ignorant of all military life, and quite impatient of all discipline, who moreover were accustomed to desert if they found service irksome, he seems to have despaired of making headway against the military force of Spain. At first he had considerable success. Having established his headquarters in Valencia he twice repelled, victoriously, determined attacks made by Monteverde, who for all that did not abandon the siege. After three months of fighting Miranda was forced back to a position near a place called La Victoria.

Just at that moment news reached him that Caracas was in danger owing to a revolt of the negroes under a partisan called Curiepe, set on it is said by the chief merchants of the place, and some of the rich cattle-farmers. As at that time there were about sixty-two thousand slaves in Venezuela,* forty-two thousand of whom were in the province of Caracas, the danger was not slight. Luckily the revolt had little consequences; but the unrest in Merida and Trujillo, the miserable state of the patriots' finances, and above all the loss of Puerto Cabello the best port of the republic through the treachery of Rafael Hermoso and Francisco Hernandez Vinoni all contributed to make Miranda throw up his cards. So on the 12th of July, 1812, Miranda capitulated to Monteverde, and the first republic fell.

Then came a black page in the life of Bolivar.

*Historia de Venezuela por H.N.M. Escuelas Cristianas, Caracas 1927, page 76.

Miranda had arranged to go on board the *Sapho*, a vessel that was in the port and just about to sail for La Guaira, at which place he hoped to join the patriots. Unluckily for him, a rich English merchant had entrusted twenty thousand dollars to the captain. The rumour got about that it was the price of Miranda's treachery. Bolivar unfortunately listened to it, and thinking that Miranda was a traitor to the cause, had him arrested on arrival in La Guaira and given up to the royalist authorities. They had him sent to Puerto Rico, and from thence to Spain. There he was confined in the Castle of the Seven Towers,* at the arsenal of La Carraca in the Bay of Cadiz. Shamefully treated, and kept in chains, he died in 1816.

Thus perished miserably the initiator of the first republic in Venezuela, a man to whom his country lay under a heavy debt, and who since 1806 had never ceased from working to free his native land. His first attempt was made from England where he had fixed his residence.

A wealthy shipowner, Mr. Samuel Ogden, fitted out an expedition under Miranda's command. He placed two hundred men at his disposal, and in three vessels, the *Leander*, the *Bacchus* and the *Bee* he put aboard arms and munitions sufficient to equip a considerable force. The expedition arrived safely at a port called Ocumare, with Miranda in the *Leander* a small corvette. As they were proceeding to disembark the arms, two Spanish men of war, the *Argus* and the *Coloso* suddenly appeared. After a smart action, the *Bacchus* and the *Bee* were taken, and the *Leander*, badly damaged, had to put to sea. Ten of the prisoners were at once executed, and a price of thirty thousand dollars put on Miranda's head.

In 1806, he made a second venture, having obtained

*El Castillo de Las Siete Torres.

from Admiral Cochrane,* the loan of fifteen ships. With these he landed, sailing from Trinidad, to which island he had retired after his first failure, and landing at La Vela de Coro took the port and forced the royalist forces to retire. Finding but little sympathy amongst the people, who did not rise to help him, as he expected they would do, he was forced to re-embark.

He returned to England, and after much persuasion the British Government consented to fit out an expedition for Venezuela with General Wellesley in command.

His usual ill luck dogged him. Shortly before the expedition was to have set out, the British Government changed its destination, and it was sent to Portugal, to fight against the French.

What might have been had it but landed in Venezuela under Sir Arthur Wellesley, is difficult to say. Probably instead of dying miserably in La Carraca, lying on straw, and deprived almost of the necessaries of life, Miranda would have occupied the place, in the affections of the Venezuelans, that Bolivar holds to-day.

With varying fortunes the war dragged on during the years 1812 and 1813. Little by little Bolivar made his name after having been forced to flee for refuge to Colombia. There he obtained command of a small army, recrossed the Venezuelan frontier, and defeated the Spanish General Correa at Cúenca. On the 6th of August, he triumphantly re-entered his native town Caracas, amidst the applause and acclamation of the citizens. On the 8th of August, 1813, he announced the re-establishment of the republic.

After a brief campaign in which at Las Trincheras, he forced Monteverde to shut himself up in Puerto Cabello, Bolivar came back to the capital. There on the 14th of October the municipality conferred on him the title of Liberator of Venezuela. This title of Liberator, per-

*Afterwards Lord Dundonald.

haps the most glorious that mankind has in its power to bestow on anyone, he bore with honour, till his death, crossing the Andes, to liberate Peru, and threading the passes of the mountains to free Bogotá.

Upon the seaboard and in Caracas, the patriot cause was popular, but in the Llanos, the wild Llaneros who afterwards with Páez did so much to free their country, were still royalists. Most probably they hardly understood what was really taking place, or how much was at stake. Lost in their solitudes, far from the world, and perfectly content with the wild life they led, the only life in their esteem fit for a free man, they looked upon the struggle as something quite outside their purview. Still there were great potentialities in these wild horsemen, so remote from the world, who had preserved some of the virtues and most of the defects of barbarism. The hope of plunder, and a wild wandering life was certain to appeal to them. All that they wanted was a leader to unite them and wield together what till that time had been a negligible quantity, dispersed about the plains, living like Arabs, though without the tribal system, to make them formidable. Páez was still an unknown subaltern. His time had not arrived; but the remarkable adventurer who first showed what the Llaneros could achieve, if once they had a leader, blazed the trail for him.

Most cruel and bloodthirsty men have had some redeeming streak, to mitigate their crimes. José Tomas Rodriguez Boves does not seem to have had any, except personal bravery. Born at Oviedo in 1783, he studied in the naval college of Gijon. His first voyage was to Venezuela on board a smuggling vessel in the character of mate. Caught redhanded he was condemned to eight years penal servitude in Puerto Cabello. This penalty was commuted to exile in the town of Calabozo.

This place although it had a bishop and a cathedral

and was the seat in those days of a governor, could not have been a pleasant residence. Its ardent climate, and alternating periods of droughts and floods; its distance from the outside world and lack of communications, made it a safe place enough to which to send criminals or political offenders.

Boves however was no ordinary man. Instead of giving way to despair, taking to drink, or loafing about the sandy streets, after having passed the hot hours of the day stretched in his hammock, smoking and killing the mosquitoes, whilst he cursed his fate, he turned store keeper.

His business took him to the various little towns and hamlets in the Llanos. He visited the cattle farms, buying up what are called in Spanish " fruits of the country," such as cheeses, hides, feathers and furs. No doubt in the long journeys that he took he learned to ride, and thus became the consummate horseman that his future exploits proved him. But he learned more than horsemanship. Somehow or other, he became popular with the Llaneros, who had seen in him probably only the good natured trader, for up to that time he had not manifested his real nature.

A contemporary writer* thus describes him. " Boves had fair hair, an enormous head, large, staring blue eyes, and broad, flat forehead, a thin beard and a white skin; he was of middle height, capable of undergoing extraordinary fatigue; active, bold, fearless, impetuous, rash, astute, hungry for power, cruel and sanguinary."

Happening to be in Caracas in April, 1810, he threw himself with enthusiasm, although a Spaniard, into the revolutionary movement, and soon attained the rank of captain. Whilst serving under the orders of Juan Escalona, that officer abused and struck him when he refused

---

*Quoted in La Historia de Venzuela by H.N.M., page 127. The name of the author is not given.

to do the duty of a common soldier. Boves was not a man to stand such treatment, and at once deserted, and joined the royalists under Monteverde, who named him ensign.

He soon rose to be a captain with the royalists. In 1813 the Spanish general Cajigal evacuated the town of Barcelona, and retreated into Guayana, leaving two of his officers, Boves and Morales, his ammunition and his arms. Boves, taking advantage of his knowledge of the Llaneros and their ways, retired into the Llanos, and soon raised a large army, partly by promising them the plunder of the towns, and afterwards by force.

Boves though a bloodthirsty wretch untouched by any human feeling, was a born leader. He called the force that he had raised the Infernal Legion, and certainly it merited the name. At the same time another Spaniard, Yañez by name, raised a second army of Llaneros in the plains of the Apure. These two renegades set out upon a campaign of bloodshed and of cruelty. Their followers avid for plunder needed no instigation to commit the most inhuman crimes.

Bolivar who had his hands full and had suffered several reverses, was obliged to try and stem the advancing tide of savagery. It must have been a pang to him to know that these fierce warriors who should have been fighting by his side, were his own countrymen. However at that time he had never visited the Llanos which were probably as little known in those days to the majority of Venezuelans as the Steppes of Asia.

He chose, curiously enough, another Spaniard, Campo Elias, to attack Boves. This partisan who was serving with the patriots inflicted a disastrous defeat on Boves in October, 1813, at a place known as La Sabana de Mosquitero. Boves on this occasion escaped with only sixteen followers. Campo Elias, who seems to have been no whit less bloodthirsty than Boves, entered the

DON PABLO MORILLO
Commander-in-Chief of the Royalist Forces in Venezuela.
(This picture is taken from El General Don Pablo Morillo por
Augusto C. de Santiago y Gadea. Madrid, 1911.)

little town of Calabozo in triumph. To celebrate his victory he cut the throats of the fourth part of the inhabitants. This act of terrorism exasperated the Llaneros who flocked in hundreds to the ranks of Boves, burning for revenge. Finding himself at the head of an army of seven thousand men, Boves at once marched upon Ocumare, and having taken it murdered the greater part of the population, who had taken refuge in a church. Unluckily no one has preserved any account of what his army looked like, but it must have resembled a horde of Tartars, or an invasion of the Pampa Indians in the south of the province of Buenos Aires, fifty years ago. These invasions, known as Malones, were a sight once seen, never to be forgotten.

For hours before the invading Indians actually appeared, troops of wild horses and of cattle, herds of deer and bands of ostriches, preceded them, fleeing as before a prairie fire. Then in the distance arose a cloud of dust. As it came nearer, through it flashed the heads of the lances, twenty feet in length, the Indians carried. They usually rode barebacked or on a sheepskin, yelling and striking their hands upon their mouths. This made their yells sharper and like the howling of a pack of wolves. Each Indian led a spare horse, trained to run head to head with his companion, on the offside. Their long coarse hair hung on their shoulders, only confined about the forehead by a handkerchief or a strip of hide. Around their bodies, smeared with ostrich grease, they carried three or four pairs of bolas, known to the Gauchos as Las Tres Marias.* With these Three Maries, at fifty yards, there was no pardon as the Gauchos said, that is they hardly ever failed to entangle the hind legs of a horse or the long neck of the Pampa ostrich, or to break in a Christian's skull, if one of the three balls should chance to light on it.

*The three stars in Orion were also called Las Tres Marias.

F

The Indians always rode in a great semicircle, with the chief warriors, who now and then had silver-mounted saddles and bridles heavily adorned with silver, in the middle. They used to pass so rapidly that it seemed like a dream. The looker on who generally sheltered himself in a thicket of tall Pampa grass, holding his horse, whose head was muffled in a poncho or a saddle-cloth to prevent him neighing, fast by the bridle, ready to spring into the saddle, hardly could believe that in a moment death had passed so near to him. The invaders pitilessly lanced everyone they met, sparing alone the girls they used to carry off into the "inside country,"* mounted before them on their horses' necks.

A very little ditch before a house usually made the dwellers in it safe, unless the Indians could set the thatch on fire with bunches of dried grass tied to the heads of their long spears, as they never got off their horses until a victory was won.

On their retreat from an invasion they drove before them herds of cattle and of horses, and left behind a trail of ruin and of blood. In the same cloud of dust in which they had appeared, they vanished, their horses disappearing first and then the riders' heads. Lastly the tips of their long lances glittered for a moment in the sun, then dipped out of sight, just as the topsails of a sailing ship flutter before they sink into the sea.

The Llaneros who followed Boves must have been not unlike the Pampa Indians in their appearance and accoutrements. In those days in the Llanos saddles were a luxury, and the greater part of the Llaneros rode barebacked from necessity. Possibly this was the reason that made them tie their lazos to their horses' tails, although indeed the practice originally came from

*Tierra Adentro. Inside country. The Indian territory was always thus described.

Spain.* Like the Pampa Indian a piece of hide fastened round the lower jaw took the place of a bit. The man who had a headstall of plaited† horsehair thought himself fortunate. The Llanos never having produced anything like the quantity of horses that the mild climate and perennial grasses of the Argentine fostered in such extraordinary numbers, the invasions of the followers of Boves could not possibly have been so rapid as those of the Indians. The ground was rougher and more broken up by rivers, the climate rigorous, and grass and water not always to be had, as on the Pampa. The universal amble of the Llanero horses was of necessity much slower than the Pampa gallop. Still Boves made extraordinary marches, in spite of all the difficulties.

The difference between his raids and those of the South Pampa was that Boves had to pay his troops by offering them the plunder of the towns. Such plunder would have been worthless to the Pampa Indians, who only cared for cattle, sheep and mares. Indians and the Llaneros under Boves, alike, were cruel and bloodthirsty. The Indians killed just as a tiger kills its prey, because he is a tiger. Boves on the contrary had the cold thought-out lust for cruelty and blood that usually is found only in renegades and those who have forsaken civilization and reverted back to barbarism.

After his first victory at La Puerta, Boves swept onwards like a prairie fire, destroying anything he passed by, and murdering all the prisoners that he took.‡ Curiously enough, for he was a white man himself on all four sides, he declared war to the death upon all whites.

---

*See Chapter II.

†This headstall of horsehair is still used on the Llanos, and is called a Falseta.

‡" Conservaba en medio de las matanzas su carácter indomable y fiero de marino (sic) y pasaba sin detenerse a ver como expiraban sus victimas."
Efermerides Columbianas
Luis Gonzaga.

His followers, who were generally of mixed blood, mestizos or mulatos, and sometimes zambos, were naturally delighted when he told them that all the property of the whites* would be adjudged to them after the victory. As a foretaste of this inhuman policy he murdered eighty-seven whites in Calabozo. In Cumana, two hundred more. In Araguá, two thousand who had taken refuge in a church. With varying fortunes this human tiger carried on war to the knife, always the first and foremost in the fight, for his worst enemy never accused him of any lack of courage.

What were his ultimate objects is difficult to say, for even if the royalists had been victorious in the struggle, the first thing that they must have done was to chastise and execute him, and he well knew that if the patriots gained the day there was no pardon for him. He may have dreamed of course of making himself independent of both parties and reigning in the Llanos as a king, or tiger patriarch.

After having inflicted a defeat upon Bolivar in the second battle of La Puerta, where the patriots lost over a thousand men, many of their chief officers and nearly all their ammunition, Boves detached his second in command to march upon Caracas. He himself attacked Valencia. The garrison under a brave officer, Juan Escalona, resisted until food and ammunition were exhausted and then capitulated on honourable terms. A solemn mass was celebrated on an open space between the armies as a sign that the conditions of the capitulation would be faithfully observed. Hardly had the mass finished when Boves murdered Doctor Espejo, the civil governor of the city and his chief officers. Bolivar had rarely experienced so severe a blow as that Boves inflicted

*Mulato—Child of white and negro.
Mestizo—White and Indian.
Zambo—Indian and negro.

on him. He found himself obliged to leave the capital
and try to raise fresh troops in the east province.* So
much was Boves dreaded that the greater portion of the
citizens followed the Liberator in his retreat. Most of
them died upon the road of hardships and the want of
food.†

The Liberator's misfortunes were not over, for on the
18th of August, 1814, Morales, Boves' second in command, attacked him near Barcelona with a strong force
of his Llaneros and routed him again. Luckily the
sands were nearly running out of the glass, and in
December of the same year, in the hour of victory, Boves
was slain. He died as he had lived, just as a wild boar
dies, fighting to the last. As he was rallying his men to
lead them on to the supreme attack against the weaken-
ing patriots, his horse suddenly reared with him and he
received a lance wound in the chest that stretched him
dead upon the field.‡ His lieutenant, Morales, inherited
the command and proved himself a worthy successor of
his chief. Seven of the royalist officers not having wished
to recognise his leadership he promptly executed them
and sent their heads fried in oil to Caracas. He then
fell like a thunderbolt upon the town of Maturin, where
the remains of the patriot army was attempting to re-

---

*El Oriente. In it are situated the towns of Cumaná, Barcelona, and
Carúpano.

†The episode has taken a great hold of popular imagination in Venezuela, and a fine picture exists of it by Michelena. In it, Bolivar, wrapped
in a black cloak, with his hat pulled down over his face, rides a white
horse in a storm of rain. After him stream the fugitives down a mountain
path.

‡ Su caballo indocil a la voz y el freno se encabritó." The house that
Boves occupied in Caracas still stands. It is a small old Spanish house at
the outskirts of the town close to the Foundling Hospital. Low-eaved
and with iron gratings (rejas) to the windows, it is a good example of
colonial architecture. Below the house runs the little river Catocho, that
flows into the Guaire. It is spanned by a curious, old, high-arched
bridge, that has a tablet set into the wall, stating it was built in the reign of
Charles III. From the balcony of the house, tradition says, Boves used to
view the execution of his prisoners.

organise, and destroyed them utterly. With these
disasters the patriot resistance for the time was over, and
the fall of the second republic consummated. The
Spaniards once again were masters of nearly the whole
territory.

CHAPTER V

In 1815 Spain made its final effort to reduce Venezuela once more to its authority. Ferdinand VII had ascended the Spanish throne, after Napoleon's defeat at Waterloo. Spain, freed from the yoke of the French, was able once again to turn her eyes towards America.

A powerful expedition composed of sixty ships, carrying about ten thousand men, with arms and ammunition to equip any force of royalists that might be raised in Venezuela, was despatched under the command of General Pablo Morillo. Morillo had served with distinction under Wellington, against the French, and was well known for his skill and energy. Páez and he were destined to fight a long duel in the Llanos. Both men were brave to a fault, ruthless and energetic, and neither of them at that time held human life dearer than the butt end of a smoked out cigar.

Morillo came out with supreme powers, under the title of " Pacifier* of the Mainland."

He was one of the Pacificators who make a desert and then call it peace. His first act after having assumed the governor generalship was to offer a free pardon to all those who cared to lay down their arms. Then he imposed a forced loan of two hundred thousand dollars on the capital.† Lastly he named one Salvador Moxo chief of a permanent court martial to judge all those accused of participation in the revolt. Judge, naturally meant condemn, for many of the leaders of the rebellion

---

*Pacificador de Tierra Firme.

†Caracas. The city of Caracas took its name from the Indian tribe of Los Caracas, who had their chief village, or " Rancheria," there.

73

were men of property, and after condemnation, confiscation of their estates followed as a natural corollary. All tribunals of the nature of that Morillo set up take little notice of poor rebels. They fly at higher game. Your indigent revolutionary may now and then be worth a cartridge, but rarely a legal trial.

The Spanish Inquisition, that persecuted with fervour the Moriscos and the Jews, ignored the Gypsies,* for they were not worth prosecuting.

Whilst Morillo was besieging Cartagena and his lieutenant, Juan Gabazo was attacking the patriots in the isle of Margarita, up on the Llanos del Apure, in the State of Guarico and the plains of Barcelona certain revolutionary leaders still held out at the head of guerilla bands. These were the brothers Monágas, one of whom became a rival later on of Páez for the presidency, Manuel Cedeño and Francisco Olmeda. Páez took service in the beginning of the year 1814 under a patriot commander, Ramon Garcia de Sena, who made him leader of his cavalry. From that time till full independence was achieved, Páez was first and foremost in the fight. The incidents of the campaign of the year 1814 read like a page from Malory, Froissart, or Monstrelet.

Men fight hand to hand, defy one another before their followers, prisoners are butchered in cold blood; hair-breadth escapes from imminent death abound in every page. No one would think in reading of the exploits of Páez, Bolivar, Sucre and the other paladins, that the fate of enormous territories was at stake. Still it was the case, and countries several times as large as France or Spain, or as the two joined together, depended on the issue of a battle between three or four thousand infantry and a horde of wild Llanero cavalry.

Thus General Arismendi reconquered the great island of Margarita with a force that at the beginning only

* " Pobre como cuerpo de gitano," is a Spanish saying.

counted fifty men, who had as their sole armament three muskets and a hundred and twenty cartridges.*

Páez very soon was disgusted with Garcia de Sena, who seems to have been, if not a traitor at least lukewarm to the causes. He took service under another chief, whom he refers to as Governor Paredes. This chieftain offered him a command of cavalry, but Páez who was riding a good horse of his own brand that he had come across in a place called Egido, as he says in his " Memorias," did not think they were well enough mounted to be of service against the Goths.† He therefore transferred himself and his good horse to another better mounted squadron under Captain Antonio Rangel.

The Italian condottieri and the partizans during the Thirty Years War changed sides with great impartiality, but it was usually from hope of gain.

It was reserved to Páez and his kind to change their regiments because they thought their horses would be put out of countenance by being called up to associate with lean, spavined hacks. The reason seems quite as good and as cogent as any gentleman is obliged to offer his superior officer. It certainly made warfare more amusing, if no whit less bloodthirsty.

Rangel, who was an enterprising man, set out at once against the Goths, and came up with them at a place called Bailadores. Their scouts exchanged a few shots, and Rangel retired towards the hills. Páez, who troubled little enough about discipline, remained behind alone. Coming up with the enemy in a place where

* Arismendi . . . reuñió un grupo de hombres, y el 15 de noviembre de 1815 entró en campaña, con solo 50 hombres, tres fusiles, 120 cartuchos : se apoderaron sucesivamente de toda la isla y redujó a los realistas al solo el castillo de Santa Rosa. Page 136, Historia de Venezuela, por H. N. M. Caracas.

† Los Godos. Páez always refers to the Spaniards as " Godos." Thus history repeats itself, for between Boches and Godos there is not much to choose. Godos means Goths. The Spaniards called the patriots, Chocutos, that is Croppies, from their shaven heads.

they were obliged to march in single file, he shouted, "Viva La Patria," several times in a loud voice. At every shout he changed his tone, so that the enemy thought they were attacked by a detachment. Then Páez, on his own good horse, charged them and killed a sergeant who was covering their retreat. Seeing the sergeant fall the rest fled, throwing down their arms and leaving two pieces of artillery upon the field. One man alone stood bravely, and he and Páez, after the fashion of the Homeric heroes, fought a duel to the death.

The one man who stood firm was a certain José Maria Sanchez, a paladin worthy to contend with Páez or any other champion on the patriots' side. Sanchez was renowned for his great strength. The legend ran that in a skirmish near the town of Lagunillas that when a field piece had been dismantled Sanchez had shouldered it as easily as most men would a musket and saved it from the foe. These well matched paladins, after defying one another after the fashion of Hector and Achilles, joined in mutual strife. Both were on horseback and both were Llaneros, that is, men to whom a horse was part of their existence.

Sanchez had no weapons but a short gun, that he had discharged. Páez was armed with the Llanero lance, some ten feet long and made of the Alvarico palm.* The lance was the especial arm of the Llaneros, that they all knew how to wield from their youth upwards from having practised with the cattle goad,† often a mere cane hardened in the fire, with a few rings fastened to the end by a strip of hide, whose rattle terrified the half wild cattle and made them easier to drive. In battle the Llaneros knotted their reins short and dropped them on their horses' necks, to have both hands at liberty to wield the lance.

* Onocarpus, Cubarro.
† Garrocha.

After a thrust or two Sanchez, seeing he had no chance armed as he was with but an empty gun, relying on his strength, seized the lance that Páez thrust at him with both his hands. Páez slipped off his horse and by a violent effort wrenched his lance free and gave his enemy a mortal wound that stretched him on the ground. Páez relates what follows so naïvely and so originally that to paraphrase* it would be but to disfigure what he says.

"Seeing him stretched upon the ground I tried to take off a handsome cartridge belt that he wore round his waist, and as he broke out into ill-considered words not fitting for the situation in which he found himself, I began to exhort him to make a Christian ending, and reciting the Creed aloud to stimulate him to repeat it. Luckily for me, I looked down by accident and saw that instead of accompanying me in my prayers he had half drawn the dagger that he carried in his belt.

"I confess my charity was completely chilled,† and as my indignation did not allow me to waste more time as to my adversary's future destiny, I freed him from the rage which was choking him, even more than the blood he was losing, with a lance thrust."

A curious episode, well told, forty or more years after the event. Certainly hypocrisy was not a vice that could be laid to the account of Páez. Still sympathy goes out to Sanchez, for to be wounded to the death and then "stimulated"† to repeat the creed by the man whose hand had dealt the mortal blow is enough to provoke a saint.

In a note on the same page (78), Páez says, "After the encounter with Sanchez I pursued the enemy, took prisoners eight artillerymen, a flag and two small

* "Memorias del General Páez," p. 78.
† Se amortiguó.
‡ Yo rezaba el credo en voz alta para estimularle á repetirlo.

cannons; one of these was the gift of a lady of the town of Merida, and was said to be the same that Sanchez had carried on his back at Lagunillas. Afterwards we twice lost this gun and then regained it twice."

After the affair of Sanchez, which not unnaturally gained Páez great notoriety, he joined a guerilla force under a General Urdaneta, that was operating in the country about Merida, a town in the Andean provinces.

Urdaneta finding himself hard pushed, resolved to retire into New Granada,* but Páez did not follow him, for the general of the cavalry, Chavez by name, wanted to take his horse away and give it to another man to ride. "I naturally resisted this injustice," Páez says, "but eventually complied from pure military obedience."† Obedience not being one of the chief virtues of his character, it is possible that Páez yielded up his horse under compulsion rather than from any fantastic ideas of discipline.

"Disgusted, nevertheless," he left Urdaneta's army and put into execution a scheme that he had long been pondering on. It was no less than to recross the Andes to the plains of Casanare and Apure, a journey that most men would not have affronted, as Páez did, almost alone, on foot, and with his wife and child. So set upon his project was he that he refused an offer from General Garcia Rivera before he started to command a regiment of cavalry.

The project Páez had in view seemed to all reasonable men not the least likely of success. Some of his friends told him he must be mad to think that the Llaneros, who under Boves, Yañez and Ceballos had shown themselves such fierce defenders of the monarchy, could be persuaded to turn round suddenly and espouse the other side.

---

* Now the republic of Colombia.

† " . . . por pura obediencia militar."

Moreover Páez at the time was a young man, comparatively unknown, or at least known but for his personal prowess in guerilla warfare. After a thousand perils and difficulties he arrived at Pore, the capital of the plains of Casanare. These plains, wilder and still more sparsely inhabited than those of the Apure, stretched out for several hundred miles along the Orinoco and the Meta. At the time of the war of indpendence, great troops of semi-feral cattle and even wilder horses roamed over them in prodigious numbers. The surface of the plains, as level as the ocean, was broken here and there by islets of Moriche palms, the only trees that grew upon them throughout their whole extent. Deep streams unmarked on any map intersected them, making them difficult to cross at any time, and quite impossible except in canoes during the rains. Páez had the advantage of knowing the Llanos thoroughly, and how to treat the wild inhabitants. Therefore his project of enlisting them to serve against the side that they had recently been serving was not so mad as it appeared to all his friends. Olmedilla, the general of the patriots, received him with great satisfaction, and in a few days Páez found himself at the head of a regiment of cavalry. His soldiers all brought their own horses and such arms as they could lay their hands upon. In an incredibly short time Olmedilla had collected a thousand volunteers. With this force he set out through the deserted plains of Lareñas, marching by night and resting all the day. Thus they avoided the terrific heat, and at the same time concealed their progress from the enemy. They crossed the Arauca swimming, carrying their saddles and their arms upon their heads. A fine wild sight it must have been, the naked men, riding their horses barebacked and making so much noise that the alligators and the other dangerous denizens of those waters were too scared to venture to attack. The electric eels, luckily for them, seldom frequent deep water, and so they all crossed safely, the few that could not swim being towed over in coracles made of bullocks' hide and fastened to a horse's tail. Their quickness on the march and the precaution they had taken in travelling by night enabled them to arrive before the town of Guasdualito at daybreak on the 29th of January (1814), without the royalists suspecting their approach.

They would have been surprised had not Olmedilla committed the imprudence of firing a cannon and sounding a ruffle on the drum. This gave the royalists time to stand to arms, and Páez found himself attacked upon two sides. The night was black* as a wolf's mouth. Páez charged home, directed only by the flashes of the guns. So furious was the charge of his wild horsemen that the enemy broke and fled, leaving more than two hundred dead upon the field and losing many prisoners. Páez, with a few of his men, pursued the fugitives up to the banks of the Apure.

Many of the fugitives took refuge in the woods, but three of their officers, Major Marchan and Captains Ricaurte and Guerrero boldly plunged into the broad swiftly-flowing stream. Páez who was well mounted followed them. Ricaurte and Guerrero safely reached the other side and disappeared into the woods. Páez, who had become as expert a swimmer† as a horseman, reached the bank before Marchan. As he emerged from the water, Páez called on him to surrender. He at once did so under promise of his life, to Páez's great surprise. Certainly a man with his horse up to the girths in water is at a disadvantage with a man upon the

* Oscura, como boca de lobo.

† No doubt his experience with Manuelote (see Chapter I) showed him the advisability of learning to swim. It is almost a necessity on the Llanos, as it is impossible to go anywhere without coming on a river. As to bridges, "Ni por pienso," as Sancho Panza has it.

Most of the Llaneros are expert swimmers, and they need to be, as half the year the Llanos are under water and they almost live in canoes.

bank. Still Páez was a man who loved a fair fight, and it is probable that had Marchan refused to give up his sword, Páez would not have taken him at a disadvantage.

The two men were both well mounted, and neither could expect help from anyone, as Marchan was a fugitive and Páez had left all his men upon the further bank. Páez received his sword and promised him his life. Then the two adversaries recrossed the river, swimming side by side.

The episode reads like something either from La Chanson de Roland or from Malory. It had been better for Marchan if he had fought it out and fallen in hot blood.

Páez was received with acclamation by his men, who had collected more than two hundred prisoners in his absence. He instantly set out to join his commander Olmedilla. This man was one of those savage partisans that revolutionary wars always throw up to disgrace humanity. When Páez joined he presented Marchan to him, saying that he had surrendered on the promise of his life. Olmedilla turned on him savagely, saying, "How dare you bring him before me, alive." Páez, who was not naturally bloodthirsty and who appears to have had from his youth upwards a great idea of loyalty to his pledged word, answered indignantly, "Because I have never turned my arms against a vanquished foe." Olmedilla instantly ordered one of his butchers, a certain Captain Rafael Maldonado, to cut off the prisoner's head.

So perished the unfortunate Marchan, after having twice in one day exposed his life by swimming the Apure with all its perils, and yet who lacked the spirit to spur his horse against Páez, and die or conquer like a man. Not content with the cold-blooded murder, Olmedilla had the other prisoners brought into a hollow square of troops and ordered his second in command, Francisco

Figueredo, to cut off all their heads. This ruffian chose two other captain-scoundrels, Juan Santiago Torres and Rafael Maldonado to help him in the task.

Páez, who did not know why the prisoners had been brought into the square, only took in what was about to happen when he saw the prisoners fall upon their knees before a crucifix* that the chaplain, Father Pardo, held in his left hand, whilst with his right he gave his blessing to them. The butchers fell to at once, and cut off four of the prisoners' heads. At the fifth, Páez could not contain himself, and rushing up checked his horse right in front of the executioners, shouted out that if they killed another man it was at the peril of their lives.

Frightened at his energetic attitude the butchers stopped their bloody work; but Figueredo haughtily turned on him, asking how he dared prevent him executing the orders of his chief. Páez now thoroughly aroused, told him that before he killed another man he would have to kill him first. Figueredo went off to consult Olmedilla; but Páez being on horseback arrived before him, and put before him in energetic terms the horror of his action and the bad effect it was sure to bring upon their cause. Olmedilla answered coldly that the lives of the prisoners were in Figueredo's hands. That ruffian said, " In that case they must all die at once." Luckily for the prisoners, all the men of the regiment Páez commanded stood by their commander, and Figueredo had to yield, not wishing to provoke a conflict in which he knew that he was bound to come off second best.

Páez in summing up the incident years afterwards in New York, where he was writing his recollections of the war, has the following. " Thus these unhappy men were saved, condemned to death by the bad heart of a Vandal, and thus good treatment made friends out of

* Un Santo Cristo.

these enemies, for nearly all of them took service under our flag and became faithful comrades in so many feats of arms, that if they were not still many of them living as witnesses, there would be a risk of it (the episode?) passing as a fable in the eyes of posterity, invented for their solace and entertainment.

" This is—I say it with intention—one of the acts of disobedience and insubordination with which my ill wishers accuse me. Insubordination towards Olmedilla and Figueredo! No; obedience even in its strictest military sense, does not oblige the soldier to change his sword into a hangman's knife; nor does war sanction the massacre of prisoners.

" Infinite thanks I give to the Almighty, that he has given me time, reason, and a good memory to relate these matters as they occurred, so that just men may pass the judgment on them they deserve."

Although the literary style that Páez writes is not devoid of that hyperbole that still clings to many of his compatriots in South America, and even in the north of that great continent, it speaks volumes for his heart. He shows his character better than the most conscientious biographer could show it for him, and he stands revealed, brave, simple, vainglorious 'tis true, but honest and kind-hearted to the core.

With such a man for a companion no Llanero need have feared to cross the Apure, though it ran brimming to the bank, certain that Páez would not have left him in the lurch if his horse happened to give out.

CHAPTER VI

By his interposition in favour of the wretched prisoners Páez had become popular with the army. His democratic manners, his skill in horsemanship and his generosity had from the first made him an outstanding figure amongst the wild irregulars who Olmedilla led, in the outlying province of Casanare. Little military skill was requisite in the operations, in which the brave, ill-disciplined bands of revolutionaries were engaged. A force, magniloquently designated as an army, rarely exceeded fifteen hundred or two thousand men. Fire-arms were scarce and ammunition scarcer. Many, perhaps the greater portion of the patriot soldiers, were armed but with a lance, and few had uniforms, not even all the officers. A picture of Páez almost at the height of his reputation represents him holding his horse, dressed as a Llanero. He has no outward visible sign of rank, and looks exactly what he was the whole of his campaigning life, a bold guerrilla chief.

In those days roads were non-existent in the provinces of Casanare and Apure, and in a campaign knowledge of frontier life and personal bravery was more important than a theoretic education in military tactics. Páez was born with a good eye for a country, and with that personal magnetism, no more to be acquired than is a sense of colour by a painter, or is style by a writer, that gives a man greater influence with his fellows than all the prestige that rank and money can bestow.

This is apparent by an incident that took place the very

morning after he had saved the prisoners. His commander, Olmedilla, gave him the charge of passing the prisoners over the Apure river. As there were more than two hundred of them and but one small canoe the operation took all night to execute.

The first thing that he heard when daylight broke was that Olmedilla was massacring seventy of the prisoners. His officers implored him once more to save the miserable men. It was too late, and the whole batch was massacred in cold blood. This action of the officers shows how highly Páez was beginning to be held. Then came an incident that gave him the opportunity to show his frontier craft.

The Spanish commander General Calzada was in considerable force, not very far from where the patriots were encamped.

Olmedilla, after the affair of the prisoners, marched to a place called Cuiloto and there, declaring he was disgusted with the patriot government, resigned his command and retired deeper into the province of Casanare. Before he left he named Figueredo, his lieutenant, commander of the little army.

This Figueredo, the same who had shown himself so eager to massacre the prisoners, seems to have been a man unused to warfare on the frontier, a warfare in which cavalry played so great a part. He camped his men upon the bank of the Cuiloto river and sent the horses out to graze upon a plain close to the enemy. Páez and the other officers who had been brought up on the plains at once perceived the danger. The enemy had only to send out a few well mounted men, stampede the horses, and the whole patriot force would have been left afoot. To be afoot upon the Llanos meant to be reduced to immobility. Páez and the other officers waited on Figueredo to remonstrate with him. They did not care particularly for the commission, for they

knew Figueredo was a hard, capricious man, and hated
Páez for his share in the release of the prisoners.

The four young men were shown into Figueredo's
room and placed their swords upon the table.   Páez,
who in all such affairs seems to have been recognised as
the natural leader, laid their complaint before the
general.   He dwelt upon the danger that the horses ran,
close to the enemy, and asked that they should all be
sent into the rear and the approaches to them strongly
guarded.   Figueredo answered that the horses were safe
enough, and after all he, and he alone was responsible.

" My general,"* Páez answered, " that is not so, for
every officer has his share of responsibility."

Figueredo instantly opened the door and calling to
his lieutenant, Juan Antonio Mirabal, said, " Arrest
Major† Páez, and put a pair of irons on him."

Páez knew well enough the class of men he had to
deal with, so taking up his sword he told Figueredo he
would die fighting rather than be ironed.   So saying he
left the room, and getting on his horse galloped towards
his men.   Figueredo, knowing his popularity with the
soldiers, immediately revoked his order and begged the
other officers to talk him over, for he feared Páez had
gone to start a mutiny.   Nothing was further from his
mind.

As soon as Figueredo thought the danger past, he
began swaggering again, and said he would give Páez
his discharge and a free pass to go to anywhere he chose.
Páez took him at his word and left him.   In four and
twenty hours most of the men deserted, and left their
general almost alone.

Both officers appealed and laid their case before the
patriot government. They approved Páez's conduct and
deposed Figueredo from his command, giving it to an

* Mi general.
† Comandante.

officer, by name Guerrero, who afterwards rose to celebrity.

Páez went on to Pore the capital of Casanare, where he found Olmedilla, who at once sent for him. Olmedilla though a brave man and one who had given proofs of valour in the field, had become convinced that the unequal contest could not be maintained much longer, and that the country would fall again into the hands of Spain. The collapse of the republic and the rumours of the great force that Spain was sending out, had very possibly shaken his nerve, or there may have been some other cause, that had not appeared, to make him take the resolution that he imparted to Páez at their interview.

After signifying to him that he thought the revolutionary cause was lost, he said he was going to retire with all his family to a place called Vichava on the river Meta, amongst the Indians.

These Indians chiefly Guahibos and Chiricoas to-day roam the great forests on the Meta, living almost entirely by the chase, although they cultivate a little Indian corn about their huts. Their arms are bows and arrows and a long blowpipe, with which they shoot a dart dipped in Curare and make good shooting up to forty yards.

" They wander " says Father Gumilla* in his great work on the Orinoco and its Indians, " from one river to another. Whilst the Indians fish or hunt deer, wild beasts, or snakes, for food, their women pull up roots. . . . These roots serve them for bread; and anything they find, as boa-constrictors, tigers or lions,† all is the same to them, and palatable to these two tribes." He adds their huts only serve them for a day or two and

---

* " El Orinoco Ilustrado," por El. P. Joseph Gumilla, Madrid, 1741, page 188. Gumilla calls the Guahibos, Guajivos, but by their position on the Meta, and their habits, they must be the same.

† Tigres y leones, *i.e.*, Jaguars and Pumas.

thus their lives are hardly better than the wild beasts of the woods.

Contact with civilization has brought them several diseases unknown to them when Father Gumilla wrote his monumental book, and also brought gunpowder and gin. However they still wander from one river to another and use the weapons, blowpipes and bows and arrows, that they used in the good Jesuit's days.

Amongst these savages Olmedilla was going to retire, with all his family. He had persuaded several of his friends to accompany him, and thought he had, in Páez a trump card to play, for he intended to make a settlement upon the river Meta's banks, rather than to submit again to Spanish rule.

"Commandant Páez" he said, "return at once to the army and choose out two or three hundred men, you can rely on, with horses for them. I will start with my family, for the river Meta, and get ready as many boats as I can find and load them up with salt, an indispensable commodity in those parts. I shall also take a priest with me to minister to us.

"As you pass by Pore,* you can take all the gold and silver vessels in the church, and gather up by force all the money you can find amongst the citizens. At any rate it would fall later on into the Spaniards' hands." Páez was struck dumb with astonishment, but knowing Olmedilla's character, and seeing that he himself was all alone, he asked leave to think the proposition over, before he gave an answer to it. After an hour or two of pseudo consideration, he refused Olmedilla's request. Páez was ordered back to take command of his regiment, and on the same day Olmedilla with his family set out for San Juan de Los Llanos, a frontier town in what is now Colombian territory.

In the town of El Puerto, Páez fell in with Solano,

* The capital of the district of Casanare.

the new patriot governor of Casanare. Casanare being
so inaccessible and sparsely inhabited, served as a secure
refuge for the patriots after a defeat. Solano when he
learned of Olmedilla's desertion was furious, and sent
Páez to arrest and bring him back again. Nothing could
well have been more disagreeable to Páez, who had
served under Olmedilla's orders and had enjoyed his
confidence. He saw at once that Olmedilla would
charge him with the revelation of his plans. However
he was obliged to obey his orders, and set out at once
with four officers and their orderlies. After five days
of forced and uninterrupted marches, he came up with
him in the province of San Martin. A forced march
in the Llanos, judging from the journeys the Llaneros
make to-day, would be some sixty miles a day. Not
a bad march, considering the climate and the fact that
they would probably be obliged to swim several rivers.
They would travel at the fast artificial gait, known as
the pasitrote, at which a horse makes about six miles
an hour. Their horses would find nothing but grass
to feed upon, and the riders must have carried their
provisions with them, for they could have had no time
to hunt, upon the way. Their food probably was jerked
beef, which they moistened at a stream. Their drink
was water.

Starting long before daylight to avoid the heat, they
would travel on to about eleven o'clock, when the
" enemy," the sun, became too powerful for them to
continue riding in its full glare. If by chance, and not
a very good chance, they came upon a rancho or
" Caney "* they would ask for, or take hospitality, and
pass the hottest hours of the day. If they passed, as was
most likely, no human habitation they would halt in

* A Caney is a roof on four posts. It has no sides, and the owners'
hammocks are slung from the beams. The word is supposed to be of
Carib origin, for the earliest conquerors mention it in their accounts of
Cuba, Santo Domingo and Puerto Rico.

some Mata* of Moriche palms and take their siesta there, after securely hobbling their horses, who strayed about the Mata, picking up what grass they could.

The travellers certainly made a fire of grass and palm leaves to keep off the mosquitoes, and dozed and smoked till it was time to start again. If they had time before the siesta, they probably led down their horses to the water, if there was any handy, and bathed them, to refresh and cool their backs, and keep off saddle galls.

Mounting again at about three o'clock, they would ride till sundown, passing through marshes where myriads of birds flew up, scared at their passage, and solemn cranes stood fishing, with one leg tucked up beneath their wing. Herds of deer scurried off before them, and bands of cattle and of horses scarcely less wild than deer, after gazing for an instant, with heads erect, and tails lashing their sides, snorted and disappeared, raising a cloud of dust upon the open plain, or in the marshes scattering the water in showers in the disordered gallop of their flight.

Páez found Olmedilla in a rancho with his family and a few followers, who immediately stood to arms. Olmedilla himself with his sword in one hand and a carbine in the other stood in the door. Who goes there, he cried. To which Páez replied, " Free America."†
When Olmedilla read the order of the governor charging Páez to capture him dead or alive, he tried to talk him over, proposing several alternatives. When he saw Páez was inflexible, he threw the order on the table and shouted, " You may take my dead body, but living I will never go with you." Then going inside the cottage he barred the door and turning to his wife and children said, " I will die, before he takes me back

* A Mata is a grove of trees, almost always of Moriche palms, on the Llanos.
† La America Libre.

alive." His wife encouraged him, saying, " You would do well, to die. I would rather see you weltering in your blood than humiliated and a prisoner."

Páez got off his horse, and tried to argue with the Spartan lady; but all her answer to his arguments, was she would rather see her husband dead than taken prisoner. At last he gave his sword to Páez, on the promise of his life, his wife and children weeping with rage, rather (as Páez says) than grief. It seems to have been a trial of will, and in the contest Páez wore his adversary down.

On the way back Olmedilla repeatedly pulled up his horse, exclaiming, " how can I have been so cowardly." It was a vain regret for he was quite alone amongst his enemies. When they arrived at Pore, Governor Solano had two pairs of irons riveted on him, and told him to prepare for death. Páez and several other officers in conjunction with one Father Mendez, afterwards Archbishop of Caracas, with difficulty procured his pardon, and left him free to prosecute his journey to the wilds. There he passed many hardships. His settlement soon came to nothing and he, driven by extremity of hunger was forced to eat the body of his son, to preserve his miserable life. How he died no one knew with certainty, but probably the Indians killed him seeing him without defence.

A wretched death after much suffering brought about by one of those strange miscalculations to which humanity is subject. Had he but persevered a little longer, he might have left an honourable name, for after having ebbed down to the lowest depths, the patriot cause was destined to flow on to victory. In fact there were not wanting indications that the tide had turned.

Though General Morillo was carrying everything before him in New Granada, had taken Cartagena, and had occupied the capital Bogotá, then more generally

known as Santa Fé, in Casanare and Apure, the guerrilla warfare that Páez, Yañez and Guerrero had
organised, was meeting with success.

The Spanish General Calzada, with three thousand
men, considered in those days and in such a country as
the Llanos a formidable force, was defeated at a place
called Banco de Chire by the patriot General Ricaurte,
under whose orders Páez fought. So primitive was the
warfare of the times, especially in such outlying places
as the plains of Casanare, the patriot forces which may
have numbered fifteen hundred men, had scarcely ninety
carbines. The rest were armed with lances, sabres, or
whatever weapon they could find.

A skirmish or a battle took place upon the 31st of
December, 1815, in which the Spaniards were completely
routed, and only saved themselves from annihilation by
taking refuge in the interior of New Granada. On this
occasion Páez had one of those curious nervous attacks,
to which he in the future was always subject before a
battle. His men seeing the state that he was in, supported him in the saddle, until they were forced to
charge. Páez then pulled himself together and shouting " charge," mounted his horse and the attack passed
off.

Several contemporary writers and notably the celebrated General O'Leary, Bolivar's aide-de-camp, have
noticed these strange seizures. Some put them down
to epilepsy, others to a violent excitement of the nerves.

One thing is certain, that for the time being, he used
to behave like a man possessed, brandishing his lance,
and foaming at the mouth, till he fell off his horse.
In pursuit of the flying enemy, Páez who could not
have recovered entirely from his attack, for it was not
the place of a commanding officer to leave his men and
pursue the enemy unaccompanied, found himself alone.
He at once perceived the danger that he ran from

falling into the hands of a body of the fugitives. Trying to come back on his trail, his horse gave out with him. Luckily he came across another horse, and as he says, was able to get hold of him, not without difficulty. The difficulty is only to be measured by those who have found themselves in the same plight.*

Upon the Llanos and the Pampas of the Argentine, few indeed of the horses let themselves be approached by anyone on foot. Páez could not have lassoed the loose horse, for his horse was tired and could hardly drag itself along. Either he edged the horse against the river bank and putting all his fortune in one throw, lassoed him, or else he may have driven him into a marsh or thicket of high bush. In any case, few but an expert Llanero or a Gaucho would have managed it. Mounted upon the horse he had so providentially managed to catch, he rode till midnight. Then seeing a camp fire rode up to it and to his joy found himself amongst his friends. Next morning in a miserable state he reported his escape to General Ricaurte. He must indeed have looked a wretched object, from his own description, barefooted, with a pair of green cloth trousers, so torn and tattered that they flapped about his knees like fringes. His general congratulated him on his escape, and then in the true spirit of the military pedant, reproached him for appearing before him " in the dress of a medicant." The general did not offer Páez a new uniform, and barefooted in his wretched rags he returned to his regiment. If this was the condition of a commandant, the common soldiers must have looked like a regiment of scarecrows.

All through the year 1816, the war continued in the Llanos, inclining on the whole toward the patriot side. After his success in Chire, Páez surprised a detachment of the royalists, and took from them an immense

* Con no poco Trabajo.

booty in cattle and in horses and about eighty prisoners.
He drove the rest of the detachment into the river
Arauca, where most of them were drowned. Only their
commander Juan Vicente Peña escaped with five and
twenty followers and took refuge in the town of Guasdualito, with Colonel Arce and a strong Spanish force.
Arce not judging the town defensible evacuated it, and
it was instantly occupied by Páez.

The Spanish commander had gone on to a place called
Quintero which Páez determined to surprise. As it was
distant only sixty miles from Guasdualito, the enterprise was not so difficult. Spies brought him notice that
his intention had got wind, and that a strong detachment under Vicente Peña was waiting for him ambushed
at the fort of Palmarite on the Apure. Páez before he
marched prepared a quantity of meat, dried in the sun,
or roasted, so as to avoid being obliged to kill cattle
by the way. His reason was one that would not have
occurred to anyone not a Llanero.

Upon the Llanos, when an animal is killed, although
not a single vulture is to be seen, no sooner is the offal
spread out on the ground, than from the four quarters
of the sky vultures appear in hundreds to prey upon it.
These vultures, known in Venezuela as Zamuros,* are
thought by naturalists, not as was formerly supposed to
direct themselves by smell, but sight. As they pass
many hours of every day soaring about searching for
their prey, one of them sights a dead animal, and darts
down upon it. The nearest to him, seeing his movement
follow him, and so by a primeval system of wireless
telegraphy, the news is brought to the whole flock.
Travellers upon the Llanos, when they see vultures
arriving over a certain spot, and then soaring down, can
tell with certainty that a dead animal is there.

* They are known by various names in the different republics, as in
Colombia, Gallinazos ; in Mexico, Zopilotes, and the Argentine Republic,
Urubus.

In the guerrilla warfare on the frontier, where safety depends on eyesight and upon intense and accurate observation of natural phenomena, a faculty so difficult to acquire by those born in the sheltered life of cities, that practically it is unacquirable, the wisdom of not killing any animal on a surprise march was at once apparent.

All took place as Páez hoped, and so unwarned by vultures, or by the smoke of cooking fires, he fell upon the Spaniards, who had been placed in ambush to surprise him, like a thunderbolt. Most of the Spaniards taken completely by surprise were taken prisoners. Amongst them was their chief Vicente Peña. Brought before Páez he disdained to beg for life, and only asked to be allowed a few hours respite to take leave of his wife. Páez who always rose to the occasion, when he was confronted by a really brave man, answered him saying, " We are not assassins. After the victory we are always merciful." He says himself, "The bravery and calm of the man* who well knew what to expect, in that implacable war to the death, moved me extraordinarily."

Wishing to save his life, Páez tried hard to make him join the patriot army, a change in those days men often made, not necessarily to save their lives, but because of personal motives, such as a quarrel with their superior officers, or the mere love of change. Peña however was not one of those, and steadily refused to change his party, even to save his life. Páez who did not wish to execute him, hit on the plan of sending him a prisoner to the patriot headquarters, with injunctions to the other leaders to do their best to win him to their cause. So well they argued that at last Peña consented to join the patriots. In debates of such a nature, a drawn sword

* "La arrogancia y severidad del hombre que bien debia conocer la suerte que le esperaba en aquella epoca de implacable guerra me llámaron extraordinariamente atencion." Memorias de Páez ,page 101.

suspended by a hair, or in this instance the metaphor perhaps should be, by a strip of hide, over the debater's head, is apt to prove a powerful argument. It is not to be forgotten either that a large percentage of the royalist forces was composed of men born in the colony.*

It was only the heroic efforts of Bolivar, ably seconded by Sucre, Santander, McGregor,† Páez, O'Leary, Piar and others of his generals continued for years, that rallied the bulk of the native population, to the revolutionary cause.

The declaration of War to the Death, that is that all prisoners should be butchered, declared by Bolivar and taken up and acted upon by the Spanish commander in chief, Morillo, just as energetically, may also have contributed to their change of attitude, for it became evident that the greatest sufferers were those whose every interest lay in the country that was drenched with blood. For all that there was a strong royalist feeling in the

* Una de las glorias de la Revolucion Venezolana fué de haber Tenido que haber durante ocho años no solo contra España, sino contra las dos terceras partes de la poblacion de Venezuela. Los ejercitos de Cajigal, Ceballos, Boves, Morales, Antoñanzas, etc., eran compuestos en su totalidad de Venezolanos. La caballeria llanera de Morillo era Venezolana. "Estudios Historicos," page 170, Aristides Rojas, Caracas, 1926.

† Gregor McGregor, known to the Venezuelans as Gregorio McGregor, was descended from an old Highland family settled in the district of Breadalbane. In his youth he served a short time in the British Army. In the year 1811 he went to Caracas to join the revolutionists. There he married a Venezuelan lady, Doña Josepha Lonera. Entering the public service, he rose to be Colonel and Adjutant-General to the unfortunate Miranda. After his fall, he joined Bolivar, served with distinction and conducted the celebrated retreat from Ocumare to Barcelona in 1815. He was present at the battles of Chaguaramas and Juncal. In 1817 Bolivar made him a general and received him into the order of the Libertadores, specially thanking him for his services. In 1819 he took Puerto Cabello, but was surprised and forced to fly, saving his life by swimming to a ship. In 1821 he quitted the Venezuelan service and settled on the Mosquito Coast, making himself Cacique of the Poyais Indians under the title of His Highness Gregor. He encouraged trade and agriculture and founded a bank, having the notes engraved by the well-known engraver William Hine Lizars. He then went to London to raise a loan, but failed in the attempt. Falling on evil days, in 1839 he petitioned the Venezuelan Government to be reinstated in a general's rank and pay. His request was granted on account of his services to the Republic. He died a few years later in Caracas.

colony, especially in the province of Coro which in
spite of Bolivar's great victory at Carabobo still held out
for Spain.   Even after Peña had said he would change
sides his life was still in danger.   They sent him back
to Páez with strict orders to have him executed at once,
as they did not believe in his sincerity.

Páez tried his best to convince them, but without
success.   He was forced to make preparations for the
execution, but at the last minute, after Peña was already
at the place where he was to suffer, Páez took a sudden
resolution and had him taken back, having decided to
take every responsibility rather than shoot a man in cold
blood.   He says during that agonizing time, Peña*
remained unmoved.

At last, after having pledged his honour that he
would respond for Peña's fidelity, he was saved at the
last hour.   Hardly was Peña snatched from the jaws of
death, and when he and Páez were resting in a hut, an
Indian soldier serving on the Spanish side rode up to
the door.   Páez he could not have known by sight, but
Peña he knew well.   Not having heard that Peña had
changed sides he reported to him that not far away
there was a company of soldiers under a captain lying
in ambush ready to attack.   Peña and Páez got him to
lead them to where they were lying hid and captured
all of them except the captain, who had disappeared.
They searched for him without success and were just
giving up the search, when a soldier saw his feet dangling through the leaves of a tall palm tree, right above
their heads.   Summoned to come down he did so instantly, remarking wittily that at the fight of Guasdualito
he had escaped by the skin of his teeth,† but that this
time even Our Lady of the Palm Tree‡ could not save

* " Peña permanecia impasible."
† " . . . escapé en alas del conejo."
‡ Nuestra Señora del Cogollo.

him. His boldness and his pawky humour probably saved his life, for Páez laughed at the jest and sent the jester a prisoner to Bogotá.

In these instances Páez revealed the goodness of his heart and a chivalric hatred of cold-blooded murder, for what is after all the shooting of a prisoner but murder of an aggravated kind. He had however much of the ferocity of his times and bringing up, and civil warfare always brings out ferocity.

The following episode recounted by a man who saw everything in Venezuela with a jaundiced eye and yet fell under the magnetic spell Páez exerted in those who came in contact with him, shows up the darker and more savage side of a character not wanting in noble traits or generosity.

GENERAL JOSÉ ANTONIO PÁEZ.

CHAPTER VII

THE Llanos were so vast, and the contending armies so relatively small, that it was possible to march and countermarch for days, without coming into contact with one another. This was the case in regard to the celebrated battle of La Mata de la Miel, that bulks so largely in Venezuelan history. At it, for the first time, the Llaneros routed regular soldiers, furnished with artillery. Páez first really emerged from his obscurity by his skilful leadership, and gained the rank of lieutenant colonel. He had been left in command of the little army that was defending Guasdualito, by the defection of its commander, General Guerrero, who, hearing that the Spaniards were advancing with superior forces and with artillery, had taken flight and with his staff and several companies of soldiers recrossed the Arauca and marched to Casanare, the usual refuge of the patriots, when they were overmatched.

Páez was left with but five hundred men, all of whom were cavalry. He at once set out to find the enemy. The first sign that alarmed him, was a dense cloud of dust that hung above a palm wood known as La Mata de la Miel. This was the first thing that showed him the enemy was near. Signs such as rising dust, the flight of birds and the way the grass is bent by the passing through it of animals or men, are the books of the Llaneros, which all of them can read. Páez advanced to reconnoitre and luckily for him, was followed by an officer with ten or twelve dragoons.

So little had the warfare of those days in Venezuela

99

changed from that carried on under the walls of Troy, that having fallen upon an outpost of the enemy some six hundred yards in advance of their main body, Páez and the officer of the detachment shouted out insults to one another. Páez having challenged him to single combat, quite in the style of Hector and Achilles, advanced to meet him, when a shot from the enemy's picket, entered his horse's eye and stretched it dead upon the ground.

So sudden was the horse's fall that it caught one of Páez's legs beneath it, and had not his lieutenant charged with the dragoons that he had with him, Páez must have been taken prisoner. When he got his leg free and mounted a fresh horse, he shouted quite in the vein of the heroes of the Iliad: " Friends, they have killed my good horse, if you will not help me to revenge him, I will go alone." Naturally all his men answered: " We will follow you." As night was coming on the other officers wished to suspend the attack till daylight, but Páez very wisely judging that a battle in the dark would be to the advantage of the weaker side, ordered an immediate advance.

His innate instinct for guerrilla warfare, stood him and the patriot cause in good stead on this occasion. Night was approaching and the dreaded fire of the artillery was rendered almost innocuous, by the sudden change, for in those latitudes, twilight is unknown. As they swept down on the artillerymen and infantry, a shot struck Páez's horse, which at once plunged violently, and broke the girths. Páez with the saddle still between his knees, found himself on the ground and the whole of his own squadron passed over him, with a thunderous noise. He arose unhurt, and mounting another horse that a friend offered him, hurried to rally his second squadron that had been thrown into confusion by the artillery fire. By that time night had fallen and the charge of the Llaneros was so impetuous that the royalist cavalry broke and fled into the dark.* Many were lanced by their pursuers before the darkness shrouded them from pursuit.

The infantry that probably either was composed of Spaniards, or stiffened by a leaven of Spaniards, true to the traditions of their infantry, one of the most stubborn in the world, especially under defeat, all kept together and retired sullenly through the darkness of the night. When Páez overtook them in the morning they had found shelter in the woods on the Apure and were unattackable.

Such was the well known, much written of affair of La Mata de la Miel, in which the royalists lost four hundred killed, five hundred prisoners, much stores and ammunition and, what was possibly a greater loss than all to them, more than three thousand horses. These horses, an enormous quantity for such an inconsiderable body of troops were what is known as La Remuda,† that

* " In the charge they lay their hands close along the right (off) side of the horse's neck with the lance poised in the right hand ready to plunge into their antagonist. At a distance the rider is not discernible and on a nearer approach it is very difficult to take aim at them so close do they crouch to their horses' backs. Their charge is furious, nor will the most dreadful fire deter them from approaching. During the charge they make most horrid yells."—" History of the Revolution of Caracas," page 110, Major Flinter, London, 1819.

Both the Indians of the South Pampas of the Argentine and the Apaches and Comanches of North America charged in the same manner, lying along their horses' sides, with only an arm and a foot visible.

† Faltaban caballos, y como estos con un elemento indispensable del soldado Llanero era preciso ante todo buscarlos.—" Historia de Venezuela." Baralt.

He gives an interesting picture of the breaking in of the horses by the soldiers, most of whom were Llaneros, and thus able to ride wild horses from their youth.

" The horses that were always used there, were tamed in the Llanero fashion (a la usanza Llanera) by squadrons. It was a curious sight to see five or six hundred soldiers struggling at the same time with these wild animals. All round the place where the breeding was going on mounted men were posted riding tame horses, not to assist the rough-riders who fell, but to pursue the horses that had thrown them to prevent their escaping with the saddles, although these saddles were but a wooden tree, with a few strips of raw-hide hanging to them."—" Historia de Venezuela," Baralt.

is the reserve, and were driven loose tended by herdsmen. The loss of them prevented the royalists from
equipping cavalry* for a considerable time and seriously
interfered with their mobility.

Upon the other hand, Páez was able to mount all his
men upon fresh horses and could extend his raids and
reconnaissances unchecked. The government of New
Granada sent him his brevet of lieutenant colonelcy, and
from that time his name was known throughout the
country. Either through policy or by the natural
humanity of his disposition, for in spite of his occasional
fits of savageness he was not inhumane at heart, he
treated all his prisoners so well, giving them liberty to
return to their homes unmolested, that after they had
done so many returned to join his ranks.

As they were all Venezuelans, and as at that time
there was no middle course between a friend and open
enemy, they acted wisely and preserved their lives and
property. Páez's conduct made a good impression in
the country and convinced the waverers of the justice of
his cause, which in the minds of many had been preju-
diced by the cruelty of some of the patriot officers.
The army then, after the fashion of a Roman army
when in some distant province they raised their commander on their shields, saluting him as Emperor by
acclamation, made Páez their general.

With commendable prudence he refused the honour,

---

* Horses at the time of the Independence War were worth about five
dollars a head in the Llanos. This price was probably for unbroken colts.

In 1848, Ramon Páez, the general's son, says they were worth from
eighty to a hundred dollars. They are rather cheaper now, as the disease
called Derrengadera that attacks their kidneys has lessened their numbers
considerably. This disease first appeared in the forest of San Camilo on
the head waters of the Apure about 1840. It never attacked cattle, but
monkeys and other wild animals died of it. Many of the inhabitants were
infected by it and died. From that time dates the depopulation of the Llanos,
of which the disease was one of the chief causes.—" Wild Scenes in South
America, or Life in the Llanos of Venezuela," p. 81. Ramon Páez, London,
1863.

not in the spirit of " Nolo episcopari," or like Old Noll
putting the crown aside that it might be pressed upon
him, but because all his life he had an odd feeling of
military discipline that, though he outraged it at times
when pushed by personal resentment or by the knowledge of the incapacity of his superior officers, always
asserted itself when he had time to think.

On this occasion he did wisely to let it influence him
and allow General Guerrero who now, the victory won,
returned from Casanare, to continue in command. His
moderation was rewarded by the recall of Guerrero by
the patriot government of Casanare. This left Páez
without any competitor for the chief command in Guasdualito, which he immediately assumed.

, At the battle of La Mata de la Miel he was ably
seconded by his lieutenants, Nonato Perez, Antolin
Mugica, Gregorio Brito, and others of his officers, who
it may be supposed had enjoyed no more military training than himself. Over these the young commander
exercised an enormous influence, by his personal prowess
and his disinterestedness. Besides these qualities, which
many another general has shared with him, he endeared
himself to his men not only by partaking of their food
and sleeping on the ground amongst them with his
saddle for a pillow, but by being able to tame a wild
horse with the best and having really little more education than his followers.

Hippisley,* an officer who had served under Wellington and came to Venezuela at the head of a regiment
that he raised to fight against the Spaniards, although he
hated everything in the country and failed to see the
genius of Bolivar, admired Páez greatly. " Páez is
self taught and sprang up all of a sudden from nothing
during the revolution. . . . His courage, intrepidity,

* " A Narrative of the Expedition to the Rivers Orinoco and Apure."
By G. Hippisley. London, John Murray, 1819, p. 416.

repeated successes and the number of his followers speedily gained him a name. His followers too were all so many Páezes, looking up to their general as a superior being . . . On the parade or in the field, Páez was their general, and supreme. In the hours of rest from the fatigues of a long and rapid march, or from conquest over the adversary, and the retaliation rigidly executed Páez would be seen dancing with his people in the ring formed for that purpose, smoking with them, drinking from the same cup, and lighting the fresh segar from the one in the mouth of his fellow soldier."

Such conduct was the only way to endear himself to such a following. Democracy in South America has much of the inherited democratic feeling of the Arabs that was derived through the Spaniards. Arabs and Spaniards alike speak to a duke or to a sultan as if he were their equal. Of course he is so as regards his humanity. Accident may have raised duke or sultan politically and economically above the tribesman or the peasant, nature has made them all of the same flesh. Something, no doubt, Spanish Americans have derived from the occasional mixture of Indian blood.

Amongst the wild Indian tribes, from Nootka Sound down to Cape Horn, the most absolute equality exists, and always did exist except in Mexico and Peru. Most of them had no hereditary chiefs, and when obliged to elect a war chief, when war was over his authority was gone, that is, all but the authority that a man of special powers always has wielded and must ever wield. Thus throughout the republics, except the great gold-standardized republic of the north, where everyone it often seems is held inferior to his fellow, absolute equality, beneath the Sun, prevails. Manners are easy and without restraint, and everyone holds himself to be a gentleman. Hence the hail fellow well met attitude, so like the attitude of two dogs meeting in the street, is quite unknown, and slappings on the back, mental or physical, make their perpetrator odious.

Nothing can make this plainer than the passage in which Hippisley says, " in the field Páez was supreme," and then depicts him dancing with his followers. This was the attitude of chiefs amongst the Blackfeet and the Sioux, so difficult to imitate by men who by the fact of some slight smattering of science or of literature think themselves demi-gods.

All through the year 1816 and the beginning of 1817 the war on the Llanos of Apure, Barinas and Casanare dragged on, but gradually more and more of the country people flocked to Páez. He became so popular that, four months after the battle of La Mata de la Miel, when many patriots flying from New Granada where the troops of Morillo were operating, assembled in Guasdualito and named General Santander commander-in-chief, the Llaneros refused to recognise him. To appease them the provisional government of Guasdualito promoted Páez to the rank of General of Brigade, with special powers over the forces raised in the Apure district.

This measure gave great satisfaction to the Llaneros who only would be led by such a man as Páez, one of their own calibre and who understood their ways. His men all spoke of him as Tio (uncle) and as they marched sang a rude verse,* in the style of the fescennine verses, the Roman soldiers used to sing.

Only in the Llanos was the patriot cause progressing, for at this juncture Bolivar, defeated at Clarines and forced to abandon the city of Barcelona, had determined to transfer his efforts to the wild province of Guayana upon the far side of the Orinoco. His objective was

---

* " De los generales cual es el méjor
Mi general José con su Guardia de Honor."

the town of Angostura,* and as its name implies situated
on the narrows of the great river Orinoco, that had
remained open to navigation, under the royalists. By
it the Spaniards received arms and reinforcements
direct from Spain.

The patriots had organised a squadron of " flecheras,"
a kind of fishing boat with a gun mounted in the bow.
This squadron was surprised by a Spanish war vessel,
and Bolivar with all his staff were forced to save themselves by jumping overboard and swimming to the bank.
Luckily for the patriot cause the Venezuelan admiral,
Brion, arrived, and having defeated the Spanish squadron, laid siege to Angostura. After a vigorous defence
under its Governor, Fitzgerald, it fell on the 17th of
July, 1817, and passed into the patriot's hands.

This was almost their first considerable success, outside the Llanos of Apure. Bolivar fixed the provisional
residence of the authorities at Angostura, and named it
the capital of Venezuela. Then came the unfortunate
conspiracy of Generals Mariño, Bermudez and Piar
against the authority of the Liberator. Mariño and Bermudez managed to reconcile themselves with Bolivar,
but Piar though pardoned and granted a passport to
the West Indian Islands, instead of going there, returned to Angostura and tried to stir up strife. Taken
and brought to a court martial, he was condemned and
shot.

The house where he passed his last night " en capilla "
is situated at the eastern angle of the square, opposite
to the cathedral. The actual room that was used as
the chapel† is on the level of the street. The plaza
where he suffered has a garden with a fountain splashing eternally underneath the palm trees, that wave over
it. It murmurs dirges for the misguided, brave Piar,

* Now, Ciudad Bolivar.
† Capilla. See Chapter III.

the victor of the battle of San Felix, or sings a pean
for the Liberator's triumph over treachery, just as the
listener's ear is tuned. Piar may hear it; but if he does
not, it has a grateful sound to the dark visaged men
in their white clothes, who saunter round the plaza
smoking, as they talk grandiloquently about futile
matters, under the tropic stars.

Páez though he was now commander-in-chief of the
army of the Apure, and the most redoubtable leader of
cavalry in the republic on the revolutionary side, was
surrounded by a thousand difficulties. Most of his men
were mounted upon half tamed horses that had
been reduced by the violence of their breaking
and the long marches that they had endured,
and were quite unprepared for hard work. Even
the grasses of that part of the Llanos were scanty and
unwholesome. The greater part of the raw levies had
no guns, and for their only arms they carried lances
and sticks of Alvarico* palm, with their points hardened
in the fire. Even clothes were scanty and as Páez† says
the soldiers covered their nakedness with Guayucos, that
is an Indian breechclout. Hats scarcely were to be seen
in the whole army, as they had rotted in the rainy season
that lasts for several months. They had not even
blankets to supplement the want of saddles, so they had
to ride their horses barebacked, for there was not a
blanket or a sheepskin to be had in the whole army.
When they killed cattle the soldiers fought amongst
themselves for the hides to use them as a shelter during
the rainy season, as without tents they were exposed
to the full violence of the tropic rains for months together at a stretch.

Besides the want of clothing and of arms, even of the
common necessaries of life, amongst his soldiers, Páez

* Alvocarpus Cubarro.

† Memorias del General Páez, page 122.

now found himself in his capacity as commander-in-chief of the Apure forces, called on to organise and lead the emigration that became necessary by the advance of General Morillo and the Spanish troops. " More than ten thousand persons who followed the army," says Restrepo* in his History of Colombia, " were removed to Araguaquén, a distant spot, inaccessible to the Spaniards." Páez merely mentions the emigration of this great band of emigrants, in passing, in his Memoirs.

In a letter to Bolivar from his headquarters at Buron dated the 26th of February, 1819, he enters into some particulars, but chiefly on the scarcity of horses and mules to mount the fugitives. " You can imagine," he writes to Bolivar, " the amount of cares and the fatigues that I have had to undergo, and how much I have had to toil. I assure you that to maintain the army and the emigrants, it has cost me and is costing me, only what God himself can tell: the lack of horses, the scarcity of cattle in these plains, give me an infinity of work."

Whether by this time Páez had learned to read and write is quite uncertain. The author of the curious narrative entitled, " Recollections of a service of three years during the War of determination in the Republics of Venezuela and Colombia,"† says " when I served with him, Páez could neither read nor write, and until the English (that is The British Legion) came to the Llanos, had never used a knife and fork,‡ so rough and so uncultured had been his former life; but when he

---

* Vol. II, Cap. X.

† London, 1828.

‡ The Llaneros, like the Gauchos of the Argentine Pampa, lived entirely on beef. The Gauchos had a saying, " Carnero no es carne," that is mutton is not meat. They ate their beef cooked on a spit over a fire of bones, dried cowdung, or thistle stalks, cutting off pieces from the joint with knives, a foot or more in length.

The meat they held between their teeth. They cut off the piece nearest the teeth, till by degrees they got down to the end grasped in their left hand.

began to meet the officers of the British Legion he copied their way of living and their dress, modelling himself as much as possible upon them, that is, as far as his lack of education allowed.

" He measures five feet nine inches in height, is very muscular and well made, and possesses great agility and strength. He has a handsome manly countenance, shaded by thick dark curly hair. He is of sanguine temperament.* His character is ardent, generous and affable, and his intelligence, though it has not been cultivated, shows all the virtues that adorn human nature. Sincere, frank and simple, he is a perfect friend, and as he is a stranger to all mean passions, a generous enemy." The chief testimonials to the character of Páez, at that period of his career come from Englishmen who served in the British Legion, and had ample opportunities of forming an impartial judgment. Many of their criticisms on others of the revolutionary chiefs are far less favourable.

Not all the duties of a patriot leader of those days were in the field. Páez found himself obliged to organise the life and daily occupations of the many thousand fugitives, in the remote and desert refuge they had found upon the banks of the Orinoco. His first care was to provide them with daily bread, their daily bread in this case being beef. Cattle were driven from the Llanos into this forest refuge round the lake of Cunaviche and slaughtered when necessary.

The women were set to spin, and as upon the Orinoco wild cotton was found in great abundance, they were never idle. Little by little their lives became more bearable, as they became accustomed to the solitary place. Their only fear was that some Spanish raiding party should attack them, before Páez could send men

* The author writes in the present tense, as Páez was living when he wrote and was quite young.

to their defence.   Raiders of the calibre of the Reverend
Colonel Andres Torrellas were indeed a danger.   This
priest, a furious partisan, had signalized himself by
many acts of cruelty after the fashion of the Carlist
warrior priests of later times in Spain, who not infre-
quently heard the confession of a prisoner, gave him
absolution, and confidently dispatched his soul to paradise by a pistol shot delivered by their own consecrated
hands.   Of such priests was the Reverend Colonel
Torrellas who never spared a prisoner, though it is not
related that he ever troubled to listen to their confession,
before butchering them.   He is most entitled to a niche
in history's pantheon, by the following exploit.

Páez had long wished to take the village, he calls it
city in his Memoirs, of Achuguas.   With that design he
dispatched an officer, one Rangel, with about two hundred men.   With him was Captain Antolin Múgica, a
brave young man, who had distinguished himself
greatly against the Spaniards. Rangel, Múgica and their
men, came down the river Apure in canoes.   Inside the
village, Colonel the Reverend Andres Torrellas was
known to have but a few men with him, from a report
brought by his scouts to Páez a day or two before.
Unknown to them, the reverend warrrior had received
strong reinforcements, and was prepared for the attack.
Silently, as day broke, the attacking party thinking to
take the garrison asleep, made a dash on the town.
Rangel who saw his error drew off his men though with
considerable loss, his horsemen covering his retreat.
Antolin Múgica, like Sir Gilles de Argenté at Bannock-
burn, saying that he would rather die than return to
Páez bringing the news of a defeat, with a few followers
advanced to the attack.

During the skirmish that took place, his horse fell
with him in a jaguéy, that is a shallow reservoir formed
in the plain to preserve water for the cattle during a

time of drought. Made prisoner and brought before
Torrellas, he was shot instantly. The ruffian presbyter
had his head fried in oil and sent it to the town of
Calabozo, where it remained stuck on a hook, as heads
were stuck over the gates of Fez, but a few years since,
and as our pious ancestors used to have them stuck on
Temple Bar, two hundred years ago, " ad majorem Dei
gloriam."

CHAPTER VIII

PAEZ, a general, and with his name recognised as the first patriot leader in the Llanos, was now called upon to meet a foeman worthy of his steel. Curiously enough the career of the man with whom he was destined to wage so long a struggle, was not unlike his own.

Pablo Morillo, Conde de Cartagena and Marques de la Puerta, when he arrived in Venezuela in the year 1815, had seen much fighting and was an experienced commander. Born at the little town of Fuentesecas in the province of Zamora, he had been a shepherd boy.* At thirteen years of age he enlisted in the army. Then he drifted into the marines, and was present at the sieges of Toulon and at the battle of Cape St. Vincent.

Both Bolivar and Morillo were easily moved to admiration by heroic deeds. At the fight in the valley of Carache a patriot soldier had his horse killed under him. Standing behind its body he kept off with his lance a group of Spanish horsemen and although wounded, killed two of them. Morillo saw him and called out to his men to spare his life and to take him prisoner. When he had recovered of his wounds Morillo sent him under the care of General O'Leary, without conditions, to the Liberator. Bolivar, not to be outdone in generosity,† returned eight Spanish soldiers of the Barbastro regiment in exchange for him.

* Francisco Pizarro had been a swineherd, and Belalcazar a donkey boy. Thus Pablo Morillo, had a sort of apostolic succession from the conquistadores of America. He himself was not destined to be a conquistador, although he had their ruthless energy, and their indomitable will.

† "Memorias del General Rafael Urdaneta," page 144. Madrid, 1916. Prologo de Don Rufino Blanco Fombona.

The incident shows that both chiefs respected one another and valued gallant deeds.

At Trafalgar, Morillo was a sergeant of marines, and distinguished himself by jumping overboard to save a flag that had been shot away. Transferred to the land forces, he served with great distinction at the battle of Bailén, where the French under Dupont* were routed utterly. Promoted to be colonel in 1809, he was at the battle of Vittoria serving with Wellington, and rose to be a general in 1812. Wellington thought so highly of him, that he recommended him to the Spanish government, for the command in Venezuela. His choice was certainly judicious, for probably no other soldier in the peninsula could have achieved so much. He failed, as he was bound to fail, confronted with the uprising of a population aroused to fury by centuries of bad government. Still he did not fail ignominiously, and it is pleasing to recall that he passed two days amicably with Bolivar, and that when peace was settled they parted, if not friends, at least with mutual respect. The Liberator and Morillo were ruthless, faithful, even to the shedding of blood, that is the blood of other people, for what they thought the right. Certainly they were not lambs, but in comparison with other generals, upon either side, it can be said that when they waded deep in blood, as they did upon occasion, it was not from mere love of bloodshed, but from mistaken views of patriotism.

Páez was in a different category. Bolivar had been born in the purple, well educated, rich and descended from a long line of wealthy and highly placed ancestors, one of whom had been amongst the first settlers in the country. Morillo, though born poor, had become by his long service in the Spanish army, an educated man,

* Dupont capitulated with 20,000 men. The battle was fought on 16th July, 1808, at Bailen, near La Carolina, in the province of Jaén. The Spanish Generals were Rodriguez and Corpigni.

and a skilled commander in whom Wellington himself had confidence.

Bolivar as his history shows had an innate genius for command. Páez had none of these advantages. He must have been over twenty years of age before he learned to read and write. Though a born leader of guerrilla bands, he had no special military gifts for generalship. General O'Leary* the biographer of Bolivar, describes him thus. " He was of middle height, robust and well made, although the lower portion of his body was not in due proportion† to his bust. His chest and shoulders were broad; his thick, short neck supported a large head, covered with dark, crisp, chestnut hair; his eyes were brown and lively; his nose straight, with wide nostrils; his lips thick and his chin round. His clear skin showed his good health, and would have been very white had he not been sunburned. Caution and suspicion were the distinctive traits of his countenance. Born of humble parentage he owed nothing to his education.

" In the presence of those he thought better educated than himself he was silent and almost timid, and abstained from taking part in conversation. With his inferiors he was loquacious, and not averse to practical jokes.‡ He was fond of talking of his military exploits. Entirely illiterate, he was quite ignorant of the theory of the profession that he practised, and did not know the simplest terms of the art. Even although he had received a careful military education, he would have

* Memorias del General O'Leary.

† This of course was caused by his early life in the saddle, and is often to be observed in the Gauchos of the Argentine Republic, the Mexican vaqueros, the Western Cowboys and other races, who pass their lives in the saddle, and walk but little.

‡ Juegos de Manos. The proverb says, " Juegos de manos, juegos de villanos," that is, Practical jokes are jokes for clowns. A truth greater than a house, as Spaniards are fond of saying in regard to that rarest of all qualities.

never been a first rate captain, for the slightest contra-
diction or emotion brought on convulsions that took
away his senses for the moment, and were followed by
fits of physical and moral weakness.

"As a chief of guerrilla warfare, he had no rival.
Bold, active, brave, and full of stratagems, quick to conceive, resolute and rapid in his movements, he was
always most to be feared, when he commanded but few
followers. A thousand men would have embarrassed
him, especially if part of them were composed of
infantry."

In 1815 and 1816, Morillo carried all before him.
His well armed and disciplined troops won easy victories
over the hastily raised ill-disciplined, patriot levies.
He took the town of Cartagena, and shot in cold blood
many of the leading citizens. Then he proceeded up
the Magdalena, to Bogotá, where he committed many
atrocities, shooting, amongst his six hundred victims, the
celebrated naturalist Francisco Caldas. He then re-
passed the Andes, marched through the plains of
Casanare and occupied the town of Guasdualito.

For the first time Páez and Morillo were face to
face upon the plains. Páez had on his side, his popularity, his intimate acquaintance with frontier life, and
the great size and difficulty of the country. Lastly he
had as his most powerful ally, the climate, that rendered
marching almost insupportable to Europeans, and
exposed them to the constant risk of fevers, of which
they died like flies.* The fate of the revolutionary
cause in Venezuela was to be decided on the Llanos, a
theatre in which the natural advantages were on the
patriots' side. After he had taken the town of Angostura, now called Ciudad Bolivar, in his honour, the

---

* The Spanish equivalent is, " Morir como chinches," to die like bugs·
Bugs, no doubt, exist as well as flies, but the tendency of the Nordic mind
is to ignore disagreeable insects and pretend they do not exist. Still, they
raise ugly lumps upon the flesh.

I

Liberator for the first time seems to have bethought himself of Páez and the war that he was carrying on, almost without assistance from the other patriots. Up to this date (1818) Páez and Bolivar had never met each other.

Morillo, by this time master of Guasdualito and at the head of greater forces than the patriots could muster, was a formidable adversary. If he could have made himself complete master of the Llanos de Apure, he would have had a source from which to draw almost unlimited supplies of horses and of cattle. These were not plentiful in other parts of Venezuela. Moreover loyalty to the nascent cause of the republic was in a fluid state. The Llaneros who so recently had followed Boves with enthusiasm, might possibly have been detached from Páez, in which event the fate of the republic was sealed.

Morillo well understood the position of affairs, and when he thought that all resistance was at an end in New Granada, on several occasions tried to occupy the plains. The only bulwark that the patriot cause possessed against him, was that set up by Páez and his wild horsemen. Knowing that Morillo would try to crush him with his superior forces, before Bolivar had had time to join him, Páez sent off his wounded and his great band of emigrants to a place of safety in a cattle farm, called El Yagual.

Páez had about eleven hundred men under his command, all of them cavalry. Morillo who had been reinforced by General Calzada, and must at that time have disposed of a relatively large force, detached General Latorre one of his lieutenants with three thousand infantry and about fifteen hundred horsemen to attack the patriots. Páez awaited him not far from Mucuritas, a place whose name is now a household word in Venezuelan history. General Latorre passed the night at a place known as El Hato del Frio, about a league away from Mucuritas, the spot that Páez had selected for his stand. At sunrise he was under arms, and by a rapid movement got to windward of the Spanish forces. In those days on the Llanos, before arms of precision had come into being, a position on the weather side of the antagonist was nearly as great an advantage as it would have been at sea.

Much galloping upon the plains in a short time raises a cloud of dust that, carried down the wind, is as good as a smoke screen to an attacking enemy. More danger-ous to the leeward army even than the dust, is the chance of a prairie fire, often occasioned in those days by the burning wadding of the guns, and sometimes as was to be the case on this occasion, when the dry grass is set on fire deliberately. The flames advance with incon-ceivable rapidity, heralded by billowing waves of smoke. The sun-dried grass takes fire like tinder. Nothing escapes the passage of the conflagration. Cattle and the wild animals rush desperately before it, and if they cannot reach the shelter of a river or lagoon in which to plunge, their charred bones show when the fire has passed, their miserable fate.

A man on a good horse, riding as men ride on such occasions, stretched out flat upon its neck, spurring and yelling words of encouragement to the animal that is to the full as well aware of its dire peril as himself, has but a chance of being able to escape. If he has time, and matches, and can gain a little on the con-flagration, he dismounts and muffling up his horse's head in a thick poncho, rapidly sets the grass on fire to leeward of him. Then, if so Allah wills it, and there is time, he finds himself on a oasis of burnt grass, over which the fire has passed already, and the pur-suing flames cannot advance. In that oasis he remains trembling and sweating, patting his horse and speaking to it in the words it is accustomed to, for should it break away his chance of life is small. Then when the ground begins to cool, he mounts, and seeks a place of safety, knowing that he will never have a closer call, but once, throughout his pilgrimage.

Páez on this occasion having got the weather-gage used it with as much effect as Nelson at Trafalgar.

The Spanish general Latorre confident in his superior forces advanced to within gunshot, which probably at that time was under a hundred yards. Before they had time to dress their lines the Llanero cavalry swept down upon them like a hurricane, throwing them into some confusion, but the stubborn Spanish infantry withstood the shock.

The custom of the Llaneros, if their first charge proved unsucessful, was to break and retire as single units and then reform when out of fire. This they called a retreat " en barajuste," and though it would probably have been disastrous if put into execution by drilled and disciplined troops, with them, was usually successful in avoiding casualties. This manœuvre was as old as the Parthians and comes quite naturally to most irregulars such as the Arabs, Cossacks and the Indian tribes of North America.

Although the infantry stood firm, Páez's charge was quite successful on the Spaniards right wing. Their cavalry, mostly composed of Venezuelans, instead of moving out to meet their assailants, stood to await the charge, a fatal thing to do, as charging horsemen invariably break through the ranks of cavalry drawn up and standing still. So it proved on this occasion, and after a brief skirmish the wild Llaneros drove the royalist cavalry from the field. Only some two hundred Spanish hussars, veterans of the Peninsular wars, stood firm, presenting a grim front to all attacks.

Dressed in their yellow uniforms, that in America

earned them the name of Tamarindos, their Hungarian
pelisses hanging from one shoulder, and their tall
hussar caps, secured by a cord of yellow braid, they
sullenly retired upon the infantry, keeping their formation as if they had been on parade.

It is most probable that the attack of the Llanero
cavalry would have been unable to break the ranks of
the Spanish infantry, and that covered by the hussars
they would have gained the shelter of the woods, practically unharmed, except for the loss of their irregulars
who had dispersed and fled. However Páez had not
gained the weather-gage for nothing. Detaching fifty
men whom he had held in readiness, he gave them
orders to set the grass on fire, over a wide front. The
flames rolled down upon the massed infantry, drawn
up in close formation, with a terrific roar. Had it not
been that four days before, the grass had been set alight
upon the other side of a depression in the plain, they
must have perished to the last man, reduced to ashes
where they stood. As it was, through the scorching
heat, and clouds of dust, they gained the other side
of the "Cañada,"* where they found water and
marched along refreshed. Time after time the cavalry
of Páez, led by himself, swooped down upon them,
jumping their mounts across the flames. For a long
league (a mortal league) the pursuit went on, until the
infantry reached the forest about The Cold Ford,† on
the Apure, and took shelter in the woods. The royalists
lost all their artillery and ammunition, and many of
their arms, that they had thrown away to escape the
fire fell into the patriots hands.

Though not decisive, the battle of Mucuritas was a
moral victory, in that the patriots' loss was very small

* A Canada is a dry valley corresponding to the Indian Nullah, or Arabi
Guadi.

† El Paso del frio.

compared to that of their opponents. Moreover it was the first reverse that the troops of Morillo had sustained since 1815, when they landed in America.*

Páez rose in the public estimation as a skilful leader, and many who had been kept away from the patriot cause, by its apparent hopelessnesss, flocked to his standard.

Morillo who himself in Spain had probably resorted to almost the self same guerrilla tactics, employed by Páez and the rest of the Llanero leaders, saw at once, that for the first time since his coming to America, that he had met with adversaries that had to be taken seriously. Writing to the King to report on the battle of Mucuritas, he gives the following testimony to the courage and the tenacity of the Llanero cavalry. "Fourteen consecutive charges on my wearied battalions, showed me that those men were not a scanty band of cowards, as I had been informed, but organised troops, able to compete with the best in the service of Your Majesty."

As a man brought up to arms from earliest youth, he saw at once that the problem he was called upon to solve was to prove arduous. He showed moreover that he had an open mind, for at that time, the absurd opinion prevailed in Europe, that men and the domestic animals became degenerate, when born in the New World. So serious did Morillo think the state of his affairs, that on receipt of the bad news, he instantly joined Latorre's shattered forces, at the Cold Pass on the Apure River. Marching along the line of forest on the river bank, he reached the town of San Fernando, which he occupied in force.

Páez hung on his flanks, but was not strong enough to venture an attack. From San Fernando, Morillo sent off Latorre, to the province of Guayana, and leaving San Fernando strongly garrisoned marched on to Barce-

* The battle of Mucuritas was fought on the 28th of January, 1817.

lona to attack the patriots in the great island of
Margarita where they were strongly entrenched. This
left Páez almost the undisputed master of the Llanos,
although the towns and villages mostly remained in the
possession of the royalists.

The province of Casanare Páez cleared entirely of
the Spaniards, taking the capital Pore by a strange
stratagem. Having surprised a detachment of the
royalists asleep, he dispatched them all and having
dressed his men in their uniforms, marched on at once,
and entered the little town of Pore flying the Spanish
colours and with a military band. The garrison thinking they were a Spanish force coming to join them,
made no resistance, and were taken prisoners to a man.

If Páez had not the qualities of a great general,* he
certainly displayed thus early in his career, an aptitude
for statesmanship.

As there was an absolute and complete dearth of
money in the Llanos, he set up his own mint in San
Fernando, the first and probably the last that the Llanos
have possessed. " Páez then established a mint in San
Fernando de Apure having collected all the silver he
could lay hands on, bits, stirrups, scabbards and silver
mounted gear. A smith† and his son ran the silver into
bars and hammered them out thin. This money had no
particular shape, and was stamped with a home made
die, so that it resembled the coins known in the West
Indies, as Cut Money."‡ The money Páez issued must
have been very like the old Spanish money, chiefly
coined at Potosi, called " Moneda recortada," which
had so many corners, that Cervantes, speaking of a thin

* See the judgment of O'Leary, in his Memorias quoted *Supra*.

† His name was Anzola, Páez says in his Memoirs, but passes over the
whole episode casually, as if coining money was an ordinary duty of a leader
of irregular cavalry.

‡ " Campaigns and Cruises in Venezuela and New Granada," London,
1831.

horse, said it had " as many corners as a real piece."
The Llanos took this strange currency, without mis-
givings, for Páez promised to call it in when he was
able. This promise he faithfully redeemed, but for
years afterwards, his Cut Money was faithfully taken
and received, throughout the Llanos.

Páez was now in a position of authority, and though
he passed his days on horseback, for skirmishes between
the royalists and the republicans were increasing, he
yet had time, as he sets down with pride, to keep an
eye upon the cattle, and to give orders that they should
not be recklessly destroyed. So well his orders were
obeyed, that though both armies looked for their
maintenance to the vast herds of cattle on the plains,
when it was over, they were still plentiful.

Up to this time Páez and Bolivar were personally
unknown to one another. Whilst from the province of
Guayana Bolivar's forces were advancing to join those
of Páez's, he was not idle. At the beginning of
the year 1818, in spite of the rains that had begun to
inundate the country, he set out to take Pedraza, a town
upon the other side of the Apure in which place
Morillo, most of whose forces lay either at Calabozo
or Barinas, had placed a garrison. Páez himself
headed the expedition, with all his "Guard of Honour"
mounted upon white horses and with a thousand horses
in reserve. White horses he explains are the best
swimmers, " as the Llaneros and I myself* believe."
This superstition founded as are most other superstitions
upon submerged facts, obtains in almost every part of
South America.† Pedraza proved an easy capture, and
Páez was able to clothe some portion of his men out of
the booty.

* " Memorias," page 162.

† The author agrees with Páez and the Llaneros. He has always found
white horses the best swimmers, and owned one in Paraguay that was

By one of those rapid raids he so much excelled in, swimming at the head of his cavalry, carrying their saddles on their heads, the Rivers Canagua and Paguëy, each of them at least a quarter of a mile in width, he suddenly appeared before Barinas, surprised the garrison, killed some of them and took many prisoners. As he had no boats at his disposal and his men were encumbered by the plunder of the stores in Barinas, he placed it in hide boats like coracles and passed successfully. These boats he formed by cutting holes all round the outside edge of a cow's hide and running a strip of hide through the holes, so as to form a kind of coracle. The articles to be transported he put inside, and then tightening the strip of hide so as to make a bag of the cow's hide, launched it tied to a lasso. Then a man swimming towed it across the river, holding the lasso in his teeth.

His various exploits and the popularity he had achieved by them, and by his frank and open manners with his wild followers, the only method possible to conciliate them, he had become a power in the Apure district and throughout the plains. No one contested his nomination to the chief command, and so great was the confidence the inhabitants reposed in him that they placed all the horses and the cattle at his disposal. At that time he says there were about a million head of cattle and five hundred thousand horses in the province, and of the latter about forty thousand broken in and fit for service* in the wars.

---

renowned for his prowess. He always swam with his back well out of the water, and his head erect, like a water snake. The author hopes . . . the Central Americans have a saying, "When the Mocking Bird sings, the Indian dies, I don't believe it, but it happens" . . . that "El Blanco" is now in some equine paradise, where there is always good grass and water where saddles are unknown, and where exists "no cruel spur to mak' him weary."

* When Páez says that they were "broken in and fit for service," he means for a Llanero, though in all probability, they would have proved not

Páez at that time (1818) was about eight and twenty years of age, he could not read and write, according to the testimony of several of the officers who knew him intimately when they served in the British Legion. His natural abilities, his bravery and his undoubted talents as a guerrilla leader, had placed him in command. His men adored him, and certainly his services to the patriot cause had been considerable, inferior alone to those Bolivar had achieved, though in a smaller theatre. He was a man who always chafed against authority, never having been accustomed to it. Yet when Bolivar sent Colonels Manuel Manrique and Vicente Parejo with a proposal that he should recognise him as the Supreme Chief* of the Republic, he at once fell in with it.

Only the purest patriotic motives could have moved him, for at that time he had not met Bolivar and had not fallen beneath the spell the Liberator seems to have exercised over all those who came in contact with him. Had he been influenced by a base ambition and a dislike to take the second place, this was the moment for him to have rebelled against Bolivar, as many others of his officers rebelled on similar occasions, bringing the patriot cause almost to ruin by their treachery. Páez at once disclosed his resolution to his army, alleging that Bolivar had superior claims and that his talents and his prestige entitled him to take supreme command. That he was right in his decision and judged the situation wisely cannot be doubted, for after all he was unknown outside the limits of his province, and by that time Bolivar had a world-wide reputation and had given proofs of his good generalship in a far wider field.

So when Páez knew Bolivar had left Angostura and

---

very reassuring mounts for Europeans. " This horse is quiet enough, for an Englishman to ride," was a phrase often to be heard amongst the Gauchos of the Argentine.

* Jefe Supremo.

was on the march to meet him at the town of San Juan
de Payara, he too set out to keep the tryst. Upon his
way he beat up the quarters of Morillo, who had advanced and occupied San Fernando de Apure. Although
he made only a false attack, more with the object of
frightening the enemy than of defeating him, the
Spanish forces fell into the trap and in a panic recrossed
the rivers Apurito and the Portuguesa, and never
stopped in their retreat until they reached the town of
Calabozo, where Morillo was encamped.

On this occasion Páez had several hundred Cunaviche Indians with him. Their arms were bows and
arrows, and they marched naked but for the breechclout, with feathers on their heads. Their chief, Linache,
Páez made their general, and fearing that the whistling
of the musket balls about their ears would cause a panic
in their ranks, he primed them with a good dose of
aguardiente before they marched to the attack. This fire
water, to which they probably were strangers, had the
desired effect. Cutting their tongues with the points
of their arrows they bathed their faces in the blood, and
rushed like lions to the fight. One of the captains,
who bore the name of " Twopence "* that the Spaniards
had given him, not being able to pronounce his own,
advanced so far beyond his followers under the influence of the aguardiente that he arrived alone before the
Spanish trenches and was cut to pieces instantly, dying
a hero's death for a cause that he could not possibly
have known much about, except that fate had given him
the chance of killing some of the white tyrants who had
enslaved his countrymen.

The attack over, the Spaniards in retreat, and the
Indians perhaps recovered from the effects of the un-
familiar stimulant, Páez advanced to meet the Liberator. Some four leagues from San Juan de Payara they

* Dos Reales.

encountered one another.   Getting off their horses they embraced, holding each other for a moment in their arms, with their heads looking over one another's shoulders, in the same way the patriarchs embraced in the Old Testament.

CHAPTER IX

THE historic meeting between the two remarkable men, so unlike in almost all respects, except in the desire for the independence of their country, took place at the cattle farm of Cañafistola, near San Juan de Páyara, upon the thirty-first of January, 1818. Bolivar had received a careful education, for his family was one of the richest in Venezuela at that time. His biographer, General Daniel Florence O'Leary,* says of him, " he spoke and wrote French correctly and Italian pretty well, of English he knew little, hardly sufficient to understand what he read. He knew the Greek and Latin classics thoroughly, for he had studied them and liked to read them in the best French translations."

Páez had only the rudiments of primary education beaten† into him by the hedge school mistress, Gregoria Diaz. What the rudiments‡ consisted of it is difficult to say, for at the time of his first meeting with Bolivar, in 1818, he was quite illiterate, as all the officers who served with the British Legion testify. His university had been the Llanos, and his tutor Manuelote, the negro capataz.§ At that time Páez had never even visited Caracas.

Bolivar had travelled extensively, had married in Madrid, had lost his wife after a year, had lived in Paris, visited London and Rome, and frequented good society in England, Italy and France.

Páez was a centaur, accustomed to break wild horses, an expert with the lazo and the lance, and a complete frontiersman at all points.

* " Memorias del General O'Leary."

† " A fuerza de azotes." See Chapter I.

‡ " Aprendi los primeros rudimentos de uña enseñanza demasiado circunscrita." Memorias de Páez.

§ Overseer.

Bolivar rode well and was remarkable for his endurance in the saddle, so much so that later in life he earned the nickname of " El Culo de hierro," which may be rendered " Copper bottomed." O'Leary says he did not look very well on horseback; but then beauty is often in the eye of him who sees it; and the reverse is true. Still O'Leary had an intense admiration for Bolivar, as his voluminous biography amply testifies. Probably there was all the difference between the horsemanship of Páez and Bolivar that exists between the natural and the taught horseman; a gulf never to be bridged.

How the Liberator struck Páez the following passage shows: " Hardly had he seen me, from a good distance off, than he got on his horse to go out to receive me. When we met we both dismounted and gave one another a warm embrace. I told him that I thought it of good augury for the patriot cause to see him in the Llanos, and hoped that from his talent and experience we should find out new means of using the resources that we put at his disposition, to launch the thunderbolts* of destruction against the enemy.

" With a generosity that characterized him, he answered me in flattering words, dwelling upon my constancy in resisting the dangers and the hardships of all kinds with which I had had to wrestle in defence of the Fatherland, and assuring me that by our mutual efforts we should be able to finish with the enemy who was oppressing us.†

---

* It is to be remembered that Páez was writing in Spanish, and phrases of that kind, were so ordinary as to be almost colourless in the Venezuela of those days.

† Readers who may find this passage flowery, have never listened to a speech in South America. There public discourses rarely are delivered to persuade. Their object is to raise enthusiasm. To northern Europeans they would no doubt seem full of hyperbole and devoid of commonsense ; but then to South Americans, perhaps our nordic eloquence would serve but as an opiate.

Bolivar was then in the flower of his youth and in the full enjoyment of the strength, such as it is, that comes from city life. His stature, without being heroic, was nevertheless sufficient for a sculptor who wished to represent a hero; his two principal distinctions consisted in the extreme mobility of his body and the brilliance of his eyes, which were black, lively and penetrating as those of an eagle. His skin, though burned by the sun of the tropics, still preserved its clearness and its lustre, in spite of all the many and violent changes of climate he had undergone in his campaigns. For those who think a warrior must be an athlete, Bolivar would have lost, when he was seen, all they had imagined him to be; but the artist at first sight and at a glance, could not but have discovered in Bolivar, those external signs that characterize a man strong in will power and fit to carry out any enterprise that requires great intelligence and great tenacity.

In spite of the arduous life that he had lived, sufficient to break down the rudest constitution, he was full of health and vigour. His temperament was gay and jovial. In private life he was most agreeable, impetuous and dominating when he had some important enterprise in view; thus he united both the courtier and the warrior in himself. He was fond of dancing, gallant and much addicted to ladies' society, and skilful in the management of his horse. He used to like to gallop across the plains of the Apure after the deer that abound there. In camp he kept his spirits up with witty jokes; but on the march he was always somewhat restless, and tried to fight against his impatience by singing patriotic songs. He was perhaps too fond of fighting, but whilst the battle lasted he was always calm. In rallying fugitives he neither spared example nor his voice and sword.

The exterior appearance of Bolivar, weak physically

and accustomed to all the comforts of a luxurious home
from his early years, formed a great contrast to the
dwellers on the Llanos, robust athletes who had never
known any other kind of life but a continued struggle
with the elements and wild animals." This description
of Bolivar, written when Páez was an old man in New
York, depicts him as well, or better, than the accounts
that have come down to us from the pens of educated
writers, in the same way that now and then inferior
painters catch a likeness that escapes better graced
artists.

Bolivar was anxious at all hazards to take Caracas,
for he saw what prestige it would give the patriot cause.
Páez and his Llaneros, not unnaturally saw nothing but
the Llanos, and it was his ambition to destroy Morillo's
army that occupied the town of Calabozo, and make
himself master of the plains. Either plan had something to be said for it, for against the prestige that the
possession of the capital would give, especially in
foreign countries, the mastery of the Llanos assured the
patriots of the great breeding grounds for horses and
for cattle, elements almost indispensable for warfare
in the Venezuela of those days. It was at this juncture
that Páez performed perhaps the most amazing feat of
his extraordinary life.

To march upon Caracas, Bolivar was obliged to cross
the Apure, for the town of San Juan de Payara is on
the west side of it. The river is about a quarter of a
mile in width, with a strong current of some four miles
an hour. The patriots had no boats, and in the middle
of the river the Spaniards had a squadron of armed
launches that barred the passage in one place, where
troops could land upon the other side.

Three or four days Bolivar meditated on his position,
not knowing what to do. All the time Páez was endeavouring to get him on the march, assuring him that

he would provide the necessary boats. At last Bolivar
made up his mind to march. When they got within a
mile of the river, Bolivar asked Páez where the boats
were that he had promised to provide. Pointing to
where the launches lay out in the middle of the stream,
Páez said, " there they are." " I see them," said Bolivar, " but what I do not see is how to take them." Páez
said smiling, " with our cavalry." " Where is this
water cavalry then? " Bolivar said, and Páez, pointing
to his Guard* of Honour, answered, " here."

With fifty of his Guard of Honour, riding with their
girths and cruppers loosened,† Páez galloped to the
bank. Then, letting their saddles slide down to the
ground, without dismounting they plunged into the
stream. They held their lances in their mouths, and
kept their horses' heads against the current by splashing
water in their faces with their hands. Those on the
bank kept up a constant yelling to scare away the alligators, whilst Bolivar and his staff anxiously watched
the swimmers in their desperate enterprise.

One of those panics that now and then seize men
confronted with a situation that they cannot possibly
have dreamed of took possession of the soldiers in the
boats. After an irregular discharge that did no damage,
for all they had to aim at were the horses' heads and the
men, naked from their waists upwards, they took to
their canoes and fled. The horsemen, from the horses'
backs, leaped on board the boats after a bloodless
victory. Turning their horses loose, who at once swam
back again to the same bank that they had left, without
a single loss, Páez in triumph brought the launches
back to where Bolivar and his staff were sitting like
equestrian statues, hardly daring to believe their eyes.

It was possibly the first time in recorded history that

* Su Guardia de Honor.

† Cruppers are in universal use, in the Llanos of Venezuela.

K

cavalry had fought a skirmish in the water, and certainly the last. Only men such as the Llaneros of those days, mounted on horses accustomed by the exigencies of the six months inundations of the country to take to water almost as readily as Newfoundland dogs, could have accomplished such a feat. Even they would scarcely have attempted it without a Páez swimming, as he would have said, " in the point* of them." His men all knew him by the familiar name of " Tio " (uncle), and when he shouted " Who will follow me? " the water must have boiled as the wild horsemen jostled one another, all eager to be first. Such men had but scant need to fight for liberty, for they were all born free of the Llanos, where, had they known it, they were far better off than their descendants, who have freedom to elect a pinchbeck Cæsar called a president to take tithe of their anise and their cumin and make them render up to him all that he thinks his due.

It was about this time that Páez first came into contact with the various British officers who had arrived to join Bolivar in his struggle for independence against Spain. Laval† Chesterton says, " When I set out towards Barinas some of the inhabitants told me that Bolivar had his camp only a few miles from that city, in the direction of the town of Arauca. Therefore I went to join him at that place. The brave general Páez, although he did not know me, received me with the greatest cordiality. Seeing me weak in consequence of a wound I had received in a skirmish with the Spaniards, he offered generously to afford me the few comforts that he disposed of until I was completely cured of my wound. Only to nature does this heroic man owe his virtues and his ideas.

" Brought up in a completely savage country, without

* En la punta.
† " Recollections of a service of three years during the war of extermination in the Republics of Venezuela and Colombia." London, 1828.

the advantages either of birth or fortune, and only by his personal merit, his prowess and indomitable courage shown in the various actions where he has been present during the revolutionary war, have raised him to the position of leader of the native levies that have been of so much help in all the territory of the republic. When the first revolutionary movement took place he was quite young, and served as a common soldier in one of the irregular bands that rose up in the Llanos; but even in such a humble position he soon found means to distinguish himself amongst his comrades.

" His strength and courage always gave him the victory in the gymnastic exercises the Llaneros practise. The skill he had acquired with the lance, their favourite weapon, gave him the advantage in all disputes. With it (the lance) he had put hors de combat so many of the enemy in the skirmishes in which he had been engaged that he gained the respect of all his companions, whilst his affable and unpretentious bearing ensured their friendship. He is much attached to the English, whom he styles his brothers,.and has always insisted that the gratitude of the country was due to them. His valour makes him dear to them, and with the exception of Mariño, Páez is the leader in Colombia* who is most popular amongst the English.†

" Nature has endowed Páez with surprising strength. Sometimes, and only as an exercise, when his men are catching wild cattle with the lazo, he will single out a bull, and pursuing it on horseback seize it by the tail,‡ and with a sharp jerk bring it to the ground. If on any of their excursions he comes across a

---

* Colombia and Venezuela were then one republic joined together, under the name of Colombia.

† Chesterton refers to the English who were serving with Bolivar at the time.

‡ The sport is known in Venezuela under the name of Tailing (coleando) a bull. It requires knack rather than strength.

tiger or a wild boar he instantly transfixes it with his lance.

"General Páez suffers from epileptic attacks, when his nervous system is excited, and then his soldiers have to support him during the combat or after it. When the attack comes on Páez is so convulsed that he falls from his horse, but it is so well trained that when he falls it never moves away until some of the soldiers come to lift him up. Then they carry him to the rear and sprinkle water on his face. Sometimes they dip him into water and shake him violently. After these fits, which have often put him in great danger from the enemy, he is generally very weak for several days. As soon as he is able to mount his horse he returns to the combat, although on some occasions the attack has been so severe as to deprive him of the power of speech."

Chesterton sums up his estimate of Páez by saying " He is a sincere patriot and certainly a brilliant ornament to his country, which owes him the chief means of continuing as a republic." In this judgment his admirer clearly was in error, for despite all the qualities of leadership Páez displayed, they never rose above the talents of a chief of irregular cavalry.

The continuance of the republic depended at that time upon Bolivar, and upon him alone. Many of his generals were able men, as Arismendi, Santander, Mariño, Piar, Anzoategui and Sucre. They stood to him in the same relation as his marshals stood to Napoleon. Páez was Bolivar's Murat. The most of the others were as anxious to supplant him as were Napoleon's generals to oust him from the supreme command. Sucre alone, whom Bolivar loved and trusted, never rebelled against him. Sucre, the first president of what is now Bolivia, might have carried on Bolivar's work, had he not fallen by the hand of assassins at the height of his career.

When they had crossed the river Apure in the launches Páez had procured with his marine cavalry, Bolivar set out for the capital. Páez, who had camped on the right bank of the River Oritua near a ford known as Los Tres Moriches, threatened Morillo, who thought himself secure in Calabozo, the capital of the Llanos and a considerable town. It lies in a flat plain covered with wiry grass. For leagues around it there is nothing to be seen but grass and sky. To the eastward, the distant hills are visible; the twin peaks known as Los Morros de San Juan, faintly discernible, looking like two blue clouds. The plaza with its shady Paraiso trees and its stucco seats, its flowers and fountain, makes an oasis in the sea of overwhelming heat. The great cathedral, relic of Spanish rule, fills up one side of the square. Its doors are always open like the doors of a mosque. Only in northern climates do we keep our churches under lock and key.

The prison,* from which the town is said to take its name, also built by the Spaniards, in the solid style in which all that they built in South America was done, as if they thought their empire was to be eternal, flanks the cathedral. Low-roofed, but substantial houses of the colonial period, their windows guarded by wrought iron gratings, their doors studded with iron nails, give an air as of a southern Spanish town transplanted to a still more ardent climate. Rings for hitching horses fixed into the walls of all the houses, planted at a height sufficient to prevent the animal fastened to them getting his feet over the halter, show that the men who placed them in the walls were horsemen.

The streets, unpaved and sandy, are mere Moorish ramblas,† too sun-scorched even for yellow dogs to lie

---

* Calabozo — prison. Hence, calaboose

† Ramel in Arabic means sand   The Spanish word Rambla is a corruption of it.

and bask in them, as they do in southern European towns.

Morillo probably occupied the Spanish governor's palace on the west side of the great plaza. It stands to-day, somewhat shorn of its former splendour, a memorial of Spain's greatness in the Indies. The solid walls, the great flagged patios, the windows secured by wrought-iron gratings, probably forged in Spain, light and artistic, but still strong enough to resist attacks from the outside, the innumerable rooms round the quadrangle, almost all communicating with each other, the carved wooden ceilings fashioned in squares and gilt, the vast reception room, all tell of a grandeur that has disappeared.

To-day the mansion serves as a residence for the governor of the state of Guarico. He camps rather than occupies the house. Hammocks swing in the great unfurnished rooms. The Spanish furniture, made like their houses to resist the march of time, has long since mouldered through neglect, or been exchanged for modern gimcracks from " Paris de Francia."

The streets, after the style of most towns in South America, lose themselves in the plain, as rivers flow into the sea. The houses for a square or two outside the plaza, all the towns are built in squares with straight streets cutting one another at right angles, gradually get smaller. Then they turn to ranchos, each with its plot of ground, planted with bananas, papaws or orange trees. All have their mangy-looking chickens, that are never fed, but pick up a precarious living as God wills it. Generally a donkey or a mule is tied under a shed with a rough thatch of palm leaves, or a horse always kept saddled during the day stands nodding, fastened beneath a tree. Then the huts grow scarcer, and the plain has eaten up the town. From the last rancho the occupants look out over the Llanos, as a sailor looks out on the sea.

Páez who had passed the night with a detachment of his cavalry only three leagues from Calabozo, was on the move at four o'clock, before the false dawn cheats the sleeper, in hopes to carry off the cattle of the garrison. These were shut up in a corral at the outside of the town, so as to be near their grazing ground. As the first rays of the rising sun broke through the night, Páez and his men quickly opened the corral and drove the cattle off, for as no enemy was known to be about they were not guarded or the guards were sound asleep.

As they moved off driving the " creagh," as a herd of stolen animals used to be called upon the Highland border, where many an operation such as Páez had performed* took place, they were seen by the soldiers of the garrison. News was brought to Morillo, who was in bed, that an army had appeared before the town, for scouts in those days (and in these) when suddenly confronted by the appearance of an unexpected enemy, are apt to magnify his strength.

Morillo, who was not easily alarmed, sprang from his bed exclaiming, " What army can be here, unless it came by air." Then calling for his horse he mounted and, followed by his staff, rode through the sandy streets towards the plain. Fortunately for him as it turned out, he had the foresight to leave a body of two hundred infantry in a strategic position to cover his retreat.

---

* The writer's great-great-grandfather, Nicol Graham of Gartmore, was the only proprietor on that part of the Highland border who always refused to pay blackmail to Rob Roy.

He and the redoubtable Rab Ruadh, were a couple worthy of each other. On one occasion it is said Laird Nicol took Rob prisoner and confined him in the old castle of Gartarton and would certainly have hanged him, for he was no stickler for the sanctity of human life, had not Rob taken " las de villadiego " during the night.

When Páez saw the glittering uniforms of the staff officers he at once judged it was Morillo who had come out to see what was afoot. Without a moment's pause he charged them, forcing them slowly back upon the town.

Morillo who was covering his staff's retreat, owed his life to the devotion of one of his staff officers, who seeing a Llanero about to pierce his general with his lance, for he had got a little separated from his retreating officers, threw himself bravely before him, and received a mortal wound. Only this hero's Christian name, Carlos, has been preserved. Without his devotion Morillo certainly would have finished his adventurous career upon that sandy street. As it was, being both a brave man and a fine rider, he spurred his horse, and in a bound or two rejoined his officers. At the same moment the infantry that had been left in ambuscade opened a hot fire, and Páez was obliged to draw his men off, having only missed by the merest chance striking Spain a blow which at that time would certainly have brought the struggle to an end. The infantry that had just saved Morillo had a tragic ending to the day, being cut off to the last man before they had the time to seek the shelter of the town.

Bolivar who was camped five or six miles off had heard the firing and rushed up reinforcements who got between the city and the Spanish infantry. They formed a square and showed a bold front to the repeated charges of Bolivar's cavalry. Morillo was unable to relieve them, for a strong force, that Páez estimates at two thousand infantry and as many cavalry, made an attack upon the town. At last the two hundred men of the retreating infantry were reduced to four. These refused all offers made to them of quarter and continued firing whilst they had ammunition. Then standing back to back, the nameless heroes met death with their faces to the foe.

Páez laments their fate, and says his men over their fires at night spoke of them with admiration, saying that they fought to the last, " culo con culo," a phrase that Spanish scholars may easily translate.

CHAPTER X

AFTER this success the first of the differences of opinion between Páez and the Liberator took place at a conference in which they met at a village called El Rastro, three leagues from Calabozo, to discuss their future plans.

Morillo had at that time provisions only sufficient for a week, and in effect was in considerable straits, but possibly not in such a desperate state as Páez thought. From the first Bolivar had put before all else the capture of the capital, for reasons that would commend themselves to a man of far embracing views. He saw of course the increase of prestige that his cause would gain, not only in Venezuela but in other countries, if he could date his correspondence from the capital. Above all else he desired the recognition of the United States. This he was not likely to receive if he was only known as the commander of guerrilla force wandering about the plains.

Páez, upon the other hand, naturally put the possession of the plains in the first place. There was something to be said for his view of the position. Could he have forced Morillo to surrender, or defeated him, everyone in the Llanos would have flocked to him, and he would soon have seen himself at the head of a considerable force. Enormous herds of horses and of cattle would have been at his command.

As the Llanos served for a refuge in defeat to royalists and patriots alike, where they were safe from pursuit, could rest, supply themselves with remounts for

their cavalry, and from their recesses sally out upon the
enemy, to close them to the defeated royalists would be
to force them to the coast, where they could find assistance from their fleet.   Thus certainly a point would
have been gained and the interior of the country freed
from the enemy.

The conference was long and heated, so much so that,
as Páez says, " those who were looking on from a
distance thought we were engaged in fierce dispute."*
Probably this fierce dispute laid the first seeds of the
future animosity that took place between these two remarkable men.   There was another reason that probably
weighed powerfully with Páez in pressing to attack
Morillo at once, instead of marching on the capital.

The Llaneros were as much attached to their plains
as the Swiss to their mountains, and never liked to
leave them.   On several occasions during the Independence Wars they deserted in whole regiments as
soon as they found themselves amongst the hills.   One
of their chief reasons was that their unshod horses,
coming from the plains where stones are as unknown as
on the Pampas of the south, soon became lame and quite
unserviceable on the rough mountain roads.

George Laval Chesterton† in his most interesting
account of his adventures, has the following: " As the
roads continued to ascend, and became stony, all the
horses that were natives of the plains began to flag and
got lame.   This was actually the cause of the desertion
of an entire corps of Llaneros under Colonel Carbajal.
His men, who bore with cheerfulness their own fatigues,
could not look with indifference on the hardships and
loss of their horses and left the army in bodies at every
halt."

* " Una reñida disputa."   Memorias, Páez 186.

† " Peace, War and Adventure.   An autobiographica Memoir by
George Laval Chesterton, Captain in the Army of Colombia."   London,
1828, page 159.

He is writing of Bolivar's march across the Andes into New Granada in the year 1819.

As Páez must have been aware of the temper of his men and their reluctance to leave their plains, his opposition to Bolivar's wish to march upon the capital appears reasonable, as does his reluctance to leave a still unbeaten army in his rear. Though Páez was not a born commander, as was Bolivar,* he was on his own ground, and possibly at that moment saw the farther of the two. Next morning, before a decision had been taken one way or the other, news came that Morillo had evacuated Calabozo. Bolivar then gave orders to march at once and occupy the town, in spite of all that Páez urged to make him repass the River Guarico and cut Morillo off from the capital. On the march Páez and his light-armed, well-mounted men left the main body of Bolivar's forces at some distance in the rear.

News came to Páez through a man by the name of Pernalete, that Bolivar had been told that Páez had hurried on in front with the design of putting Calabozo to the sack. Páez was furious, and galloping up to where Bolivar and his staff had halted, protested furiously against the calumny. The Liberator, not a whit less indignant, said " Give me the name of the base traitor, and I will have him shot." Páez says he was satisfied with the threat, but did not tell the Liberator the calumniator's name, knowing Bolivar would have shot him instantly. The incident then closed and the two chiefs sat down to breakfast amicably; but without doubt the incident served to create suspicion and bad blood between them, for both the Liberator and Páez were naturally suspicious, and neither of them brooked a rival standing too near the throne.

The unexpected evacuation of Calabozo by Morillo

---

* Wellington is said to have spoken of him as a " remarkable commander," high praise from such an unenthusiastic man.

forced Bolivar's hand. He found himself obliged to
follow Páez's advice and deal with Morillo before
advancing on the capital. He was obliged to pursue
Morillo at all hazards. The Spanish general, who was
at the head of far superior forces than those of Páez and
Bolivar combined, retreated slowly, his infantry forming an impenetrable barrier to attacks by cavalry.

Páez relates with subcutaneous* satisfaction a repulse
that their forces suffered that, he hints, happened
through Bolivar's over-rashness in attack. A deserter
from the Spanish army appeared mounted on the horse
of a Spanish officer that he had stolen in order to escape,
saying he had important information to impart. Morillo
it appeared had placed in ambush some seven hundred
men, half cavalry, half infantry, sheltered behind a
high bank that overhung the ford upon the Guarico, by
which the pursuers had to pass. The deserter offered
to show a path where they could cross at another ford,
known to himself, and so avoid the ambuscade.

Bolivar, Páez says, impelled by his impetuous† character, refused to take the good advice. Advancing to
the bank he shouted " Soldiers, the enemy is there
before you," and ordered an attack. Páez says paw-
kily, " our infantry arrived at the edge of the river,
and in less than a quarter of an hour of a sharp fusillade
we were repulsed with considerable loss, especially of
officers." Generals in all ages appear to have loved
one another like Christians of different sects, and commentators aver that petty jealousies are as rife amongst
plumed, spurred, decorated and jack-booted warriors,
as in a ladies' school.

After another conference at Calabozo, Páez urged
Bolivar so strongly not to leave San Fernando de
Apure in Morillo's hands, putting before him the pro-

* Memorias, page 188.
† " Oyó mas bien los consejos de su carácter impetuoso."

bability that should they be defeated on the march to Caracas, the Llaneros of Calabozo, always inconstant in their allegiance to whatever party they belonged, might rise against them in the rear.   Thus their retreat would be cut off and the way to the Llanos barred. He pointed out that if San Fernando de Apure were once in their possession it would be easy to embark two or three thousand men, descend the Apure to the Orinoco, and wrest from the royalists the town of Angostura,* that was the key of the only channel by which they could obtain all that was necessary for carrying on the war.   The advice was good, and the local knowledge Páez possessed supplemented the military genius of Bolivar.

Páez was despatched to take San Fernando, whilst Bolivar pursued his march towards Aragua and Maracay, upon the high road to the capital.   Arrived at San Fernando, Páez three times summoned the garrison to surrender.   On their refusal he attacked the town. Night stopped the fighting and both sides lay on their arms.   At daylight, after a fierce fusillade the garrison surrendered, and the town fell into the hands of Páez and the patriots.   The affair, though important in the history of the country, was but a skirmish in reality, for the whole losses suffered by the patriots did not amount to more than twenty killed.   The amount of men engaged and the casualties received, though small, do not of necessity imply the battle was unimportant, for it is by the result of any struggle that its importance can be estimated.   On this occasion, the prestige gained by the patriots was great.

Páez recounts a curious incident that happened to him. As he rode through the chief square of San Fernando, upon a stake he found the skull of Pedro Aldao a brave patriot commander, slain by Boves, who had set it up as

---

* Angostura, now Ciudad Bolivar, is situated on a high bluff at the narrowest part of the Orinoco (hence the name), and commands the navigation of the river.

a trophy of his victory. When it was taken down to be given Christian burial, it was found that a bird had made its nest in it. In the nest were two fledgelings. When the bird fluttered out the soldiers held it for a good omen, that it was yellow, the distinctive colour of the patriots. These kind of incidents were frequent in the war of extermination that was being carried on. Neither side spared prisoners, and the ferocity of Bolivar, and of Páez, was only equalled by that of Morillo and the other royalist commanders.

The campaign on the whole at this time* was favourable to the patriots, although the taking of San Fernando de Apure, was balanced by the check Bolivar received at the River Senea where after six hours' fighting, he was beaten by General Morales and the royalists. Páez again puts down the defeat to Bolivar's own impetuosity and charges† him with having once again taken no notice of advice, given by local men. Things at that juncture looked black for the revolutionary cause.

Besides the check at Senea Bolivar had sustained a severe defeat at the battle of La Puerta, a victory for the royalists, that the Spaniards held so considerable, that Morillo was created Marquis of La Puerta, on account of it. Bolivar who had arrived at Los Tiznados, on the road to the capital, resolved to countermarch on Calabozo, and await reinforcements that were coming up the Apure from Guayana, to effect a junction with him.

He set out from San José de los Tiznados, to which place he had retired after the battle of La Puerta, for Calabozo. Once more the campaign was flowing back to the great plains. The road on which they marched, gradually descends through wooded country, till it passes out of the mountains to the plains. The vegetation becomes more scanty, and the heat increases, as the

* March, 1818.

† Memorias, page 193.

stony roads, across which great iguanas scuttle, leaving a train of dust, till it reaches Ortiz. Once a considerable town, and now almost deserted, Ortiz lies like a ruined Maya city, in the last woods that lap the edges of the plains like waves, that beat upon a desiccated sea. The houses have not been destroyed, but left abandoned, by their former owners. The powerful vegetation of the tropics writhes round their walls, opening great cracks in the masonry, and seems to press the lifeblood out of them, as the snake winds round the limbs of the Laocoon.

Páez joined the Liberator at Ortiz, bringing with him a strong contingent of his cavalry. After a sharp action, that had no decisive result on either side, Bolivar camped his forces at a place known as El Rincon de los Toros.

General Latorre at that time was the commander of the royalists, for Morillo had been wounded by a lance thrust, just at the moment of his victory at La Puerta.* Latorre's second in command was General Lopez, an energetic soldier and well accustomed to guerrilla warfare. This man conceived a plan to surprise Bolivar in the middle of his camp, a plan that only failed by a mere accident. In those days, except the regiments that came from Spain such as Valencey, Burgos or Barbastro, none had distinctive uniforms.

Thus such a plan as General Lopez had conceived, becomes more probable. He chose Captain Don Mariano Renovales and gave him eight picked men as followers. Renovales was one of those desperate men that civil war often produces. He must have known that his own chances of escape were small. His followers,† Páez allows were all brave men.

* Páez, page 192, says he was wounded by a Captain Juan Pablo Farfán, but Loraine Petrie, says by an unknown patriot who was hiding in the bush. —"Simon Bolivar." E. Loraine Petrie. London, MCMX, page 205.

† "Ocho hombres escojidos por su valor." Memorias de Páez, page 195.

Bolivar was sleeping in his hammock, which was known to be of white cotton and therefore visible at night. At four o'clock in the morning, the time that the old Spanish writers on the Conquest, so often call the " drowsy hour,"* Renovales and his eight valiant bravos, entered the revolutionary camp, pretending that they were a patrol returning from the field.

General Santander who was upon his rounds, encountered them, and thinking they were some of his own men returning back to camp from scouting, asked for the password.† They gave it readily, probably having learned it from a deserter, or a spy. On being asked where they had been, they answered, " we were sent out by the Liberator himself to ascertain the exact position of the enemy, and have returned to report." They asked the general where Bolivar was, as they had urgent news to impart. Santander innocently told them to follow him, and pointing with his whip in the faint light of early dawn, said, " there is his hammock, the white one in the middle of a group." Hardly had he spoken when nine shots rang out, all struck the white hammock in which Bolivar slept.

By one of those strange accidents that change the course of history, and make both unbelievers and believers think, at times, that fate is really the sole arbiter of man's destiny, the Liberator, was not in the hammock that was riddled by the balls. Having determined on an early start, he had had his mule saddled, and at the moment that the shots rang out, putting the whole camp into confusion, he was just about to mount. With a loud snort the mule dashed into the darkness, leaving Bolivar on the ground. As shots were flying wildly on all sides, he sought the shelter of the trees that stood about the camp.

* " El cuarto de la modorra."
† " El santo y seña."

L

In armies such as that of Páez, camp fires were seldom lighted, for they did little cooking, and in that climate, did not need fires to keep warm. Therefore Bolivar, who was no frontiersman, and probably enough felt himself bewildered by the unlooked for attack, although he tried till daylight, could never find the camp. This Páez himself, a master of all frontier craft, confesses was not strange, for as he says "the best Llanero who gets lost by night, is in the same case as a sailor in the middle of the ocean without a compass."*

Naturally the confusion in the camp was great. Some said Bolivar had been killed, others that he was taken prisoner. It was still too dark to look for him. As they were waiting for the dawn, at the first light the royalists attacked them violently. Without their leaders, for Páez did not come up with them till much later, and still suffering from the panic into which they had been thrown they suffered heavily, losing a quantity of men and many officers. The royalists satisfied with what they had done retired; but with the loss of General Lopez himself a Venezuelan, and the best officer of cavalry the royalists possessed.

General Cedeño, one of the patriot leaders, who was camped some distance off, hurried up when he heard the firing in the night. When he arrived at the place where the Liberator had been encamped it was deserted. Both friends and enemies had disappeared. The royalists had fallen back on their main body. The patriots, in disorder were trying to regain Calabozo, to reorganise their ranks. Bolivar still could not be found; but as

---

* "The Llaneros of those days, when on a journey and overtaken on the plains, always lay down with their faces turned to the point towards which they were journeying. For otherwise from the great sameness of the desert they would be bewildered and lose their way."—A History of the Revolution of Caracas, page 122. Major Flinters. London, 1819.

The gauchos of the Argentine Pampas on the south frontier had the same custom fifty years ago, for in crossing the trackless Pampas, he who lost himself perished. Hence their saying: "Quien se pierde, perece."

they struggled on, they found him sitting beneath a palm tree and hopelessly lost. As one of the fugitives had caught the Spanish general's horse, he gave it to Bolivar, who must have felt as he was mounting it, that the stars in their course indeed had fought for him.

Had he fallen at that juncture, it is difficult to see what would have been the fate of Venezuela and Colombia. The patriot generals were hopelessly at variance with one another. Santander, Mariño and Páez were able men, but the two first were of a disposition that made it difficult for anyone to work with them. Páez was incomparable in the Llanos with his wild cavalry, but had no experience of large armies, was without military training, could speak no language but his own, and at that time was quite illiterate.

Sucre,* by far the finest character of all the revolutionary leaders, was young, but little known, and had not had the chance to show the military talents that he afterwards displayed. Morillo, with Bolivar out of the field, would certainly have proved too strong an adversary for the patriots.

The war might have dragged on for years, especially in the Llanos, for Páez by this time had made his name there, wanted no commissariat, and was as difficult to capture or to bring to a decisive action, in which Morillo's knowledge and superior forces would have given him an easy victory, as it would be to lazo a wild horse on foot, upon the plains.

In the long run, Europe or the United States, prob-

---

* Sucre afterwards gained the great battle of Ayacucho, against the Spaniards in Peru, in which he took the Viceroy La Serna prisoner. For this victory he received the title of Gran Mariscal de Ayacucho, from the patriot Congress of Peru. He became the first president of Bolivia, which he governed wisely and humanely. He was, however, driven out by the intrigues of General Obando and basely assassinated on his way to Pasto on a solitary mountain road, by bravos sent by the same miscreant. Sucre alone was faithful to Bolivar to the last, and never stirred up strife against him.

ably might have interfered, and the advance of education and liberal ideas sooner or later, would have brought about the same result. Still independence would certainly have been put back for a generation, and the two colonies been exposed to a long period of devastating strife.

CHAPTER XI

ALL through the latter part of the year 1818, Bolivar was in Angostura, and Páez left alone in Casanare and Apure had to take decisions that were more properly in the province of the commander-in-chief. He was one of those born with ample confidence in his own abilities, and the warfare that he had to conduct was of the kind he understood. He exercised his powers mercilessly, but on the whole with impartiality, that is as he saw justice, for justice, as is truth, is rarely absolute, but as it seems in the mind of the man who has to face the problem.

Thus when a Major Villasana, a personal friend and a good leader, together with Garrido a valiant captain of his guard, and others had committed depredations on the property of non-combatants, he promptly shot them, together with a sergeant, an " alferez "* and several soldiers. Dealing with the men he had to deal with, he was forced to be as ruthless, both in the field and as to points of discipline, as he was easy going in his social intercourse with his wild followers. An Englishman who knew him well at that time, gives this interesting picture of the Llanero leader and his men.

" It was quite usual to see one of these rascals (the Llaneros) come up to Páez, calling him uncle or " compadre,"† and ask for anything he wanted, certain that

* Alferez — Ensign. It is an Arabic word meaning " The Horseman " originally.

† Compadre — Godfather, and is much used in Spanish as a familiar greeting amongst friends. Possibly the Elizabethan word " Gossip " gives the best rendering of the term used as a friendly appellation.

out of his good nature, he would not refuse him what
he asked. If he was absent when they came to see him,
they would search all the camp or town, shouting his
name in stentorian tones, until he heard them. At other
times when he was eating (which he always did in the
encampment), if any of them took a fancy to a piece
of jerked beef* or anything else he happened to be eating they would go behind him, and snatch it from his
hand. Then he would laugh and say, ' all right.' "†

Páez, in August 1818, had fixed his headquarters in
San Fernando de Apure. There he had been joined by
Colonel Hippisley with a regiment known as "The
First Venezuelian Hussars." This corps raised in England seems to have been composed of the off-scourings
of the streets, stiffened by a percentage of veteran
soldiers who had served with Wellington, in the Peninsular wars and at Waterloo. Hippisley himself was an
old soldier, something of a martinet, who had seen
much service in the cavalry. His officers with few
exceptions were young men of no experience and without military training, and as happens usually with those
who have but little knowledge of the world, a high
opinion of themselves. The non-commissioned officers
were all old soldiers. From the outset the expedition
had bad luck.

Bolivar's agent Don Luis Lopez Mendez‡ seems to
have been indifferent honest, and a type of the South
American financial agents of those days. He was profuse in promises, being aware no doubt that " words and
feathers are born away by the wind."§. If Hippisley
asked for anything Mendez immediately promised to

* Tasajo.

† " Recollections of Three Years Service in the Republics of Venezuela
and Colombia." London, 1828.

‡ Hippisley refers to him as " Don Mendez," which is as if in writing
of an English baronet, Sir John Smith, he had styled him Sir Smith.

§ Palabras y plumas, el viento las lleva.

give it to him, whether it was for increased pay for his men, compensation to their families in case they should be killed or rank and precedence in the Venezuelan army. He may have intended to implement his promises, or on the other hand he may have had but little money, for the patriot exchequer was not filled to overflowing. In that case he was not to blame, for it is ill takin' the breeks off a Hielanman. Hippisley however held him for a rogue and does not scruple to write it down in good set terms. What he thought of Hippisley is not recorded, but probably he took him for a punctilious fool, whom it was his duty to get out to Venezuela, to help the patriot cause.

If Mendez was a patriot himself, as Bolivar seems to have thought, for he is reported to have said that he was " the real Liberator of Colombia owing to his success in raising arms, supplies and men in England for the service of the Republic," he most likely thought as many advocates of causes, and even of religion, have occasionally held, that the end justifies the means.

Upon the voyage out, the inexperienced young men quarrelled and drank, and on arriving in the West Indian Islands, one was killed in a duel that arose out of a drunken brawl. In the Island of Grenada, Hippisley had to suppress a mutiny, covering his crew with a brass carronade and threatening to hang some of them at the yardarm in the style of Drake, or of Frobisher.

When after much delay and difficulty, they arrived in Angostura, they must have made a strange appearance accoutred as they were, in such a climate. " The established uniform of the regiment was a dark green jacket, with scarlet collar lapels and cuffs, some figured gold lace round the collar and cuff, with an ornamented Austrian knot on the arm above; a laced girdle round the waist, and two small scaled epaulettes; dark green

* " Simon Bolivar." Loraine Petrie, London, MCMX, page 214.

trousers edged with similar gold lace down the sides; chaco, etc., by way of dress clothing.

"Undress, dark green jacket with red cuff and collar, without facings trimmed with black lacings: dark green foraging cap, with grey overalls, wellington boots, etc., crimson sashes, black leather pouch, belts, silk sash, etc., etc., completed the field or morning uniform. The officers in addition had a blue camlet cloak lined with red." The normal temperature of Angostura is about 88 deg. to 90 deg. Fahrenheit, or even higher. To the inhabitants, Hippisley's first Venezuelian Hussars must have been a strange sight. No uniform less suited to the climate, could possibly have been devised.

At Angostura, Hippisley and his green jacketed and trousered regiment, met Colonel Wilson and his Red Hussars. Their uniform was even more fantastic than that of the First Venezuelians. Wilson and Hippisley as is not uncommon amongst officers of equal rank, in all the armies of the world, cordially disliked each other from the first. These fantastically tricked out warriors, were destined, their uniforms in rags, themselves hardened and braced by months of fighting on a diet of beef and water, with an occasional glass of rum, their wellingtons and chacos long discarded, to do heroic service for the Republic in the British Legion, in which they were incorporated. Neither of their colonels long remained with them. Hippisley who might have done good service, as he was an experienced officer, left Venezuela, after a few months campaigning, in disgust.

Wilson an intriguer to the core, was imprisoned by Bolivar for his share in the mutiny at San Fernando de Apure, and after several months confinement, was released and returned home in disgrace. Thus neither of the two commanders shared in the battles in which the British Legion became glorious.

Both Red and Green Hussars embarked after a brief

stay in Angostura, for San Fernando, where they joined Páez and Bolivar, who had suffered a reverse. Hippisley who had quarrelled with Bolivar at two interviews that they had had, seems to have liked Páez from the first. Wilson and Hippisley and their regiments arrived at San Fernando just at the moment it was about to be evacuated by Bolivar. By that time relations between Páez and the Liberator had become strained, and time only intensified their distrust of one another. Bolivar, General Miller says in his memoirs* was not personally popular. Though a man of greater genius it seems Bolivar had not the gift, that Páez certainly possessed, of a magnetic personality. All the British officers who came into personal contact with Páez, with one exception, have left enthusiastic descriptions of him.

The sole exception was Daniel Florence O'Leary,† the writer of the most authentic record of Bolivar, who from the first seems to have disliked Páez heartily. The reason that he gave for leaving Páez when almost all the Red Hussars remained with him, was his disgust at the way prisoners were massacred. If that was so and only he and Hippisley lay this charge to the account of Páez, in following Bolivar, he had but changed one butcher for another. It was Bolivar who proclaimed war to the death, and carried‡ out what he proclaimed, by ordering on several occasions a wholesale butchery.

* " Memoirs of General Miller." However Miller is almost alone in his estimate of the Liberator's personal charm.

† " Memorias Publicadas, por T. B. O'Leary." London, 1879—88.

‡ See his own report on the slaughter of prisoners during his advance on Caracas in 1813, his massacre in February 1814, and the many other massacres of defenceless prisoners which up to 1820 Bolivar never checked. It was at Achaguas, not very far from San Fernando, that Chesterton, the author of " Peace, War and Adventure, an Autobiographical Memoir," saw Páez and his men at the feast of St. John riding about in their shirts playing on guitars and calling on everyone to come out and dance. Those who refused were pulled out and rolled in the mud. The streets were muddy, and the joke (*sic*) consisted in making everybody as muddy as themselves.

During the month of August 1818, a curious movement took place in San Fernando de Apure, to promote Páez* to be Captain General. Bolivar had evacuated the town and set sail for Angostura. Páez was left in sole command, for Cedeño† whose life he had just saved rescuing him the indignant soldiers who accused him of cowardice, counted for little in the army, and Santander had been ordered by Bolivar to proceed to New Granada to initiate a campaign against the royalists. Both Larrazabal‡ and Baralt,§ insinuate that Páez instigated the movement secretly. He himself in his " Memoirs "¶ denies this hotly.

The " Acta," that is the certificate of his election to the office of commander-in-chief, was signed by everyone in the army, with the exception of the garrison of Achaguas and his own Guardia de Honor. At the time he received it he was at Achaguas a few leagues distant. At once he proceeded to San Fernando, where he called a meeting of all the officers and rebuked them for having taken such a step without authority. Colonel Wilson of the Red Hussars seems to have been one of the chief promoters of the movement. He was one of the few British officers who could speak Spanish, and was a violent tempered and ambitious man, who thought apparently that under Páez he would have more freedom, than with the Liberator. His men instigated, as

---

In the evening Páez and his men rode into the river to wash themselves. A gargantuan banquet followed. The bill of fare consisted of ribs of beef, wild boars roasted whole, and venison from the neighbouring woods, poultry, wild ducks, fish from the river, wild pheasants, cheese, corn bread and guarapo (fermented sugar juice). A banquet fit for the digestion of hard riding heroes alone.

* At that time only Bolivar (page 387) himself, Mariño and McGregor held that rank.

† " See Hippisley's Narrative." London.

‡ " Vida de Bolivar." Felipe Larrazabal, 1865.

§ " Resumen de la Historia de Venezuela," por R. M. Baralt y Diaz, 1841.

¶ Page 203, " Memorias de Páez."

Hippisley says, by hopes of plunder, all joined the mutiny with the exception of O'Leary, who with Hippisley and the officers and men who remained uncorrupted, embarked to join Bolivar at Angostura.

It does not seem, as far as can be judged from a perusal of the conflicting authorities, that Páez really wanted to rebel. In a footnote to his " Memorias,"* he says when Bolivar had returned to San Juan de Payara early in 1819, " He then asked me if I was not afraid that the matter of the " Acta " would have had consequences. I answered, no, saying that its authors had drawn back, and having become convinced, that it was going beyond their power to take the step, had asked me to forget it. This calmed Bolivar's fears." The long drawn out duel between Páez and Bolivar, was still undecided in 1819.

Morillo had assembled a large force, that is a large force for those days in America, composed of five thousand infantry and two thousand cavalry. Páez had some four thousand men all told, many of them raw recruits. The ranks were full of civilians, lawyers, merchants, even priests, in fact every man who could be taught to ride a horse and wield a lance, was pressed into the service of the republic. The greater part of the soldiers were of course Llaneros, who by this time must have acquired some sort of discipline. That is in the field, for once the battle over, they would submit to no authority. In fact it is a problem how even Páez could have kept them so long under arms. The richer creoles who had been oppressed, that is kept out of office, and had had all government appointments closed against them, understood well enough what issues were at stake. Although the Spanish rule was never so oppressive as for example that of the English government in Ireland, or of the French in Algeria, in days gone

* Page 207.

by, yet it was galling to well educated men such as were the richer creoles, to stamp them inferior to quite uneducated men who came from Spain.

The trading classes also naturally chafed at the severe restrictions put upon their trade, for nearly all the ports were closed to European commerce, and the colonists were forced to buy inferior goods from Spain. This was the Spanish policy, modified by time and the advancement of communications, down to their expulsion from their last West Indian possession, Cuba, once the pearl of the Antilles.

To Llaneros nothing of all these things applied. They consumed little or no European merchandise, nor could they much have cared who ruled in Caracas, for whether he was a governor sent from Spain, or an elected president, he had as little power to oppress the horsemen of the plains, as if they had been seagulls, or flying fish. Liberty more absolute than that enjoyed by the Llaneros, can rarely have existed upon earth. They had no Sheikhs as had the Arabs, nor did they live in perpetual dread of invasions by the wild Indians, as did the Gauchos of the southern plains. The spirit of resistance however was strong in every class, the citizens of San Fernando de Apure did not hesitate an instant, when Páez proposed to them to burn it down to prevent it falling into Morillo's hands.

Páez refers to it as a "sublime resolution," as in effect it was, as sublime and just as glorious as the burning down of Moscow, to save it from the French. The relative size of the two towns, does not make the sacrifice greater in one case than the other. A man can only sacrifice that which he has, and it is just as sublime a resolution to set fire to a straw thatched hut as to a marble palace, although historians usually consecrate one action with fine words and pompous paragraphs, and pass the other over, with a few contemptuous* words.

Morillo is said to have doubted for the first time of his ultimate success in putting down the revolution, when from the other side of the river he watched San Fernando burn. However he crossed the river Apure, without opposition and encamped close to the beach. During the night Páez had four wild horses lassoed, and tied dry hides to their tails. Then, carefully, he had them led, under the cover of the darkness to within about a gunshot distant from Morillo's camp, and let them go, ordering a few shots to be fired at the same time. They rushed on like a hurricane amongst Morillo's sleeping soldiery, spreading as Páez says as much confusion amongst the sleeping enemy as the two thousand oxen let loose upon the Roman camp by Hannibal.†

The episode has an air as of the siege of Troy about

* This is well exemplified in a passage in Loraine Petrie's "Simon Bolivar." In July, 1814, Bolivar (London, MCMX, page 245) was obliged to head the emigration of the entire population of Caracas to save them from massacre by the inhuman Boves.

"The roads to be traversed were bad at their best ; now in the height of the rainy season, they were mere rivers of mud and slush. There was no accommodation for housing this multitude of people of all classes, all ages and both sexes. Ladies accustomed to comfortable living found themselves after a long day of tramping through a sea of mud or over rugged rocky roads, compelled to lie for the night in the open drenched by the pitiless rain without even a fire and almost starving. . . . Mothers unable to nourish or even to carry their children were seen to hurl them over precipices, rather than leave them to die by the roadside. All the horrors of the retreat from Moscow (there were no women or children in that retreat) were here, except the cold which was made up for by the rain. For twenty days this miserable "Emigration of 1814," as it was called (*sic*) dragged on until Barcelona was reached. By that time the emigrants had been terribly reduced in numbers by hardships, by famine and by fever.

From Barcelona, notwithstanding the desperate condition of his enterprise, Bolivar contemplated sending one of his commanders to London to open up relations between republican Venezuela and Great Britain. This at a time when the republic was on its last legs ! There is something here of the strange admixture of comic opera which seems to be inseparable from many things South American."

It is hard to see where any element of comic opera is to be found, in the contemplation of sufferings so dreadful. Bolivar, like the Roman Senators after Cannæ, did not despair of the Republic. All honour to him. His

it. Páez no doubt would have dragged the body of
Morillo round the outskirts of Calabozo, at his horse's
tail, with as much zeal as his prototype dragged the
dead Hector round the walls of Troy. The result of
the old world stratagem was that the Spaniards were
delayed for some days gathering up their stampeded
animals.   For several days the two guerrilla chiefs
marched and countermarched about the Llanos, Páez
always striving to drive Morillo into the desert of
Cariben, knowing that then he would be unable to
support his army.

Morillo, who had seen much guerrilla warfare in
Spain, and by that time must have been well accustomed
to colonial warfare, countermarched again, and fell back
on Achaguas where he established his headquarters.
Things were in the position that neither Páez or Morillo
could obtain any decided advantage over one another,
when at the end of March (1819), Bolivar suddenly
joined Páez with a considerable force. As usual, they
differed as to what plan they should pursue.

At that time much depended on the movements of
the patriot general Urdaneta, who with fifteen hundred
men sent from the Island of Margarita, was advancing
on the capital. The islanders of Margarita, called in
Spanish, Margariteños, were a race apart. Most of
them were fishermen or pearl divers, and nearly all of
them were of great strength and stature, inured to
hardships and to perils, from their infancy. On several

---

action rather merits the adjectives Páez uses, " glorious and sublime," than
this slighting comment, on his heroic attitude.   The relatively small numbers
of the sufferers make no essential difference to the magnitude of the calamity.
    Pope Gregory the Great refused all food for eight and forty hours when
he heard a man had been found dead of hunger in the streets of Rome.
    † It has been pointed out that Páez at that time was quite illiterate and
therefore could not have heard of Hannibal or any of the Roman generals
to whom he refers in his " Memorias." Páez was illiterate at the age of
twenty-eight.   He wrote his Memoirs at the age of seventy, in New York,
and by that time, had learned English, and had a tolerable acquaintance,
both with Italian and with French.

occasions during the war they had already given proofs, both of bravery* and ferocity.

Páez advised delay, so as to allow Urdaneta to occupy Caracas before engaging Morillo in the field. Both Páez and Bolivar were afraid Morillo would attack and overwhelm Urdaneta before they could advance to his support. They therefore crossed the Arauca at San Juan de Payara, to attack Morillo in his camp.

Morillo was encamped at a place called Las Queseras del Medio, a name destined by the events of the next day to become famous in the annals of Venezuela, perhaps more famous than its importance really deserved. Certain events and battles in the history of all wars pass into legend, and are more remembered and evoke more enthusiasm than others, which though less spectacular, have had a greater influence on history. Such was the cavalry engagement at Las Queseras del Medio. No child in Venezuela but can talk about it, no orator (and orators in general remain children all their lives) but when hard pressed to move his audience does not fall back upon it, and usually achieves success.

Páez valued himself more on account of it, than upon any of his battles, for it had everything about it, that would appeal to one of his romantic temperament. Páez was put upon his mettle by a report brought by a deserter from the royalists that Morillo had conceived a plan to capture him. Morillo had observed that Páez frequently with a few followers advanced close to his ranks and after having made a false attack, returned immediately to push home a second attack.

Morillo had a force of two hundred men mounted on picked horses, ready to pursue Páez upon his feint, and by not giving him time to turn, force him in reality to flee, whilst the main body of the army should advance

* General Juan Bautista Arismendi, the companion and friendly rival of Páez, who played so large a part in the campaign of Apure, was a Margariteño.

to cut off his retreat. Neither Morillo or Páez had much to learn from one another as to the stratagems such kind of warfare entailed. Had it not been for the warning brought by the deserter, Páez might have fallen into the trap. Being forewarned and thus forearmed, he determined to pay back Morillo in his own coin.

Having obtained permission from Bolivar to beat up Morillo's quarters, Páez crossed the river (Arauca) with a picked body of one hundred and fifty cavalry. As he knew what Morillo had determined, he made a feint and then retired. This manœuvre he repeated several times, the Llaneros as they charged lying alongside their horses, showing but the left hand and the right foot towards the enemy, after the fashion of the Pampa Indians of the south and the Apaches of the north. In the half light, for night was fast approaching, they were almost invisible.

The royalists thinking their plan was going to be successful extended a considerable force of cavalry on either side, hoping to outflank Páez and his men and render their retreat impossible. Páez confesses in his Memoirs that they had all but succeeded, and his position was perilous in the extreme. The royalist artillery now opened fire upon him, and several companies of infantry, that Morillo had placed in ambuscade, began a galling fire. Páez who in that sort of moment, was in his element, detached one of his officers, Rondon by name, to make a false attack. Morillo's cavalry blinded by the smoke of their own fire and by the failing light, thought that the whole body of the republicans was as it were corralled. They closed in on them, presenting no longer two extended lines, but a serried mass of cavalry.

Páez saw his chance, and with his body of picked men, charged home upon the mass in the half darkness and took them by surprise. Thinking that Bolivar's

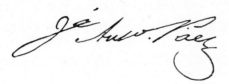

Three typical signatures of General Páez
taken from contemporary documents.

army had advanced upon them, they turned and fled. Like lightning the wild horsemen were amongst them, slaughtering them with the lance. The night, the wild yells of the Llaneros, and the dust that hung in a dense cloud, mingling with the smoke of the artillery, completed their defeat. The cavalry all turned and fled; the infantry retreated on a wood and the artillerymen, in their anxiety to save their lives abandoned all their pieces on the plain.

Morillo under cover of the night withdrew his army to his headquarters at Achaguas, influenced most probably by fear of panic spreading through his ranks, for the force he commanded outnumbered far that which both Páez and Bolivar could oppose to him. The royalists lost five hundred killed and many wounded. The loss sustained by the republicans was trifling. Such was the action, known as Las Queseras del Medio, fought on the third of April, 1819.

In Venezuela it is remembered with the same feelings as the charge of the Light Brigade at Balaclava is in England. No Venezuelan can speak of it, without a tightening of the throat and a proud sense of exultation, for it represents the acme of a heroic period, when their forefathers recoiled before no sacrifice to free their native land.

Bolivar who had watched the action from the far side of the river, unable to resist, a prey to doubt and to anxiety, issued a general proclamation to "Los Bravos de Apure." In it he thanked them, and bade them be assured of future victory. But he did more, for to each one of those who had not fallen he gave "La Cruz de los Libertadores," an order he had instituted. Páez has piously preserved the names of all of them in his Memoirs.

M

CHAPTER XII

THE result of the battle of Las Queseras del Medio, so unexpected by the Spaniards, was fatal to their morale. Morillo, hardened soldier as he was, retreated instantly with all his forces on Achaguas, pursued by Páez and Bolivar, who had joined one another after the victory. Still he retreated in good order; in such good order that Bolivar did not think fit to bring him to a general action in the plains.

When the patriots reached Achaguas, Morillo had evacuated it. Once more there was divergence of opinion between the generals, Bolivar wishing to attack Barinas, and Páez thinking it would prove a better plan to march through the plains to Casanare to New Granada, which was known to be favourable to the patriots. Just as this juncture arrived Colonel Jacinto Lara, sent by General Santander to tell Bolivar New Granada was ready to revolt.

At a general council of war, over which Bolivar personally presided, his generals unanimously approved the plan of Páez's to transfer operations to Colombia.* Once again the relations between the two chiefs were strained; but luckily Bolivar, by a tactful letter, written† in his own hand took Páez on his better side. Bolivar in his letter proposed that they should meet in Guasdualito and then determine which of them should take the command of the army destined for New Granada, and which remain upon the plains.

* Nueva Granada.
† "Escrita de su puñoy letra."

The letter must have been extraordinarily diplomatic, from the reference Páez makes to it, for it appears Bolivar wrote that if Páez were to go to New Granada, he would remain upon the Llanos, to try to form an army large enough to attack the capital. Bolivar added if he himself were chosen to command the army destined for New Granada, that he relied on Páez to hold Apure at all hazards, for he cared little what was lost, as long as it was safe. Páez who always rose to advances of that nature, met Bolivar in Guasdualito, and after thanking him for his gracious letter, left the decision to him, saying he was always ready to execute anything that Bolivar might decide. Naturally Bolivar chose to go to New Granada, where he was well known and where, for the moment, a larger field of action was open to him.

Páez remained upon the plains, his natural sphere of action, a sphere in which by his upbringing and his great influence with the Llaneros, he was more useful than the Liberator.

Bolivar instantly set out for Bogotá, marching so rapidly that he joined General Santander in the town of Arauca, upon the eleventh of June (1819) having set out upon the fourth.

The historian Baralt,* one of Bolivar's most enthusiastic admirers, blames Páez for not advancing upon the Andean town of Cúcuta to back up Bolivar. This he says he had received strict orders to undertake.

As Páez had no infantry at that time, and there were several strongly held positions on the way, it does not seem that he was blameable. As twenty leagues of bush, in which there was no pasture for his horses, lay betwixt him and the town of San Cristobal, the first of the strong positions strongly garrisoned by the Spaniards that he would have to pass, he prudently fell back upon

* "Resumen de la Historia de Venezuela," Paris, 1841.

Achaguas where he remained to organise a force of infantry.

Páez, although by disposition and by training a cavalryman, if ever such have been, thoroughly understood the necessity of infantry for operations against towns, and to oppose to the seasoned foot soldiers, brought by Morillo from the Napoleonic wars in Spain.

On several occasions he had seen them snatch victory from his grasp, and save the beaten royalists from entire destruction by their stubborn valour. The nucleus of his infantry, was the regiment known as Los Bravos de Apure, recruited in and about the city of that name. To them he joined a portion of the British Legion, and thus strongly reinforced, set out to attack El Pueblo de la Cruz a little town, the royalists had fortified, and garrisoned with some of their best troops.

Once again Páez was to learn how stubbornly the Spanish infantry could fight. Driven from the church which they defended to the last, the Spaniards fought from house to house a kind of warfare always productive of severe loss to the attacking party, exposed to galling fire, as they stood in the open streets. At last, after prodigious losses considering the smallness of the forces in the field, the remains of the Spanish infantry took shelter in an isolated house under the command of a Venezuelan corporal, who held out valiantly calling to his men to die rather than yield to the King's enemies. At nightfall Páez attacked in force, carrying the house by assault, and finding in it nothing but heaps of dead. At the last moment, the corporal and thirty men, cut their way through their enemies, and guided by another Venezuelan, one Captain Yaraza, whom Páez stigmatises, as " an ungrateful American,"* escaped into the night. Either because he was a Venezuelan, or because he really admired his courage, Páez writes of the valiant

* Ingrato Americano.

corporal in terms of eulogy. The patriots suffered so severely in this attack, that, though victorious, Páez found himself once more forced to retreat upon Achaguas, which Morillo had evacuated.

In order to avoid the town of Nutrias, which the Spaniards held,* for he feared a sally, in which case he would have been obliged to abandon all his wounded, he made a long detour through the flooded Llanos, a march in which his soldiers suffered terribly. It was the season of the rains and all the Llanos were inundated to a depth of several feet. The cattle as usual in the rainy season had migrated to the highest places they could find, and thus the line of march was quite denuded of them. The deer, and all the other wild animals, not amphibians, such as the vaquiros and tortoises had also gone for shelter to the higher† ground. The soldiers marched all day, upon their wearied horses, through the water and the mud. The men wet to the skin by the perpetual rains, shivered with their teeth chattering from the damp and cold. It was impossible to light a fire, from want of fuel. Even if fuel had been procurable there was no food to cook. The starving soldiers supported life on such fruit as the trees afforded; but even that was saturated and unpalatable. The horses' hooves softened and most of them went lame. The little store of gunpowder that they carried with them was wetted and unserviceable.

The riders' feet swelled and became so tender, that they dared not put them in the stirrups, and rode with their legs dangling, as if they had been riding barebacked. Great flocks of ducks, passed whirring over the line of march, but they had no means of shooting them. For days together the sun was hidden in a pall of mist, and that in a country where for most days in the year,

* Nutrias is on the Upper Apure, some distance from San Fernando.
† Carpinchos.

his rays pour down like molten lead upon the rider on the plains.

Reins, headstalls and hide girths shrank and were almost useless, and lazos, dangling at the saddle bows, appeared to weigh a ton.

Dried stalks of the Mastranto,* looking like gigantic mulleins just appeared above the surface of the water, their knotted stems, brushing the stirrups as the jaded horsemen wallowed through the flood. Now and then clumps of Campanilla,† its lilac flowers almost awash, shrivelled and darkened by the rain, showed where the ground was firmer underfoot. In the far distance, clumps of Moriche palms stood up like islands in the vast inland sea, and still the rain descended without intermission upon the line of scarecrows, who, encumbered with their wounded, struggled onward, their horses falling now and then, never to rise again, in some deep water hole, or bogged down in the mud.

Such were their trials by day, but when night fell and they encamped, huddled together, horses and men, in one common misery upon some patch of ground that rose above the inundation, mosquitoes, sandflies, and a thousand insect plagues, made their lives purgatory, such purgatory, that if that most humane of all the dogmas really exists, they surely must have qualified for paradise, without the intermediary stage.

At last, after swimming innumerable creeks, and enduring countless hardships, Páez reached the little town of Santa Catalina and having sent his wounded down the Apure to Achaguas, crossed over it at El Paso del Frio and once more established his headquarters at Achaguas. Even he and his iron-framed Llaneros were in need of rest after the hardships they had endured.

Moreover there was a lull in the hostilities in Vene-

* Hyptis suaveoleus.
† Contarea Hexandra.

zuela, for the chief field of operations had been transferred to New Granada (Colombia).

Almost the whole of the year 1820 Páez passed either at Achaguas or at his ranche of Yagua, employed in discipling a corp of infantry when at the former place. At Yagua, he was occupied in collecting horses, breaking in wild colts and fattening cattle, to serve him for the next campaign.

In January he made an expedition to Barinas, and by the way fell in with Bolivar on his return from New Granada. They passed a night together discussing future plans. Then, the Liberator marched on to the province of Guayana, while Páez occupied Barinas, from which the Spaniards had retired. By this time, both sides had become ashamed of the bloody war of extermination that had been waged since 1813, neither the royalists nor the revolutionaries giving quarter, but massacring their prisoners, relentlessly.

In the month of August (1820), Morillo sent an envoy to San Juan de Payara, where Páez was encamped, to propose a cessation of hostilities. With more discretion, than at that time he generally displayed, Páez returned for answer, that war or peace, were not in his hands, but depended on the patriot government. Morillo then sent commissioners to the Congress of Guayana, at that time sitting in the town of Angostura. That Congress answered that it desired above all things to re-establish peace, but only on condition that Colombia* should be recognised a sovereign state, completely freed from Spain. As Bolivar was away upon an expedition, the Congress empowered Pedro Briceño, Mendez and General Urdaneta, to bear their answer to the Spanish general.

For the time being the negotiations turned out futile,

---

* The name Colombia in those days was applied to both Venezuela and New Granada, that is the modern republic of Colombia.

Morillo not acceding to the demand for independence, although he held out as a bait, that if they recognised the sovereignty of Spain, the patriot officers, should all retain the rank they had enjoyed, during the contest.

Still contact, for the first time since the outbreak of hostilities, had been established, and shortly afterwards Bolivar wrote to Morillo, to propose a conference between them. Spaniards and patriots alike, were getting tired of the long war, and knew moreover, that the barbarities both had committed, had horrified the world. On the 28th October, Morillo wrote to Bolivar, to propose an armistice.

On the 20th of November, 1820, a date memorable in Venezuelan history, Morillo and Bolivar met, and in the semi-Andean city of Trujillo, signed a treaty that rehabilitated both of them in the eyes of the world. They agreed to treat their prisoners generously, and to exchange them, according to their rank. Better than that they promised to respect the lives and properties of the inhabitants* of the towns that either side might occupy. One clause of the treaty is remarkable, and shows a kindly spirit, that perhaps only the Latin races feel, but that the Nordic races might well copy.

" As this war originated through difference of (political) opinion, and as those who have fought so bitterly for both causes, are related intimately by many links and ties, desiring to save bloodshedding as much as possible, it is established that both soldiers and those employed in civil positions, who having served either of the generals and then deserted, shall not be liable to the death penalty, if they are taken prisoners, when fighting on the other side."

* This treaty signed in 1820, in a country swept by civil war, far off from Europe and semi-civilised, should surely give pause, if anything can pierce the armour of their self satisfaction to those who to-day " blether " about universal progress in the moral sphere.

" Blether " is a Scottish word used in a contemptuous sense, and implies not only mental drivelling, but a concomitant slavering at the mouth.

More than one hundred years have passed since Bolivar and Morillo met and set their names to a treaty that contained a clause, designed to cut the claws of politicians and of soldiers, and make the scourge of war less grievous to the world.

At the invitation of Morillo who was most anxious for a personal interview, the generals with their respective staffs met in the little town of Santa Ana. Morillo came with an escort of hussars, surrounded by his staff. General O'Leary, the Liberator's aide-de-camp, writes in his memoirs that Morillo asked him what escort the chief of the republicans would bring. On being told that Bolivar was accompanied but by ten or twelve of his officers, and had no escort, Morillo, answered, " I thought my escort small enough to guard me; but my erstwhile enemy has vanquished me in generosity." He instantly gave orders for his escort to retire.

Both generals sprang from a race quick to respond to generous appeal, to gallant bearing, and " hombria,"* that quality so difficult to render in a foreign tongue.

Morillo wore full uniform, and all his decorations. his staff was brilliant in new uniforms, their helmets, swords, lances and stirrups, shining in the sun.

When the little group of patriots appeared, Morillo asked eagerly, " which is Bolivar? " When he was pointed out, he exclaimed, " What, that little man in a blue coat, wearing a forage cap, and mounted on a mule! "

They advanced, dismounted, and embraced† each other. Then arm in arm they walked to the best house the little place afforded, where Morillo had prepared

---

* It implies fineness of character, combined with manliness.

† Men in Venezuela still embrace as did the patriarchs and the heroes of the Iliad. To those whose national method of salutation is to shake hands, or to rub noses, this custom may appear curious. For all that the Venezuelan custom has something old world and heroic in it.

a simple, tasteful, military banquet.* No banquet in South America is complete without a feast of oratory. Long residence in South America has equipped the writer with ample means to have supplied the speeches in the style of those Thucydides puts into the mouths of all his heroes.

Luckily, it is unnecessary, as Páez either has imitated the recorder of the Peloponnesian war, or, some unknown stenographer was at the banquet taking notes. At all events, the words Páez has preserved, are so much in character, that it is of but small account, if they were really uttered, or composed by the Llanero chief.

The Liberator, one of the finest speakers of his time, an orator, such as, perhaps, is only to be found in South America in these degenerate days, proposed the following toast, " I drink," he said, " to the heroic valour of the combatants of one and of the other army; to their constancy and their unequalled courage and endurance; to the worthy men who through the horrors of the war, sustained and defended liberty, to the wounded of both armies, who have manifested equal intrepidity, firmness and dignity—Eternal hatred to all those who desire carnage, and shed blood unjustly."

Morillo not to be out-done, said, " May God chastise all those not animated by the same sentiments of peace and friendship, as ourselves." His second in command General Latorre, full of enthusiasm,† said to Bolivar, " We will go down to Hell together, to pursue all tyrants."

Brave words, from men who had been butchering their prisoners in cold blood, for ten long years. Still

---

* " Un banquete militar, sencillo y delicado." Military banquets in these days are seldom simple, and not seldom tasteless ; but in El Pueblo de Santa Ana in those days simplicity was obligatory, and perhaps carried taste with it. Simplex munditiis ! Delicado in the sense of delicate, it could hardly have been.

† Lleno de entusiasmo.

oratory, like wine, mounts to the head, and without doubt all of the speakers were sincere, during their speeches, especially General Latorre, for he must have known that had he found the tyrants he was pursuing to the infernal regions, like Orpheus he would have cast a backward look, and stayed there with his friends.

After the banquet, the two generals joined in rolling to its place, a block of stone for the foundation of the monument, that Morillo had proposed should be erected, to commemorate* the day.

Páez who was a simple soul, easily moved to enthusiasm, and readily impressed by generosity, thus sums up the events of that most memorable day.

" History presents nothing more beautiful or grand. Such a spectacle proves that the human heart even although the passions harden it, always preserves a sensibility, that needs but little to make it manifest itself, in all its greatness."

To a simple heart such as his own, enshrined in a hardriding body, this seemed a truism, but then how many leagues of Llano a man would have to ride, to find a brace of them!

* It stands in the plaza of Santa Ana and presents the generals joined in a fraternal embrace, against an obelisk.

CHAPTER XIII

SOMETHING had been gained by the historic meeting, and though hostilities broke out again at the conclusion of the armistice in April 1821, from that time forth, the butchery of prisoners ceased.

In every war, each side always accuses their opponents of inhumanity. It is of course a trump card to play with the civil population, without whose backing no war can be maintained.

The war of extermination, now so happily terminated, was actually decreed by Bolivar in the town of Trujillo, on the fifteenth of June, 1813. His pretext for the sanguinary edict, was the savage massacres, that had disgraced the Spanish arms. Conceived in sweeping terms, it ran " Spaniard and Canary Islanders, reckon with death, even if you remain neutral, and do not act actively in favour of independence. Americans count upon life, even if blameworthy."* Whether such a massacre really helped him in the long run; whether it alienated many of the richer Creoles; whether it stimulated the Spaniards to greater efforts, must of necessity be left to the personal opinion of the individual man. Historians have written at great length and argued wordily about the matter, leaving as usual, their opponents unconvinced.

What the war of extermination did do most certainly, was to hold up to the opprobrium of the world, all those, on either side, who sanctioned and took part

* " Españoles y Canarios contad con la muerte aun siendo indiferentes, si no obrais activamente en favor de la independencia, Americanos contad con la vida, aun cuando séais culpables."

in it. It is not improbable that it retarded independence, by the exasperation that it caused. One thing is certain, that the warfare of to-day is just as bloodthirsty as it was then in Venezuela, a hundred years ago. Neither Bolivar nor Morillo rained death and destruction on defenceless villages from aeroplanes.

What they might have done had they possessed the means is difficult to say. The human animal yearly grows savager and more bloodthirsty. No proposition seems to have been raised to limit slaughter in the last Christian carnival of blood.

Not long before the armistice had been declared, Bolivar who had freed New Granada from the Spanish rule during his last campaign, conceived the project doomed from the start to fail, of joining Venezuela and Colombia under the same rule. When joined together, they were to be called La Gran Colombia. To make the plan still more unworkable, what is now Ecuador, was also to be joined to them, under the name of Quito and Cundinamarca.

Natural conditions, lack of communications, climate, the Indians of the various provinces, all widely differing from one another, and other causes, as the part of Spain from which the conquerors came, had in the three hundred years the Spanish rule had endured, formed national types in all three provinces. Nothing could be more widely different, in accent, habits and their mode of life, than a Llanero from the hot, humid plains of Venezuela, little above sea level, and a mountaineer, either from Colombia or Ecuador, born at high altitudes, and able to endure low temperatures.

Again the inhabitants of the coastal belt of all three countries, though nearer to each other than the first two types, were very different from them. The dwellers in the rich agricultural districts, in all three countries, formed again a different type of man.

In Quito and Cundinamarca* older traditions, more aristocratic in their tendency, prevailed. The clergy had great power both there and in Colombia, as they still have to-day.

In Ecuador, the greater portion of the people were Indians who had accepted Spanish rule, or had been forced to undergo it, but they were little different from what they had been under the Incas at the conquest.

Colombia had a percentage of tame Indians, but not enough to make much difference to the bulk of the population.

In Venezuela there were hardly any Indians of that kind. In that republic, partly on account of its being so much nearer Europe, partly because the original settlers were of a different class, ideas of liberty and self government had made more way than in what are now the other two republics. In neither of the other provinces, that were proposed to be united in one state, was there a class of men, even remotely like the Llaneros of those days. Like Paul of Tarsus, the Llaneros were born free. Nature had decreed their freedom. They wanted little, and the little that they did require, nature had placed ready for them to take with a hide rope, and use for their own benefit.

Cattle in countless herds roamed on the plains. Troops of wild horses, that any man might catch and tame, were there in thousands. All the Llanero wanted was a horse. With him he was free of the plains. Without a horse he would have been as ill prepared to face the world, as were his ancestors, the Achaguas Indians.

Such men as the Llaneros had nothing in common with the Colombian or the Ecuadorian mountaineers. This Páez, one of themselves seems to have understood from the inception of the unlucky plan. It finally

* Ecuador.

separated him from Bolivar, and even placed him in direct opposition to him.

In the capitals and larger cities of the three states, the difference of type was not so great. No matter whether the Spanish governor was called a viceroy or a captain general, around him there sprang up a little court. In Mexico and in Peru, the richest of the vice-royalties, the viceregal court was rich and stately. In the smaller states, such as Colombia and Venezuela, though less well organised, the capital still was the focus of the richer creoles, the functionaries sent from Spain, the military and the higher clergy. Cut off from communication with the other viceroyalties by the great distances, the unbridged rivers, the Andes, and in some instances by actual deserts, or at the least unpeopled* districts, each of these isolated centres developed an intense local patriotism.

Even under Spanish rule, men had begun to call themselves Venezuelans, New Granadans, Peruvians, and Mexicans.† Thus the plan of the Liberator of one great state to be called La Gran Colombia was doomed to failure from the start.

The armistice so happily concluded, and which put an end for ever to the butcheries that had disgraced both sides, came to end upon the 21st of April, 1821.

Hostilities recommenced, with a great point in favour of the patriots.

Not long after the armistice had been declared, Morillo, by far the most experienced and energetic of the commanders who had been sent from Spain, either disgusted with the turn affairs had taken, or despairing of success, returned to the peninsula. He was the only

---

* Called in Spanish, Despoblados.

† Cervantes, in Don Quixote, speaks of one of his characters riding as well as a Mexican.

Spanish officer who could hold head to Páez, in the guerrilla warfare of the plains.

With his accustomed generosity to opponents Páez sums up Morillo's character, but whilst not denying him the military talents he undoubtedly possessed, censures him for his cruelty and his neglect to restrain the bandits, who under Boves and Monteverde, laid half the country waste.

Writing in his old age in his retirement in New York, Páez reviews Morillo's tactics most skilfully. By that time Páez had become an educated man, and without doubt had studied works on military tactics. With the information that he had acquired, joined to his natural aptitude for warfare of the kind he and Morillo had been engaged in, he lays his finger on the blot. He does not hesitate to say, that if Morillo had not frittered away so much time and lost so many men in the long warfare in the plains, but marched at once to Angostura, and after occupying it, cut off communication with the outer world, by blocking navigation on the Orinoco, the patriot cause would have been jeopardised.

Páez always was singularly moderate in his judgment of his adversaries. Less so of his friends, as is natural to humanity, for our friends we invest with what we think are our own qualities, and it is usually difficult for human beings to believe that they can err. Therefore when friends act contrary to our wishes it generally seems to us that they have refused the light, which they have received from our omniscience. Thus their sin becomes one of *lese majesté* against the Holy Ghost. Páez was full of these naïve frailties that go so far to make men lovable.

Portrait of GENERAL JOSÉ ANTONIO PÁEZ
The property of
Don Lauriano Vallenilla Lanz.
The copy of a daguerreotype taken in New York.

CHAPTER XIV

THE year 1821 was the most memorable in the long struggle against Spain.

The occupation of Maracaibo by the troops of General Urdaneta caused a protest by the royalists, to which Bolivar answered by breaking off the armistice. Both sides prepared for the renewal of hostilities, and both were aware that the fate of Venezuela would be decided in the next campaign.

The renewal of hostilities was forced upon Bolivar, whose forces camped in the Llanero must have all perished ultimately of hunger or disease.

" It is my duty, either to make peace or fight," he is reported to have said, and as no peace was possible in the circumstances, he at once started his campaign.

The Spanish forces at the time numbered some fifteen thousand, but they were dispersed throughout the territory. Their commander was General Latorre, the same who at the conference proposed to go to the infernal regions* to pursue all tyrants. Latorre though a competent commander was inferior to Morillo, both in experience and ability. He had his headquarters at San Carlos not very far from the city of Valencia. With him was the main body of the infantry. The cavalry under General Morales, was stationed at the town of Calabozo, the capital of the State of Guárico. The patriots on their side were not idle.

Páez was ordered by Bolivar to join him at his head-quarters in Guanare, with all the troops under his com-

* See Chapter XIII.

N

mand. He set out on the 10th of May, 1821, with a thousand infantry and fifteen hundred horsemen, driving before them two thousand spare horses and four thousand bullocks.

No one who has not tried to take large bodies of semi-feral horses or cattle over the plains, can have the least idea of the enormous difficulty of the task. The animals cannot be driven quickly or they all lose condition and become footsore. They have to stop and graze at intervals, and drink where there are places suitable, for steep descents to rivers, or muddy water holes, are dangerous for them. On each and every one of these occasions for the first two or three days there is the chance they may stampede and break away.

The peons who are in charge of them sit on their horses, in the burning sun, the rain, or icy wind, with an eye always on the animals they drive. They must not shout, wave whips or ponchos, and above all avoid putting their horses into a sudden gallop. At night they must not light a match, for the flicker of it might alarm the herd, and alarm quickly turns to flight. If a man wishes to speak to one of his comrades he must not call to him, but ride up to his side and almost whisper in his ear.

Those who sleep round the camp fire must keep it low, never throw green wood, or boughs with leaves upon them into the flames, for they are apt to crackle and flare up, and then the herd with a loud snort is off into the night. When it stampedes, at the peril of their lives the watchers of the herd, though perhaps some of them are riding half-tamed horses that hardly know the bit, must ride like madmen, no matter how rough the ground may be, or dark the night, waving their ponchos and their whips, shouting their loudest, stretched out upon their horses necks, endeavouring to head off the cattle, and so to stem the rush. The horses

bound through the darkness like the coursers of the
Valkyrie, and in the moonlight strain every nerve, under
the whip and spur.

If a man fall in the front of the flying herd he has
scant chance of ever getting up again after a thousand
head of cattle have passed over him, too mad with the
excitement of their wild gallop to see anything. If at
last, by dint of hard riding the rush is checked, the
herdsmen ride slowly round the mob of animals, raising a melancholy chant that seems to have a wonderful
effect in soothing them. At any moment they may
begin to run again; but if they once begin to go round
in a circle, a phenomenon that cattlemen call " milling,"
they will not take to flight again, at least on the same
night.

Páez although he was a skilled Llanero, accustomed
to all the vagaries of cattle and half wild horses on the
march, dwells* on the difficulties of the task. " Every
night bands of horses broke away from us, in spite of
all the efforts of the men who watched them. Luckily
as they had been accustomed to be herded together, they
did not separate and it was easy to follow the tracks
they left on the soft ground." It was the beginning
of the rainy season and this rendered the trackers' task
far easier than it would have been when all the Llano
is parched up and dry.

Páez goes on to remark upon a fact, well known to
those who have lived the life he lived upon the plains,
that is the extraordinary sagacity animals exhibit when
they once know they can escape at night.

All through the day they graze and give but little
trouble, and to an inexperienced person it would appear
that there was no danger of a stampede. During the
night, almost at the same hour at which their fellows

* " No son de contar las molestias y trabajos que nos hizo pasar durante
nuestra marcha, la conduccion de tan crecido numero de animales."
Memorias, Cap. XIII, page 237.

have escaped the night before, they grow restless and suddenly some of them rush like a whirlwind in the direction where lies the place where they were bred. Nothing then stops them, and they take their way, just as a homing pigeon takes its way across the sky. Almost invariably they take a different road from that by which they have been driven. They never falter, needing no compass to direct them, passing through swamps and swimming rivers if they lie between them and their Querencia.*

The difficulty of crossing rivers, such as the Apure, the Arauca or La Portuguesa, all of them a quarter of a mile at least in breadth, must have been almost insuperable except to men who like Páez, were as much at home in a canoe as on a horse.

Tame horses are notoriously difficult to drive, and whilst at least as liable to stampede as wild ones, are yet more difficult to force into a river, if they know they have to swim.

The crossing of the cattle though it wanted experience and care, could not have been quite so difficult a task.

A writer† of those days relates, that if the cattle did not like to face the water, the Llaneros used to fasten a cow's horns upon the head of a good swimmer who then plunged into the river, and the cattle seeing the horns, thought it was an animal and followed obediently.

Before the campaign had definitely begun, Bolivar detached General Bermudez to occupy Caracas. This

---

* The place where an animal is reared is called in Spanish La Querencia.

† "A History of the Revolution of Caracas," page 114. Major Flinter London, 1819.

The man who to-day cross the cattle in batches of two hundred, from San Fernando de Apure to Puerto Miranda, wears no horns upon his head, other than those he may have gained in "les champs clos" of matrimony.

His sole defensive arm against the Caimanes is a short stick of hard wood, with which he taps them smartly on the snout if they attack him.

With his left hand he grasps the tail of one of his two horses, either the Chestnut or the Brown, who are in the language of the Llaneros "baquianos," at the job.

he achieved successfully, with the effect that the royalist General Morales, evacuated Calabozo and marched against Bermudez, while Latorre the Spanish commander-in-chief, abandoned his position in San Carlos and took up another on the historic plains of Carabobo. Bermudez attacked in force by Morales, was obliged to retreat towards the east, and after trifling successes at El Alto de Macuto sustained a severe defeat, at a spot on the outskirts of the capital known as El Calvario de Caracas.

This Calvary, stands where the road towards La Guaira, enters a mountain pass. Above it towers the mountain known as El Cerro de la Silla,* the deep depression in the middle forming the seat and the two rounded tops, the pommel and the cantle of the saddle.

Spread out beneath the high Calvario Caracas lies, seen as from a natural aeroplane. The slender palm trees in the gardens and squares, the houses dazzlingly white, the streets that, starting in the great square, where on his Llanero horse Bolivar rides, crucified in glory by the descendants of the men who broke his heart and drove him into exile, finish in sandy ramblas† give it an air as of the East. No pall of smoke befouls the atmosphere. So clear is it and so transparent, that church towers, domes and buildings stand up against the sky, as if the city were a model of itself cut out of cardboard.

The little Guaire running through fields of maize and sugar canes, and crossed by several efficient-looking iron bridges of the art schools of Birmingham or Pittsburg that no doubt replace old Spanish structures, not modernist enough for the artistic conscience of these

* Silla — Saddle.

† Rambla, from the Arabic Rhamel, sand, is a term often used in Spain for such streets.

later years of culture and of grace, cut off the city from the park of El Paraiso, buried in luxuriant vegetation. But for the bridges, and the motor cars, for then the worthy citizens of Santiago de Leon de Caracas, rode on their pacing mules or horses from Aragua, the city cannot have altered greatly since the battle at the Cavalry. The giant tree,* known as El Arbol de San Francisco, towered in the centre of the town, as it still towers to-day.

The cathedral tower, though probably without its clock, that seems to be a modern instance, stood up a lighthouse on the voyage to Heaven, as it does yet, although perhaps fewer mariners steer their barques by it. The mountains, the translucent skies, the luxuriant vegetation, the mild delicious climate have not varied, all the change is that the national flag with its too well assorted colours, has replaced the blood and orange standard of Castille.

The prize was worth all that the royalists and the republicans underwent to hold or to possess it, and the last check the patriot arms sustained at the Calvario de Caracas, but steeled them for the crowning mercy, that was to follow on the Carabobo plains.

The operations of General Bermudez, were of great service to the patriots, for though he was defeated at El Calvario, he yet was able to hold in check a portion of the Spanish forces and give the patriots a free hand to concentrate all their troops, at Bolivar's headquarters at San Carlos.

Páez with his Llaneros joined Bolivar, who was also joined by Urdaneta. They then returned towards Carabobo where General Latorre who had taken up a strong position was waiting for them. The opposing armies were about equal as to numbers. Neither had more than some six thousand men of every arm. With

* Either a Samaan (Mimosa gigantea) or a Ceiba (Bombyx Ceiba).

these scant numbers and a few small pieces of artillery on either side the fate of a whole continent was to be decided, for if the Spaniards were expelled from Venezuela, the nearest of their colonies to Europe, they had but little chance of holding those, such as Peru and Chile, on the Pacific coast.

Though small, the armies were composed of the best troops that either side could bring into the field. Páez had under his command the first division composed of the Llanero cavalry, the infantry that he had disciplined himself, known as Los Bravos de Apure, and the British Legion. The second division under General Cedeño comprised a Brigade of Guards, the sharpshooters and El Escuadron* Sagrado, under Colonel Arismendi, and the battalion of Boyacá and Vargas. The third division, under Colonel Plaza comprised the first Brigade of Guards, and various battalions of riflemen and grenadiers, and a regiment of cavalry under Colonel Rondon.

The royalists relied chiefly upon their infantry. Many of their regiments had served in the Peninsula against Napoleon. Worthy descendants of the celebrated Spanish infantry of the Middle Ages† they were never so stubborn or so much to be feared as in adverse circumstances and rarely to be thrown into confusion, even in retreat.

The sun-scorched wind-swept plain of Carabobo is a high plateau‡ at the south end of the Valley of Valencia. The city is some six leagues away, and the great Lake of Valencia dotted with innumerable islands, its shores a mass of tropic vegetation, its waters a pale jade, lies at one end of the valley. High mountains tower above

---

* The Sacred Squadron.

† Los Tercios de Flandes.

‡ It has been likened to a tea tray with high sides, by the historian, Blanco Fombona.

it to the east, giving it an air as of a Loch Lomond transported to the tropics.

The road to the town of San Carlos runs through the plain from north to south. Another road to the town of El Pao, crosses it laterally. At the time of the battle these roads must have been nothing but rough tracks, dusty in summer, and in winter sloughs of mud.

At daylight on the 24th of June, 1821, Bolivar's army set out to take up its position on the plain. They forded the Chirigua, passed through the broken valleys of the hills of Las Hermanas, threading first the narrow pass of Buenavista. Why they were not attacked as they passed through the defile of Buenavista is difficult to comprehend. The very nature of the ground rendered it easily defensible. The neglect to attack Bolivar's army when entangled in the hills probably cost the Spaniards the victory. It may be that loss of a detachment in Trujillo a day or two before the battle, tied the Spanish general's hands. When the patriot army emerged from the defile and formed its ranks upon the plain of Carabobo, Bolivar and his staff, posted themselves on the little hill of Buenavista. From that position he was able, as the armies engaged were of small size, with necessarily narrow fronts, to survey the field of operations.

The Spaniards awaited him with confidence, relying on their superior discipline, but without the enthusiasm that fires men fighting in defence of their own country. Although General Latorre had neglected, or been unable to attack the Venezuelan army as it marched through the hills, he had posted his best troops, to bar the roads that ran into the plain. The regiment of Valencey, the best of all the Spanish infantry, at that time serving in America, covered the road from Valencia to San Carlos. On the right were the regiments of Barbastro and Hostalrich, both of which had

served in the peninsula, and were in a high state of
discipline. Another known as El Regimiento del
Infante was posted to defend the road to El Pao. All
these four regiments were well armed and equipped,
and had seen much service, both in America and
Spain.

Four squadrons of hussars and four of carbineers
were posted at each end of the Spanish line. The regiment of Burgos, under General Morales, was held in
reserve. So confident was Latorre in the superiority of
his infantry that he sent the regiments, Navarra and
Barinas, to the aid of Colonel Lorenzo who was hard
pressed at San Felipe by the patriot commanders, Reyes
Vargas and Carillo. This was another error on his
part, destined to cost him very dearly.

Seeing the Spaniards so strongly posted, Bolivar
determined on a flank attack. Guided by a peasant, he
took the hardly practicable path known as La Pica de la
Mona. Seeing this manœuvre, Latorre changed his
front, and as the regiment of Los Bravos de Apure
emerged upon the plain it was violently attacked and
thrown into confusion by the Spanish infantry, after a
combat in which they fought hand to hand. During
the fighting, tradition says that a giant soldier of the
Apure regiment engaged a stout soldier* from Zaragoza,
of the Barbastro battalion, and that after they had
broken all their weapons they attacked each other
with their fists, after the fashion of the warriors of
the Iliad.

Páez then ordered the British Legion to advance. In
perfect order with drums beating and their colours flying they took up their position, under the command of
Colonel Farrar,† who got off his horse and ordered his

---

* " Un rudo Zaragozano de Barbastro y un soldado de Apure, rotas
as armas se dieron de puñadas."

† Páez, Baralt and other Venezuelan writers call him Farriar. Thus he
may have been called Farrar or Ferrier, but hardly Farriar.

men to kneel. Then, in the words of a Venezuelan writer, words that set the blood tingling with pride, " The British Legion ceased to be a corps like all the others, but having rooted themselves in the ground, became a granite wall."* Exposed to a murderous fire from two Spanish regiments, men fell like corn before the reapers, but as they fell, silently their comrades closed up their decimated ranks, keeping up a hot fire, as little shaken as if they had been at a field day."

Farrar fell dead, calling out with his last breath, " Stand firm."† Major Denny succeeded to the command, but in a moment he too was stretched upon the ground. Scott, a junior captain, then took command, but was killed instantly. Seeing their losses and fearing that they would be overwhelmed, Páez then gave the order for a bayonet charge. The Legion sprang to its feet, and under the command of a young lieutenant, Minchin by name, joined by the regiment of Apure, they swept the enemy away. In less than half an hour the British Legion had lost seventeen officers and almost half their men. Their firmness turned the tide. Then Páez brandishing his lance charged at the head of his Llaneros, and broke the Spanish cavalry.

The royalist regiments of Valencey and Barbastro, seeing the state of matters, sullenly fell back on the main body. Barbastro, finding itself surrounded on all sides, and without ammunition, had to surrender, and the same fate befel the Regimiento del Infante. During the charge Páez was seized by one of his strange epileptic fits and nearly taken prisoner. Seeing his danger, one Antonio Martinez, a Llanero from the town of Calabozo, though serving with the royalists, seized Páez's

---

* " Desde entonces la legion inglesa deja de ser un cuerpo como todos los otros, echa raices en la tierra, ye se convierte en muro de granito."

† " Gritando, Firme."

horse by the reins and motioning to another soldier* to support him in the saddle placed him in safety amongst his own soldiers.

The battle now was won and all the Spanish army in retreat. Only the regiment of Valencey preserved its discipline. Retreating with their faces to the foe, under the command of a brave officer Don Tomas Garcia, they resisted numberless charges of the Llaneros, and fighting stubbornly at last they gained the shelter of the forts of the seaport of Puerto Cabello, the last spot of Venezuelan soil the Spaniards possessed.

The victory was complete, after a battle furiously fought that lasted hardly an hour. It cost the patriots only two hundred losses, between killed and wounded, nearly† all of whom were members of the British Legion. The Spanish losses were not large; but the patriots captured two thousand prisoners, a great store of ammunition, and all their artillery.

After a hurried march the remains of the Spanish army gained the shelter of the forts of Puerto Cabello, where they had been preceded by the heroic regiment of Valencey. Nightfall and a violent rainstorm that swelled the rivers saved them from being taken prisoners.

The long struggle now was over and the independence of Venezuela was secure. After the battle, when Páez came to his senses, he found himself surrounded by Bolivar and his staff. Advancing amid cheers, Bolivar in the name of the Congress, promoted Páez to the rank‡ of General in Chief.

At Carabobo Páez lost a faithful follower, one Pedro Camejo, who had accompanied him for years. This

---

* What moved Antonio Morales to this action Páez said he never understood, for the man had served in the Spanish ranks, since the time of Boves.

† " Historia de Venezuela," por H. N. M. Caracas, 1927.

‡ General en jefe.

man, a negro, called from his bravery "El Negro Primero," mortally wounded, galloped towards the place where Páez sat upon his horse. "Why are you running off?" Páez shouted to him. The man did not reply till he came near, and then, opening his shirt he showed a mortal wound. "I came, my general," he said, "to say good-bye to you, for I am dying." Then he fell dead, just at his general's feet.

The laurels of the victory fell to Páez. Owing to the nature of the ground only his division was really engaged. Much was due to the heroic attitude of the British Legion, ably seconded by Los Bravos de Apure. The charge of the Llaneros, headed by Páez, finally broke the Spanish ranks. Only the regiment of Valencey resisted every attack that he launched upon it. The other regiments, less well disciplined or less well led, were either taken prisoners or fled.

Bolivar generously acknowledged the intrepidity of Páez in a proclamation that he issued shortly afterwards.

"The division of Páez composed of two battalions of infantry and fifteen hundred horsemen was enough to rout the Spanish army in three quarters of an hour. If all the patriot army had been able to engage, few of the enemy would have been able to escape upon that memorable day. At Carabobo the independence of Colombia was sealed. The indomitable courage, the activity and intrepidity of General Páez contributed above all things to the splendid victory."

Upon the 25th of June, Bolivar and Páez marched at once upon Caracas and occupied it without resistance, for General Pereira on learning of their approach evacuated and retired upon La Guaira. There, finding no ships to take him off, he was obliged to capitulate with all his followers.

Colombia and Venezuela now were both freed from

Spanish domination. This left Bolivar free to pursue the conquest of Ecuador and of Peru, towards which countries he marched in August, 1821. Páez was left with the supreme command in Venezuela, and the heroic period of the war of independence was at an end.

CHAPTER XV

NEVER again was Páez destined to occupy quite the same position in the eyes of his fellow countrymen as that he occupied for the next few months after the field of Carabobo. Years of devoted service to the patriot cause had raised him to a place second alone to that the Liberator filled. His manifold and strange adventures, his prowess in the field, his rise from humble origin, and the best gift that nature gives to man, a personality that endeared itself to everyone, without an effort on his part, had made a hero of him. Joined to the qualities of a bold guerrilla chief, he had those little failings that often make a man more popular than his more admirable qualities. His vanity, though unconcealed and patent, had nothing of conceit about it, but was of the kind inherent in a personable horse soldier, who when a band is playing and he knows he is observed, tilts up his chin a little, hollows his back, and sticking out his toes defies the thunder.

Moreover he was generous about money, when he had any; loved dancing, and was approachable and courteous, qualities without which no mortal can be popular either with Spaniards or South Americans.

Lastly and that in South America, especially in those days, he was a consummate horseman and the best lance in all the patriot army. So much it counted that it is recorded as a chief virtue of Francisco* Pizarro the conqueror of Peru, that in his day he was a renowned bull fighter with the short spear called a " rejon."

* " Pizarro mismo, tan enoblado despues, fué un rejoneador de los mas renombrados en su tiempo." Naturaleza y Civilizacion de la Grandiosa Isla de Cuba, por Miguel Gonzalez Ferrer.

He had not shown himself ambitious, nor was he sanguinary, judged by the standard of the times, still less
vindictive. His adventures in the fields of Cupid had
been moderate, and were not calculated to give public
scandal, and he was temperate in extreme in a land
where many, as the phrase went, rendered their homage
to the Tyean God. No taint of politics, that mumbo-
jumboism no one can touch without it leaving stains
upon his soul, had not yet infected him.

Gifted with a surprising memory, he was yet almost
illiterate. This in some measure accounts for the fact
that he remembered events and actions that had happened in his youth when he wrote or dictated his voluminous memoirs in his old age.

Just as an Indian sees tracks upon the ground invisible
to a white man's eye, partly because his mind is quite
unoccupied with other matters outside the actual task he
has in hand, so is a blind man, or an illiterate, forced to
rely upon his memory. Withal Páez had a sense of
humour that made him treasure up odd sayings, turns of
phrase, and curiosities of conduct and preserve them for
future generations.

His account of his faithful follower Pedro Camejo
must have come out of his own mouth, for it is difficult
to see how anyone but he himself could have related it
with so much liveliness and unconscious artistry, even if
he had received the facts to work upon.

To the end of his long life Páez never forgot his
early friends and followers. Above all of them he
valued Pedro Camejo, known as " El Negro Primero,"*
he who came dying to say farewell to him and fell dead
from his horse, at Carabobo, in the hour of victory.
Writing of the loss he had sustained at Carabobo,
amongst officers and friends, he says, " Amongst them
all I recall with most affection Camejo, then generally

* See Chapter XIV.

known by the nickname of 'El Negro Primero,' who was once a slave . . . When I came to Achaguas after the action at El Yagual, this negro presented himself before me. My soldiers from Apure advised me to enlist him, as he was a man of proved courage and a splendid lance. I liked the look of him, for he was most robust. After a little talk with him I saw he had the ingenuity of a man in a primitive condition, and was moreover one of those sympathetic characters who attract others to them.

"He was called Pedro Camejo and had been the slave of a proprietor of Apure, one Don Vicente Alfonso, who had made a soldier of him because the independent character of the negro had alarmed him.

"After the action at Araure, Camejo had become so much disgusted with military service that he went to Apure and hid himself for a long time, until he came to me after the skirmish at El Yagual. I enrolled him in my ranks, and 'always* at my side, he was a precious acquisition.' He gave many proofs of valour in all the hard fought skirmishes that we had with the enemy, and his comrades gave him the title of 'El Negro Primero.' They were all much amused with him and with his natural wit, and with the observations that he used to make on all that he had seen.

"As I knew that Bolivar was coming to meet me in Apure I told my men on no account to mention that the negro had served with the royalists. This, of course, caused them to tell Bolivar that Camejo had once been in the Spanish ranks.

"When Bolivar saw him for the first time, he complimented him upon his courage, and asked him, 'what was it moved you to serve in the ranks of our enemies?' The negro looked round at his comrades as if to re-

* "Y siempre a mi lado, fué para mi preciosa adquisicion." This phrase is translated, word for word, as above, in order to give an idea of the style that Páez wrote.

proach them for their indiscretion, and then replied,
'Sir, it was covetousness,' 'How was that?' said Bolivar to him. 'I had remarked,' the negro went on to
say, 'that everyone who went to the war, went there
without a shirt and without a penny, and came back with
a smart uniform and money in his purse. Therefore I
wished to go and seek my fortune, and more than all to
get three silver-mounted saddles, one for El Negro
Mindola, another for Juan Rafael, and one for myself.
The first battle that we had with the patriots was at
Araure; they had more than a thousand men, we had
many more, so I called out to my friend* José Felix to
give me some weapon to fight with, for I felt sure that
we should win. When I thought that the fight was
over I got off my horse and was just about to strip the
jacket off a dead white officer. At that very moment
my captain came up shouting, " To horse." What is
this, I said, is not this war over yet? It was not finished
for so many of the enemy were approaching, they
looked like a flock of turkey buzzards. There was no
remedy but flight, and so I spurred my mule. The
cursed animal gave out, and so I had to take to the woods
on foot . . ." ' They say,' Bolivar said to him, 'that
you killed other people's cattle when you were in
hiding.' 'Of course I did, or I should soon have
starved. Then came the Majordomo (Páez) and
taught me what patriotism was, and from that time I
have been a patriot.' "

Páez and Bolivar used to make him talk in this
fashion upon their marches, for he had an original and
quaint turn of mind.

The day before the battle of Carabobo, where he was
killed, Páez said he heard El Negro haranguing his
comrades in the kind of language that he (Páez)
used to use on similar occasions, and promising them

* Compadre, literally godfather, but often used in the sense of friend.

paradise if they fought bravely, and the infernal regions if they should run away.

It is not likely that Páez had any contemporary notes of this conversation between Bolivar and the negro, for at the time it took place Páez was nearly, if not quite illiterate. Therefore it must have remained dormant in the cells of his brain for more than forty years. Certainly he could not have invented it, for it bears all the stamp of truth. In all the dialogue there is no trace of patronage; but on the contrary an air of real affection breathes through it all, mingled with that half humorous, half tender criticism with which we view the foibles of our friends, who without doubt do not neglect to pay us back in kind.

Although the fight was won, and the independence of Venezuela secure for ever, there was work for Páez yet, for General Latorre with the remainder of his beaten army still held out in Puerto Cabello, and there were several roving bands of royalists, able to do much damage though not to peril the independent cause.

Páez for the first time was in supreme command and virtually dictator of the country. Bolivar having gone to Bogota, and the provincial government in Caracas quite dependent on him, Páez at once set about to reduce the remnants of the Spanish army.

Shut up in the town of Puerto Cabello with Latorre was the regiment of Valencey, that had fought heroically, and the remains of several other beaten regiments; but his chief asset was a band of almost two hundred Llaneros under the command of Colonel José Alejo Mirabal, who had served under Boves in the cavalry. This man active and energetic, skilled in the wiles of frontier warfare, not over scrupulous, and probably, having been trained in the ferocious school of Boves, cruel and bloodthirsty, was dispatched by Latorre, with the native cavalry to make a raid on Calabozo and attack the patriots in the rear.

Slipping out of the town by night, and travelling by unfrequented paths, at a place called Canoabo he surprised and massacred a detachment of the patriots. Then finding little opposition, for Páez with the bulk of the patriot forces was in Valencia, Mirabal gained the open plains. There, probably by holding out promises of plunder to the ever restless Llaneros, he soon collected a considerable force. With it he besieged the patriot commander Piñango in Calabozo, and might have compelled him to surrender had not Páez in person, by forced marches, come to his rescue at the head of his Guard of Honour.

When Mirabal heard of his approach he at once raised the siege of Calabozo and fled. Pursued by Páez he was overtaken and defeated, and after wandering alone for several days, surrendered to the governor of the town of El Pao. With him he brought Antonio Martinez* the man who had saved Páez during his epileptic* fit at Carabobo. Páez pardoned him instantly, and sent Mirabal a prisoner to his headquarters. He never reached there, for as was use and wont in those days, both in South America and Spain, he attempted to escape and was shot by the soldier who was guarding him. This, down to modern times in Spain, usually happened when bandits were being taken to be judged, and was known as " applying the law of flight to them."†

The usual procedure was to pretend to guard the prisoner carelessly. If upon passing through some place favourable for an escape he tried to get away, he was at once shot down. If knowing what was to be his fate he did not try to get away, they shot him as he

* See Chapter XIV.
† La ley de fuga.

stood.   The sergeant, corporal, or whoever was in command reported that the prisoner had attempted to escape and had attacked his guards, who had been forced to shoot him in defence of their own lives.   Thus were the law's delays avoided, for no appeal to any higher court was possible in such circumstances.

Mirabal's raid having been a failure, General Latorre, who had command of the sea, organized various sallies by land and sea, but they were all infructuous; Páez with his quick moving cavalry was able in almost every instance to stop all landings on the coast.   If by chance the Spaniards did manage to disembark, as in the case of Colonel Garcia, who slipped out of Puerto Cabello with five hundred men to attack Valencia, Páez descended on them with superior forces and forced them to retreat back to their base.

Right up to April, 1822, Puerto Cabello was not regularly besieged.

Páez resolved in the first week of May to besiege the place in form.   He hardly had begun his operations, taking a few of the small outside positions as La Vigia, Burburata and El Pueblo de Afuera, when a revolt in San Fernando de Apure called him away.   The patriot governor of the place had exasperated the inhabitants by his extortion and ill-treatment of them and had assassinated several officers.   Thus almost before the Venezuelans were quite delivered from the Spaniards, civil strife began.   It was destined to continue with brief intervals of peace for more than eighty years. Páez soon quelled the revolt and returned to the siege.

General Latorre was so hard pressed for food that he thrust outside the walls more than two hundred women, children and old men, and would have been obliged to yield the place up had he not received provisions by a Spanish ship of war, that easily brushed aside the feeble

opposition of a few small patriot vessels and anchored
in the port.

In June (1822) General Latorre, who had been
nominated Captain General of Puerto Rico, sailed to
his new post, leaving Colonel Morales to replace him
in command.

During the siege Páez, whose ideas of generalship
were of the Homeric order, exposed himself so recklessly that General Santander wrote expostulating with
him. " Once more I urge you," the general said, " not
to expose yourself unnecessarily.* Your life is precious,
and for your honour you should not expose it without
great and most urgent need. Do not be rash where
there is no occasion; I say this, for what you have done
in Puerto Cabello is mere madness, born of temerity."
Certainly Santander had ample justification for his re-
monstrance. Páez, who loved danger for its own sake,
had behaved most recklessly. Sometimes, dressed as
a common soldier, he worked under the orders of a
corporal upon the siege works. At other times, dressed
in full uniform, he would go to places under fire and
stand there, a mark for sharpshooters. Again in a
canoe he used to reconnoitre the approaches to the forts,
and draw their fire upon himself.

This though it brought him the admiration of the
soldiers, a thing that he throughout his life valued above
all else, was not exactly the duty of a general. Páez
no doubt in his calmer moods was well aware of this,
but danger was to him as morphia to drug takers, or
drink to drunkards, and he indulged his passion for it
to the full.

In spite of all his efforts and his reckless bravery, the
malignant fevers incidental to the hot, humid regions
of the Venezuelan coast had played such havoc with his

* Excerpt from a letter of General Santander, dated Bogotá, June 15,
1822.

troops, exposed to tropic rains and burning suns, whilst badly fed, that he was obliged to raise the siege and return to the better climate of Valencia. Of the three thousand three hundred men with whom he commenced the siege only one thousand had survived, and that in two short months. He was not long left unmolested. Morales, the new governor, who had replaced Latorre, sallied in force and forced him to fight several bloody skirmishes. In these, Páez though uniformly victorious suffered serious losses. There were still many sympathisers with the royalists in Venezuela. These flocked to the aid of Morales from every side, so that in a short time his forces numbered more than two thousand. He took up a strong position in the mountains between Valencia and the coast.

Páez who had been reinforced by General Anzoategui with fresh troops and cavalry, forced Morales to retire further into the hills, after inflicting considerable loss upon him. Night and the difficult nature of the ground alone saved him from being captured, as Páez, prudent for once, did not think fit to risk an ambush if he pushed on in the pursuit.

Morales remained ten or twelve days in his hill fastnesses hoping for the success of a revolt that had been organized in Calabozo, by the same Antonio Martinez who had so strangely come to the aid of Páez during his epileptic seizure at Carabobo. The revolt broke out, but was suppressed immediately. Then Morales returned to Puerto Cabello, embarked with a considerable force, sailed to Maracaibo, landed in the peninsula of La Goajira, and routed a patriot force at a place called Salina Rica. Then after having taken the castle of San Carlos, a strong fort on an island at the mouth of the entrance to the Lake of Maracaibo, he occupied the town.

This was a serious check for the patriots, for Maracaibo by its singular position was then, and always must be of the first importance to the republic.

The gulf of Maracaibo, sheltered as it is by the two peninsulas of La Goajira and Paraguana, has at its southern end a narrow passage of a few miles in length defended by the castle of San Carlos, that leads into the lake. The water on the bar only admits vessels of light draft.

Puertos de Altagracia is situated on the eastern side of the passage to the lake, and Maracaibo on the west. Once through the gut the lake spreads out, a sheet of shallow water seldom exceeding thirty feet in depth. The eastern side is low and reedy, and on the western side the land rises towards the foothills of the Andes. When the first conquerors sailed upon the waters of the lake, the reed thatched houses of the Indians standing on lofty piles caused one of them to exclaim, " this is a little Venice."* Eventually the name came to be applied to the whole country. At the south-western limit of the lake a flame at nightfall lights up a low range of hills. Its exact cause has never been satisfactorily explained. The ancient navigators called it " The Lantern of Maracaibo," and several of the first navigators refer to it in their writings. To-day it bears the name of " El Faro de Catatumbo," from a small river that runs into the lake.

Once well established in Maracaibo, Morales, who had learned nothing by experience, put out a proclamation threatening all foreigners taken in arms with death. He also most foolishly declared invalid several of the articles of the Treaty of Trujillo, to which Bolivar and Morillo had set their hands. Then after annihilating a patriot force under José Sardá, he occupied the town of Coro, further down the coast.

Páez believing that the Spanish squadron would be

* Hence, Venezuela, the Little Venice.

unable to cross the bar at Puertos de Altagracia, and
thinking that the castle of San Carlos, that had been
given up without a blow by its cowardly commander,
Colonel Natividad Villasmil, was still in the possession
of the patriots, raised a considerable force to attack
Morales, whom he was certain must capitulate, bottled
up as he was inside the passage to the lake.   Upon his
march, when he arrived at Trujillo, he received the
news of the loss of the castle of San Carlos, and also
that the Spanish squadron had passed the bar into the
inland sea.

Páez who was well aware that so long as the Spanish
fleet was in existence, that there would be constant raids
upon the coast, got together a little squadron, composed
of twenty-two vessels, and put on board them thirteen
hundred men, under the command of José Padilla. The
Spanish fleet was superior in numbers and far better
armed, but in those days of sailing ships, could not
manœuvre readily, landlocked within the shallow waters
of the lake.

Upon the 24th of July (1823) the patriot fleet
crossed the bar with a leading wind, and before the
royalists could raise their anchors, ran up and boarded
them.   After a furious fight of some three hours, ten
of the Spanish ships were taken and one sunk. Sixty-nine
officers and three hundred men were taken prisoners,
and Morales, attacked on every side, found himself
forced to capitulate, as Páez had foreseen.

On the third of August he signed a capitulation with
Padilla, the patriot admiral.   In it, as Captain General
of the Mainland,* he surrendered Maracaibo, the castle
of San Carlos, Puerto Cabello and the remainder of his
fleet.

On the 15th of August, he set sail for the Habana,
having received five thousand dollars from the patriots

* Costa Firme.

for the expenses of the voyage. Thus the last official representative of Spain had left the country, after a struggle that had lasted nearly twenty years.

General Calzada, whom Morales had left in command at Puerto Cabello, refused to recognise the capitulation which his chief had entered into with the Venezuelans, declaring that as long as one stone stood upon another he would hold the place for Spain.

Páez who was not a sanguinary man, in spite of his upbringing, wrote to Don Sebastian de la Calzada, urging him to give the place up to avoid unnecessary bloodshed, and offering him twenty-five thousand dollars to repatriate his men. He also wrote to a civilian Spaniard, Don Jacinto Iztueta, whom he knew was a sympathiser with the patriots. The letters were entrusted to two convicts in a small sailing vessel to Ocumare, and from that point they went in a canoe. Their instructions were to tell Calzada that they had escaped from the prison in La Guaira, and to make the tale appear more real the iron rings they wore round their ankles were not unriveted.

Calzada answered saying his honour and his duty did not allow him to consider such an alternative, and he reiterated his determination to hold out. His proposition not having been accepted, Páez set about to besiege the place in forms. Puerto Cabello is divided into two parts. One called " El Pueblo Interior "* forms a peninsula that is joined by a narrow neck of land to the suburb called " El Pueblo de Afuera," that is the outside town. The interior town is separated from the exterior by a channel that runs into the sea at the bottom of the bay, whose waters reach the battery called La Estacada, that with a bulwark to the eastward called El Principe, and another to the west called La Princesa, defend the place towards the south.

* Memorias del General Páez, Cap. XV, page 267.

To the east there was another battery called El Picayo, at the edge of the town. On the north side the chief defence was the battery El Corito, which with the castle of San Felipe situated on an islet at the mouth of the channel that forms the entry to the port, across which ran a massive iron chain.

The siege of Puerto Cabello was the one occasion of his life in which Páez was in supreme command in such an undertaking. Up till that moment, though he was the idol of the native Venezuelans, he had been over-shadowed by the superior genius and position of Bolivar. Now Bolivar was far away in Bogotá and there was no one left in Venezuela to overtop the Llanero general. General Soublette, his only rival, though a brave and skilled commander and an old patriot, was lacking in those qualities that commend a man to the crowd. It was only natural therefore that Páez in his Memoirs should give full prominence to all his operations in the siege. His reckless bravery and utter disregard of his own personal safety have been corroborated* by impartial witnesses.

Undoubtedly Puerto Cabello was well defended, both by its natural position and its numerous well constructed forts and batteries. Inside the walls was shut up all that remained of the heroic regiment of Valencey, and many of the soldiers who had escaped from the defeat of Carabobo, earlier in the year. General Calzada was a man of character and resolution. Moreover in the harbour there were two or three warships that not having been at Maracaibo had not been given up. Amongst them was the powerful corvette Bailen.†

Páez commenced his operations by an attack upon the

* See letters from General Santander and General Lopez, quoted on page 215.

† Named after the decisive victory gained by the Spaniards over the French at Bailen, in the Napoleonic wars. The French commanded by Dupont were forced to capitulate with twenty-five thousand men.

battery of El Trincheron, situated on the edge of a mangrove swamp and well defended by skilled artillerymen. He took it on the 7th of October. This opened up his way for a direct attack against the town. Then he constructed at a place called Los Cocos, a battery, that commanded the mouth of the river San Esteban, from which the besieged obtained the greater part of their supply of drinking water. To the east of Los Cocos he established another battery, in despite of a desperate sally of the besieged. These works allowed him to bring to bear a heavy fire on the walls of the town and the forts that defended them. The breaches that his artillery made during the day were repaired at night by the defenders. Notwithstanding that he had captured the advanced post of El Mirador de Solano, his prospects of success were none too brilliant when a mere accident opened the way to him to take the town by assault.

Some of his scouts had observed each morning fresh human tracks in the wet sand of the seashore. These led outwards from the town and back again. At first but scant attention was paid to them. Then as they frequently appeared, Páez set men hidden in the mangrove swamp to watch the beach. One night they caught a negro emerging from the waters of the swamp and took him prisoner.

Brought before Páez he said he was a slave of a rich Spaniard, who sent him out to report on the position of the guns in the besieger's batteries. Either by threats, or promise of reward, or both, Páez was able to secure the man's allegiance to him. This he obtained so absolutely that after having pointed out the ford to several officers who accompanied him, he returned to the town and went on making his nocturnal sallies, but without revealing what had happened to him.

Páez must have had a most magnetic influence over

the man, or else the negro was a sympathiser with the national cause. Being now certain that he could attack and carry Puerto Cabello, Páez sent twice to General Calzada, summoning him to capitulate in order to avoid useless bloodshed. The third time he gave him notice that if he did not either surrender or meet him to sign a capitulation in four and twenty hours, he would take the place by assault and butcher all the garrison.

Calzada answered that the town was defended by old and seasoned soldiers and in the last resort they were prepared to follow the glorious example of the defenders of Numantia and Saguntum. He added, if fortune should prove adverse, he trusted Páez would not stain the brilliance* of his sword by an act worthy of an age of barbarism.

Both of them having, no doubt, the racial love of high-sounding language, must have enjoyed the writing of the letters to the full.

To give the scene its requisite setting and proper colour, when the envoy Páez had sent was passing through the gate on his return, the Spanish soldiers lined† the walls and with loud cries called upon the Venezuelans to come and cut their throats if they were able. Hector and Achilles could have done no better beneath the walls of Troy.

In order that the Spaniards should not think he had any design of a direct assault, Páez set five hundred men at work during the night to dig trenches and turn the course of the river, as if he had intended only to tighten the blockade. During these operations he had a marvellous escape. At daybreak, as he stood directing the operations, a cannon ball struck a heap of sand

* " Aunque esperaba que yo no queria manchar el brillo de mi espada con un hecho digno de los tiempos de barbarie."

† " Cuando el parlamento salio de la plaza la tropa formada en los muros nos desafiabia con gran algaraza á que fuéremos á pasarle á cuchillo."

on which he happened to be standing and threw him down into a trench, but without doing him the slightest injury. All the day long before his contemplated assault, he kept his artillery at work in a prolonged bombardment of the town, in order to fatigue the enemy and to distract their attention from his preparations.

At ten o'clock at night upon the 7th of November he mustered his attacking force and ordered them to strip, retaining nothing but their arms and cartridge belts. Under the cover of the warm, tropic night they set out, about five hundred strong. Four hours they marched through the mangrove swamp, with the water breast high and their feet in the black mud, that always accumulates where mangroves grow. So near they passed to the battery of La Princesa that they could hear the soldiers talking and heard one of them remark that there must be vast shoals of fish upon the move that night, as the water was so agitated.

When they arrived upon dry land, having passed so near to the corvette El Bailen that they could almost touch her, they at once rushed to the assault. The Spaniards, taken by surprise, as they had no idea the mangrove swamp was passable and had kept no watch upon it, fought desperately, but seeing that the game was up, abandoned all their outer batteries and retired into the town.

At daybreak, two priests arrived to where the naked troops were bivouacking, saying that General Calzada, who had taken refuge in a church, awaited Páez, to deliver up his sword. Páez at once set out, probably wet and half naked as he was, to meet Calzada, who delivered up his sword and congratulated him on having " put the seal* upon his glories." His actual words, as Páez with some commendable pride duly recorded. Páez, not to be undone in generosity, thanked him cour-

* Felicitóme por haber puesto sello a mis glorias.

teously, and probably at some considerable length, for the occasion was not one to be neglected, and certainly it was propitious for an outpouring of high-sounding adjectives. Then the two generals went off arm in arm* to drink their coffee in the house Calzada had occupied during the recent siege.

An unlucky incident nearly marred their recently established friendly relations. The castle not having received notice that hostilities had ceased, opened fire and killed a sergeant who was close to Páez. At the same moment the commander of the corvette El Bailen blew her up, and the whole harbour was filled with a dense cloud of smoke. Páez indignantly upbraided Calzada with this act of treachery. He instantly wrote to the commander of the castle telling him the war had ceased and that he was a prisoner. The commander, either a fool or a brave, wooden-headed soldier, returned for answer that as Calzada was a prisoner his authority had ceased.

Páez not wishing to recommence hostilities, and probably knowing the kind of man he had to deal with, returned Calzada's sword to him and sent him to the castle to deal with his subordinate, who seeing his general free and with his sword at his side, recognised his authority and capitulated.

Calzada having settled with his subordinate, invited Páez to come to breakfast with him. Confiding always, as he says, in Castilian honour,† he accepted and was received with military honours and with the gallant courtesy that he expected from such valiant adversaries.

With the fall of Puerto Cabello the war of independence was at an end. The Spaniards possessed no inch

---

* Dile las gracias y tomandole familiarmente del brazo fuimos juntos á tomar café á la casa que el habia ocupado durante el sitio.

† "Fiado como siempre en la hidalguia castellana y con toda la gallarda cortesia que debia esperar de tan valientes adversarios."

of Venezuelan territory. Isolated bands of the nature of banditti rather than of soldiery still held out in distant places, and these Páez was called on to deal with and disperse.

After so many years of desperate bloodshed, massacre and warfare to the knife, it speaks well for the Spaniards that their character stood high in the estimation of such a man as Páez. His trusting faith in the " Castilian honour " shows that that honour had remained unsmirched in spite of everything.

The simple tale of the two enemies, after a bloody night of slaughter, going off arm in arm to take their early morning coffee and then breakfasting together, whilst their horses fastened to a post or to the grating of a window stood nodding in the sun, almost induces the belief that, in the words of Páez, " The human heart, no matter how the passions harden it, always preserves remains of sensibility and only needs a simple action to make it show itself in all its greatness."

CHAPTER XVI

FLUSHED with the triumph of his successful sieze, Páez was called upon almost at once to deal with some of the ferocious bandits, who masquerading under the name of royalists still pursued their operations in several isolated districts of the country. In the execution of his task, Páez displayed his usual contempt of danger and that personal magnetism that never failed in its effect even upon the wildest and most desperate characters.

In a short campaign he broke up and scattered most of the bandits, taking and executing several of their leaders. A certain José Dionisio Cisneros, secure in the deep valleys and the mountains of the Tuy district still held out. This rascal who had been a sergeant in the Spanish army, had gathered to himself a band of cut-throats, deserters from both armies, escaped slaves, and all the flotsam and the jetsam that civil warfare brings to the top like scum. He styled himself the defender of the Spanish throne.

In spite of all his crimes Cisneros seems to have been a man of desperate courage, and as events showed afterwards, not devoid of a certain generosity. For one cause or another, for the present Páez left him unmolested, though in later years he dealt with him faithfully.

Páez was soon called upon to face difficulties of a more complex nature. The very qualities that served him so well in matters such as the quelling of the bandit bands, did not so well fit him to deal with civil administration.

After the fall of Puerto Cabello, Páez set out with

Generals Mariño and Bermudez for Caracas. As might have been expected, his journey was one long triumphal march. In every town the citizens came out to greet him, and women from the balconies threw flowers on his head. The inhabitants of the newly-emancipated Republic had looked upon Puerto Cabello as the key to the Spanish power. Its exceptional position and the many forts defending it, upon which the Spanish engineers had lavished all their skill, had spread the legend that it was invulnerable. Since the year 1812 it had resisted all attacks. Now it had fallen after a short siege, with but a trifling loss to the patriot forces. Thus the joy at its fall was quite legitimate, and all his countrymen naturally saw in Páez the incarnation of their independence. Bolivar was away in New Granada, Mariño, Santander, Bermudez and the other generals had not the personal qualities Páez possessed. So for the moment he occupied a position that he enjoyed for a brief period and to which he never rose again throughout his long career.

At the same time the difficulties he had to face were great. The war once over, the necessity arose to pay the troops who had served, often for long periods, practically unpaid. The national treasury was empty, and the only way open to the government to satisfy the soldiery was to assign to them the cattle and the horses on the estates that had been taken from the royalists.

As there was no machinery existing by means of which these animals could be delivered to the soldiers to whom they were assigned, the government was forced to allow them to go and take them for themselves. This naturally was the cause of grave disorders, which some of the Venezuelan historians* have denounced as brigandage. The soldiers being entirely without money, naturally

* "Resumen de la Historia de Venezuela," Rafael Maria Baralt, Paris, 1841.

wished to turn the cattle into cash rather than sit down
and look after them. So great was the slaughter of
the unlucky animals, for the sake of their grease and
hides, that the Llaneros in many instances used their
bones to form the fences of their corrals. Páez found
himself obliged to send out regular expeditions to the
Llanos to establish order.

In May, 1825, the Congress of Caracas, alarmed by
rumours of a Spanish expedition to recover their lost
territory, and under the necessity of providing troops
for the war Bolivar was waging in Peru against the
Spaniards, who still were in possession of that country,
passed a decree to raise a force of fifty thousand men.
It was a risky experiment for a government so newly
come into existence, and that had emerged from sixteen
years of war. Moreover the rumours of a Spanish
expedition had no foundation, except mere rumour. In
fact after their great defeat at Carabobo the Spaniards
never seem to have harboured any sinister design against
Venezuela or Colombia. The decree did not give satisfaction to the people, who were all tired of war. Still
with commendable patriotism a force of over ten thousand men was equipped and embarked at Puerto Cabello
for Peru.

Unluckily for his popularity, the work of raising men
was given to Páez. No one could have well been less
suited for the task. The citizens of Caracas not having
responded to the decree in any numbers, Páez resorted
to the press-gang system, and rounded up anyone he
found upon the streets, just as he would have rounded
up wild cattle on the plains. He tells the story as if he
had been genuinely surprised that anyone should object,
and puts down the recalcitrancy of the people of Caracas
to his mildness* of procedure, that probably encouraged

* Asistieron pocos y obligado a convocarlos de nuevo . . . y como
ni aun asi obedecieron el decreto, tal vez envalentonados por la lenidad
con que yo procedia mande piquetes de los batallones, Anzoátegui

them to resist. Though this was the system that prevailed in all the South American Republics up to a few years ago, and still prevails in some of them to-day, at that time the maggots of liberty and the rights of man were breeding vigorously in the brains of the new republicans of Venezuela.

To be herded, like wild mules into the corral of the convent of San Francisco did not appeal to their ideas of republicanism. They had not the experience that later years brought to so many of the republics. As yet no general from his headquarters in the field had written home, " Thanks for the five hundred volunteers, I return the ropes."

At the uproar that ensued, Páez appears to have been genuinely amazed. He says, next day, the Intendant,* General Juan Escalona, pretending to be a zealous defender of the peoples' rights in a communication to the Executive, stigmatized the measures I had taken as abuses.

The Municipality of Caracas also protested in the same terms. Hardly was this affair over when a rebellion broke out in a town called Petare, two leagues from the capital. Páez was called on to deal with it, and in his own words, " terminated the matter in the military style." He only punished† the three leading men. This natural and military method of procedure was also made the subject of attack by a meddling deputy, one Dr. José Antonio Perez, in the senate of Caracas. These two matters might have led to disagreeable consequences for Páez, had not, luckily for him, a

---

y Apure para que trajesen al convento de San Francisco los ciudadanos que hallasen por los calles."

* An " Intendente," is the treasurer of a government, or the quartermaster general of an army.

† " Castigué." He does not say what the punishment was ; but one supposes he was too good an economist to saddle the rates of the new-born republic, with the maintenance of prisoners.

violation of the national territory chanced to occur by a French squadron. The Venezuelans were quite naturally easily alarmed at even the shadow of an attack upon the liberties that they had won at such a cost of blood.

Páez was invested with extraordinary powers by the National Executive to resist attacks from any foreign power and to deal with interior revolutions. Thus the year 1823 closed luckily for him. Although his methods in the matter of the levy had been those of the Llanero cattle man, who when a herd of bullocks will not enter a corral or cross a river, crowds in upon them with his men shouting and whirling whips and lazos in the air, and now and then not sparing to use the goad to stimulate the stragglers, he saw more clearly than any other public man that the formation of Colombia and New Granada into a single state was doomed to failure. Bolivar, far off in Peru, marching triumphantly along, in triumph, the cynosure of every eye, his fame extending over the whole world and his head filled with those heroic visions* that have filled every conqueror's head from Alexander to Napoleon, had got a little out of touch with his own country. Páez who had remained a Venezuelan pure and simple, and lived upon the spot, was well aware of the deep seated jealousy between the Venezuelans and the New Granadans.† He knew the wants and aspirations of his own people and saw quite clearly, the symptoms of the inevitable rupture that was certain to ensue.

For the present the question of separation was in abeyance, and Páez had to face the serious charge of having broken the law and outraged the persons of the citizens, by his arbitrary dealings with them in the affair of the compulsory enlistments. Accused before

* Some commentators term them Megrims.

† Colombians.

the government in Caracas, of having not only broken
the law, but having fired upon citizens who refused his
orders to enlist, and in some instances burned down
their houses, he had to face, perhaps the bitterest
moment of his life.

In a few short months to have stood on a pinnacle,
hailed as the saviour of his country, and then to find
himself accused of serious crimes, by the very government that owed its existence to his bravery, must have
been galling to him. He faced the storm with the same
courage that he had so often manifested on the battle
field.

The petty jealousies that always sour the life of
every public man, now broke out against Páez with
extreme virulence. The whole affair seems to have
been mixed up with the question of the separation of
the two republics, that was beginning to occupy the minds
of everyone. The vice-president of the executive was
General Santander, himself a New Granadan. Knowing or perhaps feeling instinctively, that Páez was no
friend to New Granada, he seems to have played a
double part, writing* to Páez in terms of friendship
and respect, and to Bolivar in another sense. After
some hesitation the Chamber of Representatives found
a true bill against Páez. The Senate after equal vacil-
lation, ratified the accusation. Páez was deprived of
his command, and to make it harder to endure, his
accuser General Escalona was appointed to it.

On this occasion Páez behaved with commendable
dignity and self respect. Although in the Llanos nothing would have been easier for him, than to defy the

---

* " Mi opinion—fue que la acusacion era ligera, y que se debian esperar
nuevas pruebas."

Extract from a letter of General Santander to Páez dated May 10th, 1826.
On the 15th of July he wrote to Bolivar condemning Páez in the strongest
terms.

This letter is contained in the sixth volume of " Los Documentos de la
Vida Publica del Libertador," page 210.

government, who had no forces at its command to send against him, he at once submitted to the decree depriving him of his command.

On the same day that General Escalona took over the command a movement broke out in Valencia favourable to Páez. The municipality passed a vote deploring the accusation against him, and registering its conviction, that he would be able to justify himself. It placed on record that all the citizens were convinced of the probity which Páez had shown in the exercise of his powers, and that he had gained the affection and respect of every one.

Unfortunately in the transports of their indignation, the people murdered two unlucky men who had had neither art nor part in the affair of the accusation and threw their bodies on to the steps of the Town Hall. Colonel Carabaño ordered the troops to barracks; but they broke out and carried Páez on their shoulders through the streets to the Municipality. In after years, Paéz regretted the step that he was forced to take, but says quite reasonably that his position was most difficult. Valencia was the town where he resided and was beloved by everybody. Upon the steps of the old Spanish House, now "El Mueso Páez," whose walls are covered with ingenuous frescoes of his exploits, his fellow citizens, so to speak, forced the crown upon him. Less hypocritical than Cromwell in like circumstances, he did not put it away from him, and on the same day that had been witness to his fall he was restored to power. He says in an unlucky* hour he resumed the command of which he had been so unjustly deprived, and that, the first step taken, it was necessary to go on with the mistake, into which he had been led.

The step may have been unfortunate for him, but

* "En hora menguada para mi, reasumi el mando de que me habia suspendido tan injustamente, y ya dado el primer paso, era necesario ser consecuente con el error cometido."—Memorias, page 330.

for his country it probably was fortunate, for civil war would certainly have broken out, had not there been a strong hand at the helm. Valencia invited all the other towns to follow its example, and to approve the movement it had initiated, in order that they should all join in maintaining Páez in command, for the sake of public order and of peace, until Bolivar should return to preside over the Convention that had been convoked for the year 1831, to deal with public difficulties.

All the towns followed the lead Valencia had given them. Even Caracas once so hostile to him, now relented, and Páez borne on a wave of popular enthusiasm, was invested with supreme authority, in civil and in military affairs.

By this turn of the wheel of fortune, Páez was once more president in all but name. It is to be supposed that some of the citizens who had been so unceremoniously corralled, were not too well pleased with the rough treatment that had been meted out to them. Probably the majority laughed at the whole affair, for the South Americans of those days did not object too strenuously, when a man in authority showed that he could rule. There were other factors in the situation that made the Venezuelans look leniently on the high handed methods Páez had employed. The question of the separation of the two countries,* though it had not yet been agitated publicly, no doubt, was uppermost in every heart. The fact that General Santander, a native of Bogotá held high office in Caracas, certainly must have made the citizens of Venezuela look upon Páez as the representative of nationalism. This probably inclined them to overlook the roughness of his recent methods, for every nation since the beginning of the world, has preferred, and rightly, indifferent govern-

* Venezuela and New Granada, *i.e.* Colombia.

ment, by one of its own citizens, to any rule, however beneficial, imposed from the outside.

Páez who knew his fellow countrymen, as instinctively as a horse knows a horseman from a " maturrango," almost before he mounts him, at once issued a proclamation, conceived in just the terms most suited to appeal to them.

All peoples have and perhaps ever will be taken with fine words, as is quite natural, for as the minds and the vocabulary of the greater portion of humanity are poorly furnished, high sounding words appear to them as coming from on high.

He began by stating he had been raised to power by the free vote of all the towns. The fact that no vote had been taken, neither weighed with him nor with his countrymen. He then went on to say, self preservation is the first law of nature, which may have seemed to the public he was addressing as a great truth Páez had discovered on the Llanos for himself.

After the necessary amount of rhetoric without which no public man from Pericles to Gladstone ever addressed the sovereign people—he came to the one grain of wheat amongst the chaff. Being an honest man and a sincere lover of his country, he could not ignore the fact, that the internal situation of Venezuela was becoming serious. He therefore told his people that he would use his influence to have the Congress, fixed for the year 1831, to be held immediately.

" The Liberator-President, will be arbiter and mediator. He will not turn a deaf ear to the complaints of his compatriots."

Old use and wont, the strongest power in the world, obliged him to conclude with a piece of cant.

" The power you have confided to me, was not given to oppress you, but to protect your liberty."

The proclamation dated 19th of May, 1826, was signed at his headquarters in Caracas.

The proclamation certainly must have had a good effect, for opinion in Caracas was rapidly becoming hostile to the central authority that sat at Bogotá, which city had been declared the capital, of what was called La Gran Colombia. Situated as it was, more than a thousand miles away and inaccessible, except by a long and arduous journey across the Andes, or by a sea voyage to Cartagena and afterwards, another journey in clumsy sailing vessels, for nine hundred miles on the Magdelena river, it is not wonderful that relations between it and Caracas easily became strained. This was the case almost immediately. The executive of Bogotá declared, the events that happened at Valencia upon the 30th of April (1820), involving as they did the election of Páez, almost to supreme power, constituted "an armed insurrection." Luckily for the peace of the two republics, secured to one another, by a bond injurious to both of them, Bolivar held a different opinion.

His secretary, General José Perez, in a speech he made to the municipality of Guayaquil, inspired of course by the Liberator, poured oil upon the waters. "His Excellency," he said, "has not yet received officially, the account of the events that took place in the month of April at Valencia, and cannot therefore form a just opinion of their character; but by reports he has received from private individuals, he understands that they have not made a breach in the Colombian Pact."*

Secretary Perez went on to say that Venezuela wanted a reform in its constitution, and that Páez had received

* This Pact was entered into by delegates from both Venezuela and Colombia, at the Town of Cucuta, upon the 6th of May, 1821. It instituted the artificial State known as La Gran Colombia, comprising Colombia, Venezuela and Ecuador. Bolivar was elected President, and the title of

promissory powers of government. "As Páez had asserted that the name of the Liberator was graven* on his heart," the secretary was certain that he harboured no ulterior motives, and that the *status quo* would be maintained until the Liberator should arrive.

The time was overdue, for the whole country was falling into anarchy. Some of the towns were in favour of the federal system, the only one in their opinion that could save the country, as if a system ever saved anything, except itself. Politicians in every age and country have always had some nostrum or another, by which all ills humanity is heir to, can be cured. What renders, and has generally rendered the matter worse, is that they have been bestially honest, in the majority of cases. Had they been rogues, there might have been some chance, for although suffering humanity is not as a rule oppressed with intellect, the logic of hard facts might to some extent have supplemented the lack of brains.

Other towns wished to have the "Bolivian Code "† adopted. This was a constitution that Bolivar had invented for the new state, that had been named after him. Like most constitutions of the kind, it looked quite feasible on paper, but was too full of high aspirations, and theories suitable rather for orphaned archangels than for ordinary men, to turn out workable.

One party wanted decentralisation, but without separation from Colombia. Lastly there was a group that wished to set up some kind of monarchy, though who they could have got to accept a throne so totter-

---

Liberator was accorded him officially. The Vice-President was General Santander, and the capital was fixed at Bogotá.—" Historia de Venezuela," p. 167, por H. N. M. Caracas, 1927.

* Este general (Páez) ha expresado que el nombre del Libertador esta escrito en el fondo de su corazon.

† El Codigo Boliviano.

ing, and a crown so thickly set with thorns, is difficult to see.

All parties were quite ready to resort to arms, to
show their love of peace and liberty and their belief in
forms as the best solvents of all difficulties.

Puerto Cabello gave its adhesion to the federal
system, upon the 8th of August (1826), and Maracaibo,
Aragua, and Cumaná soon followed its example.
Finally to make things more distracting, Quito and
Guayaquil, towns situated at the furthest limit of La
Gran Colombia, followed Valencia's lead.

Meetings and convocations came in quick succession
and Páez, more accustomed to the vagaries of wild
cattle, who at least acted upon instinct, than the ways
of over logical republicans, must have looked back
regretfully upon the days when mounted on a half wild
horse he sallied out at sunrise, for a long day upon the
plains.

On the 5th of October (1826) the federal system
was adopted at a conference held in Caracas. An
assembly of the electoral colleges arranged for a second
conference at the Convent of San Francisco to be held
at Valencia early in the following year.

All seemed to have settled down at last, when
Puerto Cabello, that had been previously a warm
adherent of the federal system, suddenly pronounced
against it, and a battalion of grenadiers, who garrisoned
the place, broke out into revolt. Páez was obliged to
send troops against them to reduce them to obedience.
He must have been driven half distracted amid all these
difficulties.

Upon the 25th of May he wrote a letter from Caracas
to Bolivar, that shows under how great a strain he
laboured. In it he begs Bolivar " to come and be the
pilot of this ship tossed on a stormy sea, to conduct it to
a safe harbour, and permit me to retire into private life

in the Llanos of Apure, there to live amongst my friends, far from invidious rivals, and forgotten by ungrateful people, who had but just commenced to serve (their country), as my career is at an end. " I had thought, he wrote, to burn my uniforms and all my decorations upon the public square, retaining only a bust of yourself as a memento. This was not merely flattery, for Páez always seems to have looked upon Bolivar with feelings almost of veneration, treating him as an elder brother, with whom his junior quarrels, but in his heart reveres.

After much correspondence between the two generals, conducted at such an enormous distance apart, as they were situated, Páez in a letter from his headquarters in Valencia, dated the third of January, 1827, assures Bolivar, that though he had vowed never again to obey the government in Bogotá, he was resolved on account of the peace and welfare of the republic, to place himself in the hands of Bolivar, to judge his actions, during his absence in Peru. Bolivar who saw his presence in Venezuela was imperative, if the distracted country was to be saved from utter anarchy, left Lima, and after a short stay in Guayaquil, upon the 14th of November arrived at Bogotá.

On the last day of 1826, he anchored in the bay of Puerto Cabello, and next day wrote to Páez confirming him in his command. The Liberator came at the right moment. Had he delayed his coming, civil warfare would have broken out; but his prestige was still so great amongst his fellow countrymen that his mere presence served to restore order and to still down civil broils.

As soon as Páez, who was at his house in Valencia, heard of the Liberator's arrival at Puerto Cabello, he rushed off to greet him. As he rode down the mountain roads, the vegetation becoming every mile more tropical,

and the heat greater as he descended, till passing Las
Trincheras with its hot springs, he reached the flat
ground near the sea, in an atmosphere close as a Turkish
bath, he must have wondered how he would be received.

The Liberator was not a man to trifle with, and his
position had become more authoritative, since the last
time they bid farewell to one another. They met at
the foot of the hill of Naguanagua some little distance
up the pass. Dismounting, they cordially embraced.
So cordially that the hilts of their swords became entangled. Bolivar, ever quick of wit, and swift to seize
an opportunity for a good effect, exclaimed, " This is a
good omen, general, for the future." When they
reached Valencia, the whole town was in the streets to
welcome them. After the customary inspection of the
troops, a ceremony that even soldiers must find weari-
some at times, they set out for the capital. The entry
of the Liberator into Caracas was the occasion for a
general outburst of relief. He was acclaimed as the
First Born of Fortune, the Creator* of the Three
Republics, The Genius of War and Peace, who from
the Temple of the Sun had come armed with an olive
branch, to restore life to the Fatherland.

Brave words indeed, no doubt sincere when uttered,
by men who in the space of two short years, were to
pass a decree of ostracism against the man they spattered
with their praise.

The Caraquenians vied with one another in doing
honour to their most illustrious citizen. Arches of palms
and willows, festooned with ribbons of the national
colours, and crowned with flags, were set up in the
streets, which the Liberator had to pass.

---

* " . . . El Primogenito de la Fortuna, El Creador de Tres Republicas,
El Genio de la Guerra y de la Paz desde el Templo del Sol viene armado con
la oliva a dar otra vez vida a la patriá." In the classic words of one who
was no mean exponent in the art of rhodomontade, hyperbole was " beaten
to a frazzle," by these stout Euphuists.

There in the naïve words of Páez, " although not
comparable to the marble arches, with which Imperial
Rome had honoured Trajan, they displayed the gratitude and the affection of those who had erected them,
a thousand fold more deeply, for they were offered
from the heart."

The flags of all the newly freed republics were
displayed, together with the star-spangled standard of
the Eagle of the North. That bird at the time had
not revealed its claws to its younger brothers in democracy, but cooed as sweetly as a pigeon when it is going
to be fed.

In the cathedral the Dioscuri heard a Te Deum and
then retired to the house prepared for their reception.
No rest awaited them, for fifteen damsels, richly dressed
and symbolising civil and military virtues, were in waiting for them. They bore two crowns of laurel.* One
of them as destined for the triumph the Liberator had
gained against the tyrants of his country. The other
for the man who had prevented civil war. Bolivar who
probably felt that two crowns of imperishable laurel
were difficult to dispose gracefully upon his brow,
presented one to Páez, placing it with his own hands on
his head, and dedicated the other to the illustrious people
of Colombia.

Banquets and balls succeeded one another in quick
succession and speeches were delivered, each one rising
nearer to Olympus than the other, and adorned so
thickly with metaphors and tropes, classical quotations
and above all with adjectives, that all the dictionaries
of Caracas must have been thoroughly well thumbed to
furnish them. The Municipality offered the troic
heroes an " Ambigu,"† at which two hundred guests
attended.

* " . . . dos coronas de inmarcesible laurel."
† Ambigu is an old-fashioned word meaning luncheon or collation.
At this Ambigu or at the banquet that followed it the writer thinks his

When it came to the turn of Páez, " to make use of speech "* he expressed himself in the following chaste words. " Gentlemen, allow me to express my sentiments of pride. I cannot keep it (his pride) in my heart, for it is a noble sentiment. Gentlemen, the Liberator has filled up the measure of his benefits, and of my glory to the full. He has given me the sword† with which he freed a world.

" If the sword of Frederick, who did no more than defend his inheritance and usurp another, was a gift of inestimable value for the Sovereign‡ of Europe, what shall I say when I see in my possession the sword that was the terror of tyrants, that sword that has redeemed the human race. . . ?

" What use shall I make of the sword? How shall I preserve its laurels, its glories and its honour?

" It adds to my duties a hundredfold, it calls for strength, that only is in Bolivar's power. It confounds me; this sword that has redeemed mankind. In my hands it will always be Bolivar's sword; my arm may wield it; but his is the directing will. I am prepared to perish a hundred times before this sword shall ever leave my hand. Fellow citizens, Bolivar's sword is in my hands; armed with it I will follow him to all eternity."

Pericles, Mark Anthony or Mirabeau, could hardly have soared to greater heights or have been more

---

maternal grandfather, Admiral, the Honourable Charles Elphinstone Fleeming, and his grandmother, Doña Catalina Paulina Jimenez y Alesandro, were present.

* Hacer uso de la palabra.

† Bolivar had presented him with a sword and a lance, inscribed with his name in gold, and also with two fine Peruvian horses and a dressing case.

‡ The allusion is wrapped in mystery. What Frederick had in his mind is as hard to explain as the proverbial way of the serpent on the rock and that other way too hard of explanation, even for Solomon himself who had travelled it so many times. The Sovereign of Europe also gives ground for speculation.

magniloquent. As stones are practically unknown throughout Los Llanos de Apure, it is to be supposed that Páez was born an orator, for it was impossible for him to have found pebbles to put into his mouth, after the example of Demosthenes, if he had stuttered at the start.

The mayor not to be outdone, raised his glass " to the inviolability of the monument* erected between the people and their Liberator. The sword and lance given to the Venezuelan Achilles never shall be employed but in the defence of Liberty." That nothing should be wanting, and that the Venezuelan Achilles and the Liberator should be justified, as it were out of the mouths of babes and sucklings, a pretty child, Maria de la Paz, pronounced a graceful allocution, and placing a palm branch in his hand, bedecked the Liberator's forehead with a wreath.

He replied shortly,† Páez says, ceded the palm branch to the army, and adjudged the wreath to the people " as a symbol of its triumph and its power."

All had been done in the way of banquets and of speeches that weak humanity could stand. The Liberator and the " Achilles of the Llanos " had done everything that could have been expected of them.

Páez set out for Apure, and Bolivar took the road to Bogotá. It was time for them to go.

* This must have been a moral monument, a quantity similar perhaps to a moral victory, for there is no record of any monument, either in Carian marble or imperishable bronze, having been erected at the time.

† This the writer takes leave to doubt, for Bolivar, though extremely eloquent, was not often brief.

CHAPTER XVII

BOLIVAR who certainly had a far seeing eye, and as the cant phrase goes, thought in continents, about this time (1827) turned his attention to the emancipation of Cuba from the Spanish domination. Páez who was no initiator, but of the stuff from which the best lieutenants are engendered, embraced the idea with enthusiasm. He saw himself, in his mind's eye, leading the Colombian army hardened by many years of warfare, to the emancipation of the Pearl of the Antilles.

This was not an unreasonable belief, for Bolivar's health was breaking down under the tremendous strain of the past years of strife. Though relatively young in years, not much over five and forty, the long campaigns, and the arduous journeys upon horseback from the hot plains of Venezuela, over the snowy Andine passes, repeated many times, had made him an old man before his time. Sucre, the only possible alternative commander was far away, acting as president of Bolivia. Santander, an able soldier, was never faithful to Bolivar, though at that time he still remained ostensibly a friend.

Mexico had promised her assistance in the enterprise. The project was not so Utopian as it seems in the light of history. Undoubtedly, the Venezuelan and New Granadan army was the best fighting force, at that time, under arms in the Americas. It had proved its valour, not only in the Venezuelan war of independence, but also Peru, which country owed its freedom mainly to

227

the armies, Bolivar with his lieutenant Sucre led with such disregard of hardships to the Pacific coast.

Páez who from the first had striven to abolish slavery at home, counted upon the vast negro population whose chains he would unloose.

Bolivar, more fertile in expedients, and with a greater vision than his lieutenant, had conceived a plan such as could only have originated in a brain so teeming with ideas as his own. It was no less than, having freed the Cuban negroes, to form an army with them, take them to Spain, as a proof of the greatness of Colombia, and free that country from the bad government that crushed it to the dust. Nothing more magnificent in the way of empire building has ever emanated from the human brain. The plan had that slight touch of ridicule about it that most great enterprises, which have not material-ised endure, viewed in the cold light of subsequent events, seen in the minds of those incapable of generous ideas. Had it succeeded, and at the time the world was going through one of those heroic periods that leave it fallow of heroism for a generation, as plants that fruit and flower to excess are barren for a season till they recuperate, Cæsar and Alexander would have been left like driftwood on the beach of history.

Páez no doubt saw himself freeing the slaves, re-dressing all injustices and framing laws, as pertinent as those that Sancho Panza wished to enact in Barataria, if the dullards who controlled his destiny had not pre-vented him.

To do Páez justice, from the beginning of his career, he had never faltered in his humanitarian ideas about the negroes.

In 1816 he had manumitted all the slaves in the Apure district, when he was but commander-in-chief of the local levies. Now with the presidency of the republic almost in his grasp, it was natural that Bolivar's

Utopian idea should have appealed to him. He writes in his Memoirs, " do not forget, no people is free that sanctions* slavery."

It was not written in the book of fate, unfortunately, so the redemption of Cubanacan† was put off for two generations. Had it occurred in the time of Páez and Bolivar, to-day Cuba might have been an independent state, instead of having merely changed one form of serfdom for another no less humiliating. The internal state of Venezuela needed more instant attention than the possible emancipation of the Antilles.

It was not to be supposed a country that for so long had been the prey to turmoil and had been devastated by constant warfare would settle down without convulsions. As a storm settles down at sea, first with tremendous waves and afterwards a long subsiding swell, so did the storms of Venezuela gradually subside.

Each military chief accustomed to almost independent command, a necessity that grew out of the great size of the territory, and the want of communications, looked on himself as the governors of tribes looked on their position in Morocco, before that country lost its independence.

Not having been accustomed to control, except under the stern rule of the Spaniards, now that the iron hand was gone, each leader of a few hundred men was ill disposed to recognise the central authority. That authority itself was weak, its resources feeble, and the army deep in arrears of pay.

All the fine speeches at the banquets in Caracas did nothing towards the pacification of the country.

The deeply seated feeling of resentment against the artificial union with New Granada, though it had as yet

* " No oliveden jamás que un pueblo no puede ser libre si mantiene esclavos en su seno."

† The original Indian name of the island.

but little open manifestation, was always growing in intensity and force. Various discontented ex-officers led bands of brigands, who masquerading under the style of royalists pillaged and plundered the country districts and made the roads unsafe. The most considerable of these, Juan Dionisio Cisneros,* defied all the attempts to capture him, safe in the rugged fastnesses of the mountains at the head of the river Tuy.

An event took place that ought to have brought home to every Venezuelan the danger of domestic turmoil. Colonel José Antonio Arizabalo, a Spanish officer, who had passed most of his life in Venezuela, collected a force of discontented ex-soldiers, escaped slaves and cattle stealers. He then wrote to the governor of Puerto Rico, General Latorre, who had fled from the rout of Carabobo, to ask for recognition and a supply of arms.

Latorre promised him support, and engaged to send strong reinforcements by the end of the year. Strengthened by the letter from Latorre, Arizabalo contrived to get the leaders of the various guerrilla bands to recognize him as their general. As he had served for long in the Spanish army as an officer of artillery and was a man of courage and enterprise, the insurgent captains readily submitted to his authority. The one exception was Cisneros, who had so long been independent that he could brook no check to his authority. Still by the adhesion of the other leaders to his cause, Arizabalo found himself at the head of a considerable force.

Nine hundred men under the command of a bandit chief by name Centeno, together with four hundred under another leader called Tazon, joined Arizabalo. These with the men he had collected on his own account made up an army of two thousand men, all of the finest flower of the rascality the country could produce.

As officers Arizabalo appointed the various bandit

* See Chapter XVI.

chiefs, Centeno, Rodriguez and Herran, all of whom had committed the most atrocious crimes. This rabble of thieves and cut-throats he dignified with the apellation of " The Defenders of the Altar and the Throne." He set about defending these revered institutions in the time-honoured way, by levying contributions to support the force that was protecting them.

This naturally made the ordinary upholder of the altar and the throne view him and his merry men with some misgiving, for to uphold an institution theoretically and to be forced to back it with one's purse are very different things. Arizabalo then wrote to Páez and proposed an armistice between the army of the church and crown and the republicans. Páez, who was not devoid of humour, laughed at his pretensions and sent a force against him.

It was high time that he did so, for Arizabalo had surprised and taken prisoners several small detachments of the soldiers of the government who were unaware that he was in the field. Flushed with these successes he had his standard blessed publicly in the town of Lezama, and dedicated it to the King of Spain. This rite duly performed, he hastened to take up a strong position till the reinforcements from Puerto Rico should arrive. With that intention he set out for the hills of Tamanuco and fortified his camp.

His brief spell of fortune soon deserted him. All his lieutenants were defeated and he himself left in his camp, with forces thinned by perpetual desertions and without any sign of the reinforcements that he expected, was almost desperate.

As a last resort he endeavoured to attract Cisneros to his cause by various promises. That rascal, seeing how matters stood, denied him even bandages for his wounded, advising him to follow his example with his own wounded followers, and cut their throats to save:

expense and time.   At last Arizabalo, seeing that no one joined him and the reinforcements on which he counted did not arrive, capitulated on honourable conditions, more favourable in fact than he deserved.

This was the last serious attempt to raise a revolt in Venezuela in favour of the King of Spain.   Cisneros, not yet subdued, had dubbed his band of some two hundred cut-throats the Royal Army, but he was confined to his hill fortresses and though he plundered and committed various atrocities they had no political significance.

Many occurrences combined to make the year 1828 one of the most unfortunate that Páez ever passed. The Treasury was empty.   Many of the soldiers were unpaid.   Ragged and half starved they roamed about, robbing or begging, according as it served their turn. Demagogues, their heads full of undigested theories that they had assimilated from translations of the writers of the French Revolution, desired at once to apply the federal system to Venezuela, pointing out that it had been successful in the United States.

Others wished for Bolivar to return and take up office as perpetual president, hoping his prestige would be the solution of their difficulties.

A few wanted to invite a foreign prince to accept the throne of Venezuela as a constitutional king.   Where they would have found a princeling ready to risk his life in such a desperate venture did not seem to trouble them.

Bolivar, whose health was now beginning to give way under the strain of the agitated life he had now lived for years, at times on horseback, ill fed and lodged for months together, at others chained to his desk, writing and dictating, and called upon to speak in public frequently, was beginning to lose hope.   He spoke of Venezuela and Colombia as " an immense desert peopled by wild beasts eager to devour each other," a phrase that in the mouth of one who for so many years had been so buoyant and self-confident showed that the iron had entered into his soul.

His popularity was waning also, and all his actions had become the theme of acrid criticism. The six years he had spent in Peru amidst the praise and adulation of the whole population had made him get a little out of touch with his own country. Rumours that probably were unfounded, that he aspired to be crowned king of La Gran Colombia, had done much harm to him and without doubt impaired his popularity.

During the years Bolivar had been absent in Peru, Páez had steadily been growing in the public estimation. The state of things both in Venezuela and New Granada was daily becoming worse. The country was the prey of factions that up to that time had refrained from a recourse to arms, although the tension was acute. One thing, and one thing alone all parties had in common. That was a desire for the reform of the constitution, that drawn up hurriedly in the stress of warfare was too inelastic. Páez no doubt was in a difficult position. The country was clamouring for a reform of the constitution, and he, no doubt feeling his lack of education, was diffident of embarking on an undertaking for which he felt himself not competent to carry through.

Moreover, though later on he was forced by circumstances and the pressure of events to declare against Bolivar, he still had the feeling of respect for him, mingled with awe, their previous relations had induced. He must have seen Bolivar as the Liberator not only of Venezuela and New Granada, but of Peru and Ecuador, with his name known throughout the world.

He knew that a new state had been called into existence and named Bolivia, after the Liberator. What wonder therefore that he looked up to a man endeared to him by dangers shared together in the field with feelings of respect. In days gone by, in every difficulty, civil or military, when things looked desperate, Bolivar had appeared, like a god descending from the sky, and settled everything by the mere prestige of his name.

In a passage in his Memoirs he gives vent to his fears in a passage that speaks volumes for his modesty. " Not daring to rely on such light as I had, and fearful of falling into error in the difficult position in which fortune's prodigality, the people's vote and the will of the Liberator* had placed me, I gathered round me the best advisers† I could find, chosen amongst the men who for their patriotism, their love of order, talent and virtue, seemed to me, and with justice passed for representatives of the most intelligent and honest of the people."

In response to the general demand for reform of the constitution a convention was appointed to be held at the little town of Ocaña. The election of delegates for convention was the occasion of the first public manifestation of hostility to the Liberator. General Santander was the chief mover in the attack, doing his utmost to get delegates returned in opposition, both to Páez and Bolivar.

When the convention assembled at the little mountain town, on the 9th of April, 1828, the deputies immediately formed themselves into two opposing parties. The partisans of the Liberator, known as Los Bolivianos, favoured a centralised republic. The opposition party, Los Santanderistas, wanted a federal form of government.

Feeling ran so high and passions were so violently aroused that Páez says the Federalists left the Jacobins‡ of the French Revolution a long way behind in violence. After much wrangling and abortive risings in various

* Detractors of his conduct, amongst his fellow countrymen, might surely read and ponder on this passage.

† Autobiografia, page 448.

‡ " La exaltacion de los federales dejó muy atras la de los Jacobinos de la revolucion francesa."

portions of the territory, the convention decreed a central government, but failed to come to a conclusion as to the reform of the constitution to an appreciable degree. Thus the chief object of the convention remained unfulfilled. The delegates separated in mutual dissatisfaction, and the state of the country became more serious than before.

Páez was desperate and wrote despondently to the Liberator, " begging* him on his knees to save the country at whatever cost." Bolivar, who had returned to Bogotá, on the 24th of June (1828) was solemnly invested with dictatorial power. In the month of September Páez swore to recognise him as Supreme Chief of La Gran Colombia. At a solemn assembly in the chief square of Bogotá, the courts of justice, corporations, the officers, and all the soldiers of the army to the number of six thousand, registered their oaths to support the Liberator in the dictatorship. All seemed in a fair way for a general settlement, but in a month's time a formidable conspiracy was formed to assassinate him.

Two Frenchmen and a Venezuelan, Pedro Corujo, possibly instigated by General Santander, or at least with his knowledge, though he had taken the precaution to be absent, planned to waylay and shoot Bolivar on an excursion it was known he was contemplating to the town of Soacha on St. Simon's† day. It is said that General Santander, not liking the plan, or being frightened of detection, put off the execution of the crime, but without warning the Liberator of his danger.

The conspirators then decided to advance the date, and fixed it for the 25th of September. At dead of night a band of ruffians made their way to the presidential palace. The building stands in a steep narrow street crossed by a considerable stream, not far from the

* " Pidiendolo de rodillas que la salve, á cualquiera costa."
† 28th of October.

chief plaza of the town. The stream is called El Arroyo San Augustin, and there still stands a high-pitched bridge across it, the bridge under which the Liberator took refuge on that memorable night.

Bolivar was sleeping with his mistress Manuela Sanz, a Quiteña* lady, who had followed him from Peru. Awakened by the noise Doña Manuela, an Amazon, who often rode dressed as a man with Bolivar's body-guard in a gold-laced scarlet dolman and white breeches, stood bravely at the door armed with the Liberator's sword. Bolivar had just time to huddle on some clothes and drop from the window into the street below. Alone and quite unarmed, for he had left his sword with the brave woman, he hid beneath the bridge.

The conspirators, after handling Doña Manuela† roughly and murdering Colonel Fergusson, who had come to her assistance, burst into the room. They found it empty, for the bird had flown. For two long hours Bolivar lay hidden, shivering with cold, for the nights in Bogotá are chilly, and in peril of his life. Over his head and in the streets the sound of battle raged, for his supporters had flown to arms and rushed on the conspirators. He dared not move, for he was ignorant as to which party had prevailed. At last, hearing continuous shouts of "Long live the Liberator," he emerged, and found the conspirators defeated and their leaders prisoners. Some of them were executed and some condemned to death, and some were pardoned.

---

* That is a native of Quito.

† Manuela Sanz was born in Quito, and was married to an Englishman, one Dr. Thorne. She first met Bolivar in Lima and at once fell in love with him. She soon left her husband and became Bolivar's mistress, and accompanied him in many of his campaigns.

In 1851 Garibaldi, on one of his voyages to Lima, saw her and left an interesting account of her. He described her as still beautiful, although paralysed and confined to her chair, but bright and intelligent, and full of stories of her adventurous days.—" Simon Bolivar," Loraine Petre, London, MCMX.

Amongst those was General Santander. For the moment this infamous attempt revived Bolivar's popularity, but he was a winged bird.

In Venezuela after the indignation at the attack upon the Liberator had subsided, things steadily got worse. The country was torn with faction, and matters seemed so little likely to improve that in the beginning of the year 1829, many of the more moderate men seem to have thought the best remedy would be to set up a constitutional monarchy.

Páez although a staunch republican, was one of those rare men in any country, but rarer still in South America in those days, who put his country's welfare above the triumph of his principles. Few men have been more dangerous, or have worked greater evil, than those who willingly would have seen the whole world descend into the abyss rather than sacrifice some megrim or another of abstract justice, as it appears before their heated brains. Possibly therefore as a last resort, especially if he had been given a strong lead by the Liberator, Páez would not have rejected the idea, whilst as is the wont of politicians the whole world over, condemning it at first.

It is not certain, for the evidence is so conflicting, whether Bolivar ever really contemplated making himself king. The historian Restrepo, who stands high in the estimation of his fellow countrymen in Bogotá, in a much commented passage in his life of Simon Bolivar, produces a strong piece of hearsay evidence, but it is only hearsay at the best. "Several of his friends had heard the Liberator say that Colombia (that is La Gran Colombia, comprising Venezuela, New Granada and Ecuador) and all Spanish America, had but one remedy by means of which to free itself from the anarchy that was preying on its people, that was to set up constitutional monarchies, and that if the inhabitants of Colombia should decide for that system of government, and should call in a foreign prince, he would be the first to submit to his authority and would support him with all his influence.* He repeated this on a subsequent occasion."

It is likely enough that Bolivar, who was very highly strung and on occasion did not weigh his words, may have said something of the kind when disgusted at the state of events, the falseness of his friends, and the self-ishness of party leaders.

Still that is no proof that he was contemplating making himself king. He would not have objected to a perpetual dictatorship, for in his message to the Congress at Guayana, he strongly recommended the adoption of the Bolivian Constitution by Venezuela. That constitution, mainly contrived and drawn up by himself for the new state of Bolivia, he frequently referred to as a " monarchy without a crown."† Restrepo observes with truth that " the project of changing republican to monarchial institutions may have been a mistake, and almost ruinous to Colombia, but it was not a crime."‡

In Bogotá, that always was both more conservative and far more clerical than Caracas, a feeling rather than an actual movement prevailed, that the one way to escape from anarchy was to call in a foreign prince.

Bolivar without doubt had he been much pressed, and seen his way for European support, might have assumed the crown. His sympathies were for order and tranquillity, and the long lease of power he had enjoyed

* Varios de sus amigos, habian oido decir el Libertador que Colombia y toda la America española no tenian otro remedio para libertar de la anarquia que devoraba á sus pueblos, sino, establecer monarquias constitucionales, y que si los habitantes de Colombia, se deciderian por este sistema de gobierno y llamarian á un principe extrangero, el seria el primero que se someteria a su autoridad y le apoyaria con su influjo. Esto mismo repitió en una epoca posterior. —"Vida de Simon Bolivar." Restrepo, Vol. IV, page 207.

† Some people no doubt would prefer a crown, without a monarchy, such as exists to-day in Great Britain, as more decorative.

‡ The difference is so slight that the action rather falls under the head of a misdemeanour than a crime.

without doubt had inclined him not to brook opposition readily.

Páez who, though afterwards he became his political opponent, still in his heart looked on him almost as a god, and would at the time have supported him to the best of his power. He may have even urged him to accept the throne, as his enemies declared; but probably only in a moment of despair.

Writing from Guayaquil to Colonel Patrick Campbell, the British Chargé d'Affaires, on the 5th of August, 1829, Bolivar in a prophetic passage shows his deep insight into political events. Speaking of the little likelihood a foreign prince would have of support, he says, " How strongly all the new American Republics would oppose him, and the United States who seem destined to plague all America in the name of liberty."*

By the beginning of 1829, Páez was so much disgusted with the state of Venezuela that he desired nothing better than to retire to his farm in Apure and wash his hands of public life.

Bolivar whose health was breaking rapidly, also at times wished to retire.

Páez addressed a letter to him that shows the goodness of his heart and his simplicity. He offered him his house in Apure and proposed that both of them should go there and pass their lives " like simple Roman citizens." It might have turned out better for both of them had the offer been accepted.

Writing from Guayaquil in September, 1829, Bolivar answered as one might answer a faithful follower, a younger brother, or an attached retainer of the family. " I remain, my beloved general, your grateful friend.

---

* " Cuanto no se opondrian los nuevos Estados Americanos, y los Estados Unidos, que parecen destinados á plagar la America de miserias a nombre de la libertad."

He seems to have foreseen the high-handed action of the United States in Cuba, Panama and Nicaragua . . . all of course in the name of Liberty.

I say grateful, for this letter that I answer is a noble and a generous letter, as regards myself. The idea has much moved me. Would to God I could enjoy private life in your companionship."*

It is not difficult to imagine how Bolivar felt in answering the simple, generous letter of his friend of early days. He must have smiled, and then drawn his hand across his eyes as the smile died away.

* " Quedo de V— amado General, su agradecido amigo, digo agradecido, pues esta carta que contesto esta muy noble y generosa para mi. Me ha enternecido la idea que V— me ha dado, y ojalá, pueda gozar con V— de la vida privada, y compañia intima."

CHAPTER XVIII

CERTAINLY few men in history have had a greater chance to seize supreme power than Páez had at this juncture of his life. That he resisted is a tribute to his character, and shows how a man almost completely destitute of primary education, exposed to flattery on every side, and without one true friend on whom he could rely for counsel and advice, still kept a level head.

In April, 1829, General José Maria Cordova, a young and gallant soldier who had distinguished himself fighting in Peru under the Liberator, had become imbued with the idea that Bolivar had monarchical designs, rose in rebellion against him. He wrote to Páez urging him to make common cause with him against the tyrant. He dwelt on the great services Páez had rendered to his country and pointed out that Bolivar owed more to him than he owed Bolivar, trying to excite his jealousy. Páez refused to listen to him and Cordova, after a brief campaign, paid for his folly with his life. Páez was now approaching the great crisis of his career.

The smouldering feeling that the constitution was no longer fitted for the times, and that the scheme by which La Gran Colombia had been created was unworkable, at length came to a head.

At a convention in Caracas, held in the month of November, 1829, Páez, who presided, had to call to order several orators who attacked the Liberator in unmeasured terms. After a long and violent discussion a note was framed, signed by the priests, fathers of families and the chief notables of Caracas and dispatched to

241

the Liberator. Though couched in courteous terms, it called explicitly for the separation of Venezuela from La Gran Colombia, and expressed their intention at once to form a separate government.

Páez was in a cruel situation. On the one hand his admiration for Bolivar and his long subjection to his will, tempted him to oppose the project. Upon the other, natural ambition, for he must have known that once Bolivar was eliminated, his mantle would fall inevitably on his own shoulders, urged him to press the claims of Venezuela to be supreme in its own boundaries.

Moreover he was a staunch republican, holding that the voice of the people was the expression of the will of God, and thus believing that the Deity had used " the priests, fathers of families and notables " as a speaking trumpet to make his wishes audible.

Lastly he was a local patriot, and knew how impossible it was La Gran Colombia could continue to exist.

At last, all Venezuela was in revolt against the union. The people looked on Páez as the standard bearer of the movement for national independence.

Curiously enough Bolivar, though a native of Caracas, had become almost hated; but in Bogotá he still was popular, although an alien. This was the more extraordinary, for local patriotism is ingrained in every member of the Spanish race. He who is not born in " my town "* is a foreigner, or at the least an outlander, for that perhaps renders best " forastero," the word the Spaniards use.

The movement for separation was not of yesterday.

Before the year 1731, the provinces of Caracas, Cumaná, Barinas, Guayana and Maracaibo were dependencies of New Granada. The viceroy lived at Bogotá. In that year (1731) owing to the enormous distance that

* Mi pueblo.

ADMIRAL THE HONBLE. CHARLES ELPHINSTONE FLEEMING
Sketch by Hayter for his large picture of The Reform Parliament,
1832.

separated the Venezuelan provinces from the capital, they were given separate status, under the title of The Captain* Generalcy of Venezuela and became independent of Bogotá.

This state of things lasted a century, in fact up to the time when the struggle began for independence from the mother country. Hence the artificial state La Gran Colombia, formed by Bolivar with the idea that it would prove a stronger barrier to resist the Spaniards, was never popular. Baralt, perhaps the most independent of the historians of Venezuela, was well aware of this. Writing on the question he says, " But what agreement† short of a prodigy, could hope to join together countries nature herself has separated? " He refers to the Pact known as " La Constitucion de Cúcuta (1821) " largely inspired by Bolivar himself.

A series of high-handed actions by officers of the Liberator, that passed unpunished, served to add fuel to the fire. They set afoot the feeling that Bolivar aspired either to a military dictatorship or a monarchy. This put the finishing touch to his unpopularity. Violent attacks appeared in the local newspapers. The foreign press instantly copied them, calling Bolivar a fallen star.

Páez, to his credit, loyally defended him. The attacks were in the main unjust. The Liberator had spent his fortune and his health in the long struggle against Spain. For twenty years he had never known repose. He had set little store upon his life, exposing himself, often recklessly. Now when his health was failing and his fortune spent, the pack that had adored him turned snapping at his heels.

As men are commonly judged rather by their words, than actions, the criticisms that Bolivar sometimes

* La Capitania General de Venezuela.

† " Mas que pacto se dirá ; podia hacer el prodigio de confundir pueblos que separa la naturaleza."—" Resumen de La Historia de Venezuela," Vol. 2, page 7. Rafael Maria Baralt. Curazao, 1887.

R

levelled at his fellow countrymen seem at that juncture
to have outweighed his brilliant services. " I have
ploughed in the sea," he said, probably when plagued
by fools, a race that he, unlike the Apostle to the Gen-
tiles, never could suffer gladly or even tolerantly.

" Spanish America is ungovernable," and again, " All
we have gained by the revolution is our independence,"
and other dicta of the same nature, did an infinity of
harm.

The mediocre men amongst whom the Liberator
moved, a veritable Triton among the minnows, never
forgave these utterances, for they all knew that they
contained a modicum of truth.

Páez though not a man of Bolivar's genius, perceived
more clearly than his chief the reason of the social
turmoil. In his own words he sets this forth with
admirable clarity. " The state* of the country was only
the legitimate consequence of all and each of the evils
that it had inherited from the ominous colonial domination."

Bolivar ought to have known this, for he said on one
occasion that Venezuela " had known nothing but chains
in infancy, and in maturity, only arms to break the
chains."

In Bogotá matters were rapidly going from bad to
worse.

In January, 1830, Bolivar resigned his power, but
was persuaded by his evil genius to resume it.

In Venezuela most of the towns, following the example of Caracas, had declared for separation. All
pointed to the election of Páez as first president. Torn
as he was between his loyalty to the Liberator and what
he thought his duty, he put out a proclamation of
which the following is the preamble. It is headed,
José Antonio Páez, Civil and Military governor of

* Autobiografia de Paéz, Vol. II, Cap. III, page 27.

Venezuela. "People of Venezuela, you have shown clearly that you desire to separate yourselves from the government of Bogotá and not to remain under the authority of His Excellency, The Liberator; you have pronounced at the same time in favour of the establishment of a sovereign, popular, elective, representative and responsible government for Venezuela. Such is the unanimity of your decision, that I should be failing in my duty to my country if I did not accept the honourable charge with which you have honoured* me."

He knew that his election to the presidential chair was certain to take place. Given the circumstances in which he found himself involved, it is difficult to see how Páez could have acted differently. Had he refused to take up power the country would have fallen into anarchy, for there was no one of sufficient note or character to take his place. If at all hazards he had remained loyal to Bolivar he would have hitched his wagon to a falling star. When the news of the events reached Bogotá, Bolivar though he must have known that separation was inevitable, still clung to the idea of union.

It was but natural. In the full plenitude of his strength and power he had created La Gran Colombia, and no doubt hoped to be remembered as the contriver of the scheme. For a short time it may have served a useful purpose, and impressed the Spaniards with the simulacrum, for it was nothing more, of a great state, able to raise large forces if provoked to war. That time, if it ever really existed, had now passed away. This a man of Bolivar's penetrating intellect should have comprehended; but vanity and a belief in a man's own mental offspring usually obfuscates judgment and it is given but to few to step down gracefully from a throne, or even from a presidential chair.

* This is the substance of his proclamation, shorn of many of its innumerable adjectives.

A state of war was nearly breaking out between Vene-zuela and New Granada, from henceforth to be known as the Republic of Colombia.

Bolivar, at the same time that he sent a mission to Caracas and wrote to several influential people there to try and bring about reconciliation between the two re-publics, dispatched his faithful friend General O'Leary in command of a considerable force to the Venezuelan frontier. Even his most fervent admirers must admit that this was a mistake in judgment and that he does not seem to have acted in a straightforward way.

Páez quite naturally was forced to take measures of defence, and wrote to General Mariño to guard the frontiers on the Orinoco carefully.

Nothing of note took place. Manifestly Bolivar could not invade his native country, and the days were passed when, had he appeared in person, all would have flocked to him. But there were stronger reasons. The Liberator's days were drawing to an end. His health had completely given way, and he who for the last twenty years had lived in the saddle had now become so weak that he could only sit two hours upon his horse.

Both parties knew that an appeal to arms would be the ruin of their countries, whose treasuries were almost empty and whose people had had more than enough of war.

Mainly to please Bolivar, a conference was called at Cúcuta between commissioners from the two countries. It broke up without doing anything but issuing a pro-tocol, that last device of the diplomatist.

Bolivar still held on obstinately to his dictatorship, impelled either by love of power or by the advice of injudicious friends. Town after town in New Granada declared against him, leaving him almost alone except for the support of Bogotá.

At last, pushed to extremities and desperately ill, he

convoked an assembly of his friends to advise him if he
should accept a nomination for the presidency at the next
election.   His friends, amongst whom was the historian
Baralt, advised him to retire.   When they communi-
cated their decision to him, Restrepo* says, there was a
painful scene.

Bolivar had so long been used to power and so much
incense had been burned in his honour that he could
hardly comprehend his star had set.

Moreover his partisans were numerous and strong.
At length he yielded to the advice of the foreign
ministers and the entreaties of his friends, who did not
wish his enemies should triumph at the election.

On the 29th of April, 1830, he sent his last message
to the congress, depositing in its hands the power that he
had held so long.

Next day he set out for Cartagena, having determined
to end his days in Europe, far from the ungrateful
country that he led to independence at the cost of his
fortune and his health.   Fate did not grant his wish
should be accomplished.   Taken ill at Cartagena, he
retired to the old-fashioned little Spanish house of San
Pedro Alejandrino, four miles from Santa Marta.   The
house still stands, sheltered by secular trees, from which
hang streamers of Spanish moss and round whose trunks
climb lianas, like the snakes that wind round Laocoon
and his two sons.   Their red and yellow flowers peep
out through the dark metallic leaves and humming birds
hang poised above their petals, outvying all the art of
jewellers in their iridescent brilliancy.

A little garden with a few neglected shrubs gives that
air of desolation that a deserted garden alone knows how
to give, speaking of departed hands that in the past
tended the withering flowers.

* " Historia de la Revolucion de Colombia."—José Manuel Restrepo.
Paris, 1827.

Above the Quinta* towers La Sierra de Santa Marta, with its snow-capped peaks.

The Liberator's body does not rest in the little quinta, for his native land, that in life spurned him ignominiously, has now raised a marble catafalque over his remains. The pity of it! Far better had they remained in the lonely little Spanish country house under the Sierra, whose peaks are seen far from the coast in passing ships by those who plough the ocean, even as he, in his own bitter words, ploughed in the sea.

Páez was now unquestionably the foremost figure in the country and his election to the presidency sure. Ecuador soon followed the example of Venezuela, and withdrew from the union. La Gran Colombia was thus dissolved into its component parts. The Liberator's great dream was over, and the three republics left to "dree their weird." It had been inevitable for several years. No citizen of either of the republics suffered by it. What had also been dissolved was the long companionship of Páez and Bolivar. Together they had ridden over so many leagues of Llanos, sweltered together in the hot plains of the Apure, plunged into so many cayman-haunted streams and charged so often with their stirrups touching, that each of them must have regretted that fell politics had made them enemies, or at least "contrarios," to use the Spanish word. Had but the Liberator been a little more unbending, the inevitable disruption of the union might have taken place more graciously, and Páez and himself remained to the end in the position they had occupied so many years, of master and disciple, or of two brothers, one of whom has been well educated, looked up to and revered.

Páez now had a fair field. His only rival in ability was General Santander in Bogotá, but he never appealed to the public, as did Páez or Bolivar.

* Country house.

In the year of the dissolution, Sucre, the victor of
Ayacucho,* the finest character either New Granada or
Venezuela had produced, was basely assassinated near
Popayán, when on a journey through the Andes. Loyal
to the core, Sucre was the only one of Bolivar's generals
who never conspired against him or ran counter to his
plans.

Páez, from the humblest origin, had now risen to be
the first citizen of the republic. The wheel of fortune
had indeed come round full centre, and he who once had
washed the negro Manuelote's feet was seated in the
presidential chair. Until the year 1847, he dominated
the public life of the republic, making and unmaking
generals at his will and ruling like a patriarch.

---

* The battle of Ayacucho was fought in the Andes of Peru, on the 9th
of December, 1824. Sucre totally defeated the Spaniards, and took La
Serna, the viceroy, prisoner. After that he became the first president of
the newly constituted state of Bolivia, a territory that previously had been
known as Alto Peru. Its capital was Cuzco.

CHAPTER XIX

ONCE seated in the presidential chair, Páez immediately began to agitate for the abolition of slavery. Years before when, as he says himself, he was quite ignorant of any theories about the rights of man, he had abolished slavery in the district of Apure, when he was only a general officer in command of the local forces.

He seems to have had an inborn sense of justice, and the fact that many negroes were fighting bravely in his ranks weighed with him when he reflected that they were imperilling their lives to free a country that denied them elementary liberty. He influenced the Congress to pass a law, not for complete abolition, but limiting the evil by various provisions, such as forbidding any slave to be sold out of the district where he was living.

The law provided for the education of the negroes and forbade the importation of fresh slaves. It certainly was a step in the right direction, and as far as he could go, with safety, at the time. He was not destined to reap the harvest he had sown, that was reserved for his great enemy General Monagas, in the years to come.

Páez was soon to find that the cares of a president are harder far to bear than those of a Llanero horsebreaker or a guerrilla chief.

The archbishop of Caracas, one of those ecclesiastics who in all ages seem to have thought that the mere fact of consecration placed them above the civil power, refused to take the oath of fealty that the constitution of Venezuela had prescribed. Páez, who throughout his life preserved the simple faith in which he had been brought up, was loath to come to extremities with the recalcitrant ecclesiastic.

His position was rendered doubly difficult by the fact that the archbishop was a man of blameless life, highly respected by his fellow countrymen, and had always been a patriot.

Twice was the oath tendered to him and refused. At the third time of asking he agreed to take it, but with what was called a " contrapisa," that is with an interpolation of his own, rendering it nugatory. The " contrapisa " ran, " I swear to respect the constitution if it contains a clause to respect the immunities of the church, that at my consecration I swore I would maintain."

After much negotiation, Páez gave him forty-eight hours in which to swear or leave the country. The archbishop chose the way of easy martyrdom, no doubt acting according to his conscience Then Páez had him put aboard a ship and sent to Curazao. As this was a Dutch island, where the faith of the accursed " Calvino " ruled, the worthy priest no doubt died daily,* in his sandy Patmos.

The archpriest having been removed, the other clergy quietly took the oath, and Little-Venice was preserved.

At the close of the eventful year the Liberator died, poor and neglected. Some say almost without the necessaries of life. No tragedy of Euripides has a more tragic ending than the Liberator's. From the highest pinnacle of fame, his name trumpeted throughout the world, fêted, beloved and adulated, he fell not as fell Lucifer, but as the Archangel Michael might have fallen, if heaven had not been populated by angels, but by men. The very house in which he died he owed

---

* He might have made a version of the Scriptures in Papiamiento to pass the time away. This jargon composed of Dutch, French and Spanish, with a few words of Carib here and there, was left in Curazao, it is thought, by the buccaneers. It flourishes both in the island and in several towns along the coast, possesses newspapers and possibly a literature well worth investigation, by those who find that Volapuk and Esperanto are not satisfying.

to the kindness of " a good Spaniard,"* Don Joaquin de Mier. The doctor who attended him in his last illness was a Frenchman, Don Alejandro Reverend. Born rich, he left no property, but his sword, his clothes and books. Of few it can be said more truly than of him, " sic transit gloria mundi." The glory passed indeed; but his name will never perish whilst the sun lights up the snow on Puracé or Sotará, caymans lie like logs awash in the Apure, and whilst the white cones of Illimani and Pichincha still tower up like lighthouses upon the course to heaven, seen by the passing mariner, far out at sea.

Páez must have felt compunction at his death, and regretted that he left no recorded protest against the defaming sentence Venezuela passed on the greatest of her sons. To brand him as a tyrant and to say he was a danger to his country, as did the congress of his native city, took nothing from his fame and left the congress poor indeed. It may be though, that politicians who so faithfully take and receive and fling about the epithets of rogue, assassin and of knave, know one another better than ordinary mortals know them.

So in a herd of wild asses on the Llanos, a few kicks endear the animals to one another, for after all " cinq ou six coups de bâton, entre gens qui s'aiment, ne font, que regaillardir l'amour." Even to-day many Vene-zuelans have not forgiven Páez, although his policy of separation was the making of their country.

Páez at least never joined in the outcry against the Liberator after his fall from power. When almost everyone abused him, Páez alone spoke of him with affection and respect.

In June (1830) he wrote to Dr. Yanes, the president

* " El dia 6 de Diciembre fué traslado a la quinta de San Pedro Alejan drino, propiedad de un buen español, Don Joaquin de Mier, que generosa-mente le brindó hospitalidad."—"Historia de Venezuela," por H. N. M. Caracas, 1827.

of the congress, recommending that an annuity of seventy thousand dollars should be voted to the Liberator as Venezuela's quota of the three hundred thousand assigned to him as President of La Gran Colombia at the Congress held at Cúcuta in 1821. He also said it was a question of the national honour to aid the Liberator in his suit for the possession of the mines of Aroa, which had been the heritage of his family.

No doubt, now that their positions were reversed, his first meeting with Bolivar, in Apure, must have risen to his memory, his admiration for him in their youth, and the long marches they had made together over the scorching plains. Those sorts of memories last longest with a man such as was Páez, and with all those who have passed long hours on horseback, hungry and parched with thirst.

Once and once only he is reported to have criticised his friend adversely, in the far off early days when both of them were young. After a fight that took place near Villa de Cura, Páez was heard to say to the Liberator, " I never lost a battle when I acted by myself and I have always been defeated when acting in concert with you, or under your command." It is true that the writer who has preserved this anecdote* was most unfavourable to the Liberator, denied him military talent, questioned his courage and impugned his honesty .

With Páez as president, the threatened war with the newly constituted state of Colombia averted and all danger of an attempt to regain power by Spain, at rest for ever, matters in Venezuela ought to have gone smoothly, and the country turned its attention to its own affairs. Fate willed it otherwise.

A guerrilla leader, rich and patriotic, General José Tadeo Monagas, who had always envied Páez in his

* " Memoirs of Bolivar." Ducoudray Holstein, London, 1830. Vol. II, page 402.

rise to power, refused to recognise the act of separation and took up arms against the government. He attracted to his cause General Mariño one of the patriot leaders, who had served bravely under the Liberator, but an intriguer to the core, who always fought for his own hand.

The movement headed by Monagas, did not result in actual warfare at the time.

At an interview between the rivals at El Valle de la Pascua, an understanding was arrived at and a general amnesty proclaimed for all offenders. Stifled for the moment, the fire still smouldered, and from this time dated the long struggle between the moderates and the liberals.

By a strange freak of fortune Páez became the leader of the aristocratic party, known as the Mantuanos. Monagas who was a man of property and well educated, became the champion of the democrats. Their rivalry cost the country untold miseries, and paved the way for the long series of civil wars that have been the curse of Venezuela, up to the commencement of the present century.

Monagas, was not the only partisan who raised the standard of revolt. Bands of semi-brigands, semi-revolutionaries, usually denominated " facciosos " in Venezuela, rose on every side.

Castañedo, Cegamón, and Alcazar all discontented officers, who had fought in the war of independence, and knew no other trade but fighting, gathered whatever rascals they could find available, and ravaged the country, plundering and pillaging, in the name of Liberty. Even General Bermudez, who had been one of Bolivar's trusted officers, always an opponent of separation from New Granada, raised the standard of revolt in the eastern province, on his own account.

Páez was kept continually on the alert, and passed

life either in the saddle, a seat probably more agreeable than the presidential chair, or in Caracas, devising means to deal with the numerous uprising of the " facciosos."

In one way or another, sometimes by force of arms, sometimes by judicious clemency he managed in a few months to reduce all the discontented officers to obedience.

Only the bandit José Dionisio Cisneros, still held out, in his inaccessible retreat amongst the hills. This rascal had collected a band of discontented soldiers, escaped slaves and highway robbers, about two hundred strong. These he had drilled and disciplined and made them into a formidable well armed force. His chief resort was in the deep valleys of the Tuy district, not many miles outside the capital. From there he used to sally forth and plunder almost to the gates of Caracas.

The Guaire river runs through the upper portion of the district. It has cut its way, during the course of centuries, deep into the mountains, and flows in a series of cascades until it joins the Tuy. Its banks are clothed with the most luxuriant tropic vegetation and are the resort of troops of monkeys and innumerable parrots and macaws. Great butterflies float across the clearings, seeming not to move their wings, as imperceptibly as owls float round the clearings of a northern wood, whilst from the tree tops comes the lamentation of the sloth.

Such country, abounding as it does in caves and hiding places and easily defensible, was an ideal refuge for a bandit chief.

Páez sent several expeditions to pursue Cisneros to his lair, but invariably without success. In one month alone the government of Caracas expended sixty thousand dollars fruitlessly, without the least result.

One of the devices Cisneros used to employ to throw his pursuers off his trail, was to make all his followers tread in the footsteps of the man who led the troop. This left a single track, and often threw the pursuers off the pursuit. Sometimes* he made them in their retreat walk backwards, so that it became impossible to follow up the trail, but to skilled trackers from the frontiers.

The horrible atrocities Cisneros committed terrorised all the villages, and forced the inhabitants on peril of their lives to become his spies.

The ruffian seems to have believed sincerely that he was the last defender of the rights of Spain, the true upholder of religion and the inspired opponent of the republicans.

The archbishop of Caracas, Dr. Mendez, besought Páez several times to rid the country of the man.

The moment was not favourable, for Páez had his hands full at the time, quelling the various revolts. Later on, in the year 1831, he took one of these resolutions that only such a man could have conceived. His plan was to attract Cisneros to him by kindness, and having got into personal relations with him, exercise over him the power of fascination, that he knew that he possessed.

It is not to be forgotten that at that time Páez was president of the republic, and that he lay under no obligation to put his life in peril by tracking bandits to their lairs. Such a consideration never troubled Páez, who if he ever thought about the matter, must have believed he was invulnerable, after the many hairbreadth escapes, and wild adventures, he had experienced.

One of the parties sent out to pursue Cisneros, happened to lay hands upon a son of his, a boy some sixteen years of age. This young orang-outang, for he was a true wild man of the woods, had never been baptized. Páez resolved to have the ceremony per-

* " Historia de Venezuela," Baralt.

formed with considerable state, serving himself as god-father to the young Christian. The ceremony of baptism in addition to the mystical import assigned to it by true believers, in Spain and South America, was held in those days, to create a spiritual relationship between the godfather and the parents of the child.

Thus, baptism duly performed, as without doubt, it was, by the archbishop of Caracas, the salt placed duly in the mouth of the neophyte, and the customary* alms bestowed, Páez and Cisneros were bound together in those unseen bonds of faith, stronger by far, as theologians tell us, than the strongest links of steel.

On the material side Páez undertook to provide for the education of the young brand snatched if not exactly from the burning, probably from the gallowstree. He then wrote to Cisneros informing him of their mystical relationship, for they were now Compadres, that is co-fathers in the Lord, of the involuntary catechumen.

Cisneros seems to have been flattered, for he answered amiably, no doubt with all the wealth of adjectives that is the common gift of statesmen, bandits, muleteers and princes of the church, in the Americas. Páez then wrote, exhorting Cisneros to leave his life of crime and "seek† the repose and the tranquillity of civilised society under the sanction of the law." He also offered him the means of livelihood beside his son, now a member both of the Catholic Church, and of a normal school.

He pointed out that it was useless to be more royalist than the king, for the King of Spain had abandoned all his rights in Venezuela. Cisneros replied in an

---

* " Trajeron el agua que esta la bendita
  La sal en la boca, soltaron la guita."
        Old Song.

† " Para buscar el reposo y tranquilidad de la vida civilizada, protegida de las leyes."

official letter, that he would never tire of serving God, and that he was an officer of the king who knew what honour was, and he would never break his word.

Páez who never hesitated to put his life in peril, both in and out of season, went to stay at a country house called Súenta, in the middle of the district where Cisneros operated. He then invited all the country people, whom he knew were in the bandit's confidence, to a series of rustic entertainments. At them he provided enormous meals of beef and of Hayacas,* a local dish consisting of meat chopped fine, spiced and rolled up in a maize leaf; the whole washed down with copious draughts of new rum from Carúpano.

These banquets always finished with a dance called El Carrizo, popular in those days in the district. Most likely Páez joined in it himself, for to extreme old age he never lost a chance of dancing, an exercise that he enjoyed almost as much as he enjoyed a fight.

By these acts, and a generous expenditure of rum, he became so popular, that Cisneros wrote to him " affectionately."† Then Páez proposed an interview. Cisneros answered " that in the name of the Holy Trinity,"‡ he would meet the president at a mountain called el Lagartijo, in the province of Caracas.

Páez set out to meet him, it is to be supposed under the same sacred ægis, for he was a devout trinitarian holding all the dogmas of the church in their entirety, only a little tinctured with the dogmas of the French Revolution, but not enough to signify. He took with him only two aide-de-camps and a horse soldier from the Llanos.

At the foot of the mountain Páez halted and sent the soldier on to tell Cisneros that he was coming to the

---

* These Hayacas are called Tamales in Mexico and are also a national dish in that republic.

† " Me llegó a cobrar afecto."

‡ " En nombre de la Santisima Trinidad."

Doña Catalina Paulina de Fleeming

tryst. In half an hour the man returned and implored
Páez to go no further, for up the pass there was a band
of brigands posted all fully armed, and that their chief
had told him Páez should be received in the way he
merited. Ordering his aide-de-camps and the soldier
to remain, and telling them if he did not return by sundown to tell the authorities in Caracas that he was dead,
Páez advanced alone. At a bend in the mountain road,
upon a little plateau he saw a body of two hundred
bandits drawn up and waiting for him.

Cisneros stood a few paces in advance leaning upon
his blunderbuss. Cisneros though fully armed and
evidently obeyed by all his followers does not appear
to have looked the part of the ideal bandit chief, in
spite of his ferocity. Short* and of a slight build, his
face was almost hidden by the mass of dangling hair
that fell on each side of his cheeks.

" President Páez," said the bandit, " what devil
brings you here? " Páez answered that he wished to
come to an understanding with him. " You see "
Cisneros said " my followers ready to shoot you at a
word from me. That you may form an idea of their
discipline, I wish you to put them through their
drill."

Quite naturally Páez thought his last moment was at
hand; however he stepped forward and put the troop
through some simple evolutions, which they performed
both with alacrity and skill. The crucial moment had
arrived. Drill finished in those days in South America
by a volley from the troops. Páez gave the customary
order to spring the ramrods previous to loading, as was
the fashion of the time. No ring of steel rang out,
for all the blunderbusses* were fully loaded, and the

---

* " Wild Scenes in South America," Ramon Páez. London, 1865.
Page 369.
† Trabucos.

S

steel ramrods, sounded dully on the wads. Take aim, he ordered, thinking he was ordering his own death.

Just as he was about to give the word to fire, Cisneros who probably had staged the scene to try his courage, gave a signal with his hand. The bandits raised their guns and fired into the air. Advancing, Cisneros exclaimed, " You have conquered, General, and from this day count on me always, either alive or dead." As the bandit cast an envious eye upon a silver mounted hanger Páez wore, he took it from his belt and gave it to him. Then they set out for Suenta, where General Ortega was waiting anxiously. When they arrived riding side by side, and followed by the greater portion of the outlaws, Ortega, using the well known Llanero allocation applied to a wild horse that has been half subdued, said " General, the Indian's ears* are hanging down."

Cisneros indeed had let his ears hang down, and was subdued.

Páez assigned him lands in the Tuy district, on which to settle with his followers. For a time he remained quiet, though now and then old habit was too strong for him, and he committed various small excesses, that Páez who plumed himself upon his exploit always overlooked. When summoned to appear before the government, he always answered in his defence, " I did not submit to any government, but to my compadre Páez, his is the only law I will obey."

On several occasions he did good service against other brigands, being employed upon the principle of set a thief to catch a thief.

All seemed to point to Cisneros ending his days as a prosperous cattle breeder, but politics were his undoing, as they have undone men more deserving then the ex-bandit chief.

* General, El Indio dejó caer la oreja.

Involved in some of the countless revolutionary movements that in those days served, as it seems, to purify the blood, as warbles on a horse's back in spring purge his gross humours, he paid the penalty and in the Spanish phrase was passed duly " through the arms."* He made an edifying ending, as befitted one who all his life, in his own estimation, had served both Majesties, God and the King.

---

* Fué pasado por las armas, *i.e.* shot.

CHAPTER XX

THE whole affair of the bandit Cisneros was an unusual experience for the president of a sovereign state to be engaged in, even in Venezuela in the year 1831. It serves to illustrate the adventurous character of the man, and no doubt appealed as much or more to the bulk of his fellow countrymen, as if he had produced a code of laws. Together with this tendency to expose his life unnecessarily, Páez affected now and then a moralising view occasionally sometimes to be found in men of action, who value themselves on qualities of prudence that they erroneously believe that they possess.

This shows delightfully when he writes of the return of General Santander to Bogotá after a period of exile consequent on his connection with the plot to assassinate the Liberator. " At this date (1831), General Santander has had his military rank and honours restored to him.

" These and many similar examples ought to serve as an example to public men not to appeal to violence when they are sacrificed to the passions and the necessities of a party. Time alone, in these cases, is the best court to which they should appeal."

An excellent counsel of perfection and one that Páez sedulously avoided following, in his own person, when his own party had been driven out. His firmness with the clergy of Caracas was rewarded with success, for at the end of 1831, the archbishop and his priests, duly repented, metaphorically in sackcloth and in ashes, and signed the constitution without " contrapisa " or any higgling. This enhanced Páez's prestige considerably, for at that time no ruler could afford to have the spiritual powers arrayed against him, even though Venezuela was a liberal state.

Still his position was hedged about with difficulties, which he was called upon to face.

Risings against the central government, on a small scale, were almost continuous. These he was able to suppress without much trouble, though a revolt of all the slaves in the republic gave him more difficulty. When he had leisure, public education was always his first care.

Almost illiterate himself at that period of his life, or at the least, but just emerging from illiteracy, he had the breadth of mind to comprehend that no people that is ignorant, can really be called free. Thus, he protected the celebrated Feliciano Montenegro in his efforts to establish primary schools, with all his influence.

The commentary Páez made upon a schoolmaster's lot show how far-seeing and comprehensive was his mind.

" Do not forget " he writes, " that teaching is the most painful career an educated man can undertake . . . it calls for the most absolute self abnegation for it is a continual hand to hand struggle, with the ignorance, the prejudice and the vices of the age."*

No one could have written more sympathetically or with more insight of a schoolmaster's daily life. It does the writer honour, not only for the qualities of intellect it shows, but of the finer feelings of the heart.

Páez had always that respect for learning, that only the most highly educated and the illiterate feel.

* " No se olvide que el magisterio es la carrera mas penosa que abraza el hombre instruido . . . ella exige la mas completa abnegacion, porque es lucha continua y á brazo partido con la ignorancia, con las preocupaciones y vicios de la epoca."

Montenegro was no common man. Thinking the revolution premature, he enlisted in the Spanish army, rose to be colonel, and when the war was over, finding his service unrecognised in Spain, returned home to Caracas. There he became the pioneer of Venezuelan education, and in the face of much ill feeling for his part in the revolutionary war, lived down all opposition, by his sincerity. He sealed his services to his country by founding El Colegio de la Independacia, in Caracas, atoning thus for the lack of patriotic spirit he had displayed in youth.

Those who have accused Páez of being hostile to Bolivar, should read his letter to Congress, dated the 23rd of January, 1833, in which he asks that public honours should be paid to the memory of the Liberator. " The name of Bolivar cannot be pronounced without admiration and merits our respect."

He goes on to say " Great deeds, magnanimous efforts, continual sacrifices, eminent patriotism go to form the history of this immortal leader, already canonised by fame."

So strong ran party feeling that an acrimonious debate took place in the Venezuelan Congress, on the proposition Páez had submitted. One deputy who had served against his country in the Spanish ranks, whose name Páez withholds, went so far as to say that neither New Granada or Venezuela had benefited by anything the Liberator had done.

This opinion natural enough, in the mouth of one who had fought for Spain against his native country, does not seem to have raised much comment at the time. Owing to the part that Páez took in the debate, the honours were accorded to the Liberator's memory but only by a small majority.

To-day, he has become a demi-God, and more statues of Bolivar exist, than those of any other national hero, with the exception, perhaps, of Garibaldi. The title of Magnanimous was added to that of Liberator. A retrospective honour is after all, that which does least damage to the receiver of it, for being dead, only the givers of it bear the ridicule.

Caracas was decreed to be renamed Ciudad Bolivar. The honorific appellation has remained in abeyance, and the city still bears the name of the Indians who at the conquest had their "rancheria," where now Caracas stands.

Páez's first term as president was drawing to a close.

In spite of all the difficulties he had had to face, his total want of experience of administration, his lack of education, and the perpetual risings that he had to contend with, he had on the whole acquitted himself well.

The country was fairly prosperous, the national finances were improving slowly, and all that Venezuela wanted to become prosperous was a long period of peace.

In 1835 Dr. José Maria Vargas was elected president, although Páez favoured the candidature of his old brother in arms, General Soublette, a veteran of the war of independence.

The following description of the General has been preserved. " He was a man, of pleasant manners, easy of access and of taking speech. Though he hears everything, he says but little; courteous by nature, and a courtier by inclination."

His accessibility and courtesy are the two qualities most insisted on in this most charming picture of a public man. Both then and now in South America, no one can win success in public life without good manners, no matter whatever other qualities he may possess.

Páez laid down the reins of government, as it would appear as willingly as he took up the reins, and the

" falseta "* of a half wild horse, on his own property of San Pablo, some two hundred miles in the
interior, and prepared to resume a cattle farmer's
life.

Only four months was he destined to remain, like
Diocletian in his retreat, not planting cabbages after
the fashion of his Roman prototype, but probably breaking in wild colts. Early one morning, as he was getting
on his horse to gallop round the cattle, a group of his
adherents arrived, bloody with spurring, from the
capital. They were charged with letters from the chief
citizens of Caracas imploring Páez to return.

A band of revolutionaries, led by one Major Pedro
Carujo, had surprised the president unguarded in his
palace, and made him prisoner. They called upon him
either to institute certain reforms that they desired, or
abdicate at once. Though threatened with instant death
if he refused, he remained obdurate, saying such conduct was not consistent with his dignity, or that of the
nation, that the first magistrate, duly elected should
yield to force of arms. As to the reforms, he said, he
would bring them to the attention of the Congress; further he would not go. Carujo, with a drawn sword in his
hand, said " Doctor, the world is to the bold." Vargas,
quite undismayed, rejoined, " You are mistaken, the
world is the heritage of honest men." His constancy
was admirable, and his faith in mankind sufficient to
have piled Aconcagua upon Cotopaxi, considering the
world† in which he lived. The revolutionaries put him
by force on board a schooner and shipped him off to the
island of St. Thomas, and then proclaimed General

---

* " La falseta " is a headstall and reins made of horsehair, used for a
wild horse before he has been bitted, and generally in the Llanos for almost
any horse as an additional security. When used on a tame horse, the rope
that forms the reins is used only as a halter.

† It remains but little altered, and honest men do not seem as yet to
have received the stamped conveyance of their heritage.

Mariño, Supreme Chief* of the republic. As a sop to the army Páez was appointed to the command. The reforms demanded, were to establish the federal system, and to make Catholicism the national faith by statute. Lastly to place the country under military law.

Páez had no troops at his command, with the exception of a feeble bodyguard of friends. Hastily he got together a band of countrymen, armed only with machetes and with sticks. A body of thirty or forty horsemen from Villa de Cura arrived to help him. With this inadequate force he set out towards Maracay and was joined on the way by various bodies of his old soldiery. By a dash he took Valencia; then marched upon the capital, his forces growing larger every day. General Alcantara faced him at a place called Lagunitas and there ensued a curious and primitive scene. Determined at all hazards to prevent bloodshed, he called a conference with Alcantara, and so worked on his better feelings that he persuaded him to lay down his arms. Then he cried out in a loud voice, to friends and foes alike, to give thanks to the Almighty for having saved them from the crime of civil strife. After this simple prayer both sides knelt down and rendered thanks to God.

* The whole episode is almost similar to that which happened to President Leguia of Peru only a few years ago. Seated in Lima in the presidential residence, he was surprised, just as was Vargas, a hundred years ago. Threatened with death if he refused to abdicate, he refused bravely, as his prototype had done. Dragged to the plaza by a tumultuous crowd of revolutionaries, he still held out, though a gigantic negro with a great stone uplifted in his hands stood on the pedestal of a statue, ready to dash his brains out at a given signal. The troops were all in barracks, some say in ignorance of what was going on, others because they had been won over by the revolutionaries. In the midst of the altercation, a party with a quick firing gun, quite unaware of the danger of the president, was returning after practice with their gun. The revolutionaries opened fire upon the machine gun party, thinking they had come to rescue the president. The officer in command got his gun into action and mowed the revolutionaries down like wheat. Those who remained alive fled to conceal themselves. Then from amongst a heap of bodies the president, who at the first discharge had thrown himself upon his face, pretending to be dead, arose unharmed and, getting on a horse that someone brought to him, mounted and rode back to the palace, quite unharmed amidst the " Vivas " of the populace.

A strange and a pathetic spectacle it must have been, as they knelt down and prayed. The wild surroundings, the ill armed country levies and half wild horses, made up a scene that must have left the God of Battles, half pleased, half angry, that so much blood he looked on as a libation he was entitled to, had been reserved for an occasion more congenial to him.

For fourteen days Páez and his ever increasing forces ranged through the country, receiving the submission of the revolutionary leaders, who had regretted their precipitancy. When he approached Caracas, the rebels left the town by night, and he entered unopposed. Then, quiet restored, he sent to bring back Dr. Vargas from his exile, and reinstated him. It was a real moral triumph, unlike the usual moral victory, in which the victory generally is the prize of the stronger side, and the morality consoles the victim.

The revolutionary party had not known how to play its cards. All the trumps had been in its hands, the army, treasury, all the old officers of the independence wars, and all the warships, such as they were, at anchor in the ports. Páez had his name alone and for sole backing, public opinion, for it was on his side.

Although the capital was pacified, the revolutionary party still had considerable sympathy in the provinces. Páez pardoned all the insurgents, with his usual generosity. At this period of his career, he seems to have been a little over lenient, for clemency was but ill understood in those days, and usually was put down as weakness, by those who certainly would not have exercised it, had they been the conquerors.

The National Congress passed a vote of thanks to him and furthermore bestowed upon him the title of Illustrious Citizen,* a reward that certainly did not deplete the national exchequer, and added little to the

* Ciudadano Esclarecido.

weight, the charger Páez rode, had to support on a long day.

Páez no doubt was gratified by the honorific adjective. Those who invented it must have been pleased with their imaginative powers, and after all the appellation was more justifiable than are the war medals civilian ministers award themselves for issuing protocols.

General Monagas still was the chief opponent Páez had to face. José Tadeo Monagas was a rich cattle owner in Barcelona, where his family had been long established, and had served with credit under the Liberator. Tall and of powerful build he passed for the best lance that Venezuela had in the independence wars. Tolerably educated and rich, he was possessed by an insatiable thirst for power.

He is said never to have been able to look the man that he was speaking to in the face, which made him shifty looking, and took away from the air of distinction that he otherwise possessed.

Well over six feet in height, his features were expressive of great determination, and though he had attained the age of sixty-two, at the time* when Ramon Páez writes of him, he looked scarce fifty, for his hair and beard were black.

His jealousy of Páez amounted almost to an obsession, although at one time they had been friends, and had served long together under Bolivar.

Both were great horsemen and wielders of the lance, and both were frontiersmen skilled in the methods of guerrilla warfare, avid of popular applause, ambitious, brave to a fault, not valuing human life at a brass boddle, and careless of their own. In the comparatively narrow field of Venezuela, there was no room for two such bright particular stars in the same firmament.

Monagas seems to have been honest in his wish to

* " Wild Scenes in South America," Ramon Páez, page 575

re-establish the paper union between New Granada and
Venezuela, a wish that showed him inferior to Páez
as a statesman, and a poor judge of political events.
A proclamation Monagas put out in 1835 shows his
mentality. "Citizens, we must re-establish the republic
of La Gran Colombia and the federal system, in order
to deliver Venezuela from the narrow circle in which
she is situated. The Catholic Apostolic Roman faith is
the religion of the republic. All public offices should
be filled by old patriots, the founders of our liberties."

As all religions and rebellions have their moral status
through the offertory, for without money neither
religion nor rebellion can endure, Monagas as his first
step towards liberty made a forced levy on the citizens
of two hundred thousand dollars, for which no doubt
he issued bonds, payable when he was president.

As usual, civil war soon became sanguinary, for liberty
has to be watered well with blood before it thrives.
No citizen could call his life his own, between the various
bands of patriots who went about the country, saving
free institutions and cutting throats.

Páez, who had a real horror of civil strife, proposed
a conference between delegates from either side.
Monagas offered to disband his troops if Páez would
summon a congress immediately, to pass the various
reforms that he desired. The chief of these was in
relation to the law under which elections had been held.
His second proposition was that a complete amnesty
should be given to everyone who had taken part in the
revolt, and that his officers should retain their rank
and property.

These two propositions, to which unfortunately Páez
agreed, perhaps because he was unsure of his position,
have been the curse of Venezuela, as they have been of
Mexico, down to the present day. Once certain of
security to life and property after defeat, no revolu-

tionary abstained from trying odds with fortune, for if he lost the game, there was no penalty.

Páez was criticised severely for his mistaken clemency, both in the tribune and the Press; but criticisms were of the nature of the Spanish adage, " pay and appeal," that is appeal after you are forced to pay.

Puerto Cabello still held out for the revolution under a Major Pedro Carujo, who for years past had had a hand in every plot against the government.

Páez determined at all hazards to reduce the town. On Christmas Day (1835) he attacked in force, entered the town and took it after a sharp struggle in which Pedro Carujo mortally wounded was taken prisoner, and in a day or two expired. His death removed one of the most turbulent and determined disturbers of the land.

Once again peace, that ignis-fatuus of Venezuela, fluttered her wings over the blood-stained land, but hardly could be said to soar, for in a month or two Páez was called to meet an insurrection in his own territory of Apure.

Two brothers, Juan Pablo and Francisco Farfan, Llaneros of gigantic stature, brave to the point of ferocity, and knowing no other law but force, had raised the standard of revolt.

Their plea was the same as that Monagas had advanced, the re-institution of La Gran Colombia, and the defence of the Catholic Church, which church had never been attacked.

These two defenders of the Catholic Apostolic and Roman faith. had been brave, but unmanageable officers of Páez in the independence wars. They had both frequently deserted and joined the Royalists when anything occurred to put them out of conceit with the Republicans. They had served under General Yañez and Morillo, only rejoining Páez when he offered to promote to the rank of captain, anyone who should join him at the head of forty followers.

Just before the fight at Mucuritas* they had again deserted, and come back again. Páez tired of their insubordination had expelled them from his army, swearing that if they ventured to return again they should be executed. For several years they had remained living quietly in the Llanos on their own properties; but all the time swearing to take revenge on Páez if the opportunity occurred.

Páez saw the necessity for speed. He knew his fellow countrymen of the Llanos, and how readily they joined any adventurer who raised the standard of revolt, no matter in what cause.

Their wandering life, pastoral pursuits, and the abundance of horses on the plains, caused them to look on revolution as a sort of picnic, in which, whilst they saw little danger, they could enjoy an adventurous life, and if the cause they followed should succeed, their fortune was assured. If it should fail, they were sure of amnesty. Even without it, all they had to do was to go home, bury their arms in some convenient place and reassume their ordinary life, for distances were so enormous, it was impossible to pursue them, on the illimitable plains.

Gathering up rapidly some sixty of his best mounted followers, Páez crossed the Apure, swimming it by moonlight, a feat few but himself and his Llanero followers would have cared to attempt. The caymans and the other pests that haunt the waters of the Apure, are just as vigilant by night as day, and far more difficult to see.

At daybreak he pushed on at top speed, after the brothers Farfan. Crossing the Payara a deep, muddy stream, haunted by alligators, he came up with the

* Mucuritas was one of Páez's early victories.

rebels at the little town of the same name.* They numbered some four hundred, but Páez instantly resolved to fight, although the odds were great. His horses could not have been very fresh, after their long swim and their night march, but that did not prevent him from charging the four hundred horsemen opposed to him, at once.

So hot the struggle was, and for a time his chances seemed so exiguous, that Páez always spoke of the fight on the Payara, as the most desperate of his life.

Juan Pablo Farfan, the elder of the brothers, sought out Páez and attacked him fiercely with his lance, but was slain instantly by a servant Páez had called Rafael Solimas, who transfixed him with his spear.

Francisco, the younger brother owed his life to the swiftness of his horse after he had cut his way through his enemies.

The rebels left nearly two hundred dead upon the field, whilst Páez only lost three dead and seven wounded.

This feat of arms gained him the title of the Lion of Payara, a name by which he is often styled, even to-day, amongst his countrymen.

Once more Páez became popular, admired and looked upon as the accomplished type of a Llanero warrior.

He was now forty seven years of age, at the height of his powers, mental and physical.† For nearly ten years, his was the controlling influence in Venezuela, although his popularity began to wane, after his second term as president.

In 1835, he set on foot negotiations, through his minister in London, Don Alejo Fortique,‡ for the recog-

* San Juan de Payara.

† The action of Payara was fought in 1837.

‡ Don Alejo Fortique was a friend of the writer's maternal grandfather, Admiral Fleeming, and of his grandmother, during his residence in England. His name was a household word to the writer in his childhood.

nition of the independence of Venezuela by the mother country. The negotiations turned out infructuous, for Spain was not a country that accepted the inevitable, without a struggle against destiny. Fate decreed that in old age during his second occupancy of the presidency, in the year 1838, Páez should have the honour of conducting the negotiations that placed Spain and Venezuela on a level as sovereign states, not interdependent on each other.

Writing to Queen Cristina, Páez offers Spain the position of most favoured nation, and goes on to say, nature, religion and language point out that Spain and Venezuela should be friends. In a noble passage he adjures Cristina to bow to the decree of providence, " in order that the New World, that owed to Isabel I of glorious* memory, the discovery of its existence to the older world, shall owe to the august mother of Isabel II, the ratification of its national existence." It was reserved for the humbly born Llanero to write to princes on an equality.

Bolivar had seen the promised land from afar off like Moses, but Páez rode into the heart of it, on his Llanero Pegasus.

---

* " El decreto de la Providencia esta cumplido . . . reconozcale. V. M. para que el nuevo mundo que debío á Isabel I, de gloriosa memoria el discubrimiento de su existencie á la faz del antiguo, deba ahora á la augusta madre de Isabel II la ratificacion de su existencia nacional."

CHAPTER XXI

By this time the name of Páez had become known throughout the world.

William IV* sent him a sword of honour, in the year 1837. The inscription on it, did the king's discrimination honour, and is a proof that he had more imagination than he has been credited with, by his historians. The inscription ran, " from William IV to General Páez as a proof of his admiration for his character, and for the disinterested patriotism that has distinguished his brilliant and victorious career."

As the constitution of Venezuela did not permit any Venezuelan to accept a gift from a foreign potentate, without previous permission from the Congress, Páez asked Congress† to accept the sword, and place it in his house beside the rustic arms that he had used in the War of Independence.

Both king and patriot were honoured in the presentation and acceptance of the gift.

In 1838 Páez was elected president for a second term of office, by two hundred and twelve votes, out of a total voting list of two hundred and twenty two qualified electors of the whole republic. Congress awarded him a sword of honour, on his election.

Writing in exile in his old age he says pathetically, " This sword one of the few objects I have saved out of the shipwreck of my fortune, is made of gold. On the hilt is a statuette of Victory, inscribed, ' To the

* Our well beloved, Silly Billy.

† " En mi hogar al lado de las toscas armas que me dieron la victoria en las lides de la Independencia."

Illustrious Citizen, defender of the constitution and of his country's laws.' "

His second term of office was far more peaceful than the first.

Not so much disturbed by revolutionary risings, he had time to devote himself to the encouragement of agriculture, which had been sadly neglected during the independence and the civil wars. It was to Páez that the first roads made in the republic since the expulsion of the Spaniards, were due.

His efforts, were only tentative, but the national revenue was small, the population scanty and wheeled vehicles were few. Throughout his second term of office, Peace, that unusual visitor to Venezuela, remained, as one might say, the guest of the republic. With a broad vision, hardly to be expected from one of his up-bringing, throughout his second administration, Páez endeavoured to bring about good relations between Venezuela and foreign governments.

The long drawn out question of the limitation of the frontier betwixt British and Venezuelan Guayana, nearly brought on a war with England. It was not settled, finally, till 1899 and even now, the frontier posts, lost in the vast unexplored territory, maintain a malevolent neutrality to one another.

Without an army, or a fleet, with little money in the treasury, Páez governed almost like a patriarch, relying on his personal prestige to keep order in the enormous territory over which he ruled.

The greatest moment of his civil life was now approaching. The three republics, Venezuela, Colombia and Ecuador, all of whom owed their independence to the Liberator, Simon Bolivar, and all of whom had turned against him in his life, branding him as a danger to free institutions, bethought themselves that the time had arrived to make amends and bring his body back,

to lie weighed down with marble in the Caracas, where
he was born, and that had cast him out with ignominy.

Posthumous honours, perhaps salve the conscience of
the honourers, and are well typified in the Spanish saying, pithy and pawky as it is, " when the ass dies, put
barley underneath his tail."

Such credit as there was, belongs in the first place to
Páez, who since the Liberator's death had never ceased
importuning congress to bring back the Liberator's bones.
With great pomp and circumstance, representatives of
the three republics, brought back the mortal remains of
the immortal Liberator, and with all due ceremony they
were deposited under a splendid marble hearse in the
Pantheon at Caracas.

Honour was satisfied, and to-day, the Liberator's
tomb is a place of pilgrimage.

Páez rests under a simple marble slab, inscribed but
with his name. The Venezuelans seem in the main, to
have reversed their judgment on their two Liberators,
Páez and Bolivar, and whilst the one is justly honoured
for his heroic life, Páez, who saved his country from
the position of a mere adjunct of the greater state of
New Granada,* has not a monument, worthy of his
fame.

His second term of office over, Páez retired to private
life, but still continued to be the arbiter of his country's
destiny. He had perhaps been wiser, to have settled
in the Llanos and resumed his old life of a cattle farmer.

From that time his influence declined. At the election
for the presidency, General Carlos Soublette, an old
officer of the Liberator's and a man of the highest character, was practically the nominee of Páez. He
governed well and wisely, but the opposition attacked
Páez fiercely, through his nominee. There was some
truth in their allegation that the electors were not con-

* To-day, Colombia.

sulted and that Soublette owed his place to a few oligarchs.

Although Páez's influence at home was waning, his fame abroad was at its height. On his retirement from the presidency, Louis Philippe sent him the grand cross of the Legion of Honour. The King of Sweden and Norway made him commendator of the Order of the Sword. In 1845, Spain recognised Venezuelan Independence, and Congress specially thanked Páez not only as a soldier of the Liberator, but as the initiator of the negotiations with the mother country, now crowned with success.

Peace had now reigned for sixteen years in Venezuela, an unprecedented term.

Soublette, whose time of office was drawing to a close, had governed wisely, and the finances of the country were slowly mending, but as the Spanish phrase runs, " goats always seek the mountains,"* and in the year 1846, General Leocadio Guzman once more raised the standard of revolt.

Almost in a moment the country fell back into its old ways. Armed bands appeared on every hand and set about their usual game of pillaging the country people, in the name, as usual, of the reuniting of La Gran Colombia, of liberty, religion, and the other war cries that throughout the world have brought such misery upon the human race.

Monagas, usually the first to take advantage of the turmoil, well understanding that the troubled water is the time for the adventurous fisherman† to throw in his line, rallied to the government. Appointed second in command of the army, he assisted Páez ably till the revolutionary movement was suffocated.

Páez himself, who was living quietly in Maracay,

* La Cabra tira al monte.
† Rio revuelto, ganancia de pescadores.

hoping, it may be imagined, for a little rest from warfare, was suffering from fever at the time.

On hearing that Leocadio Guzman was in the field he left his bed at once, mounted his horse and set out for the province of Barinas, where " factions " had risen under an Indian called Rangél.

As he passed through the little town of Magdalena, a man fired a blunderbuss at him out of a window, so close that it singed* his clothes.

Páez seems to have borne a charmed life, as sometimes is the case with those who take little precaution for their safety.

The would be murderer was seized at once and brought before his intended victim. Páez told him he was a miserable shot and set him free at once. Most generals of those times, and perhaps some of these, would have set him with his back to the wall to face a firing party. In all such matters Páez always exhibited a humanity that does him credit and shows his native generosity. Although not sanguinary by nature, he must have seen and ordered so many military executions in the independence wars that it is wonderful his character had not been warped by the sight of continual bloodshed.

The Indian Rangél was routed at a place called El Rincon del Limon by General Guerrero, acting for the government.

Monagas dispersed the other bands, and in any other country peace would have seemed secure. Soublette's term of office finished in 1846, and as Monagas had done good service against the rebels in the recent troubles, Páez supported his candidature for the presidency, and of course, with such a backer, he was elected.

As peace appeared secure, and Páez for a long time

* á boca de jarro. This was really a case of " á quema ropa," though Páez's son refers to it as " a boca de jarro." Both phrases mean, point blank.

had neglected his own interests, he set out with his son Ramon for the State of Guarico, where he had several cattle farms.   It was the last time he was fated to enjoy the wild life of his native Llanos free from the cares of state.

On a fine morning in December, 1846, Páez journeyed to Maracay, for his last visit to the plains.

In those days a trip to the Llanos required as many preparations as a journey in Morocco thirty years ago, or as a journey from San Antonio Texas to the city of Mexico in the last century.   As the plains afforded no provisions but meat, and to get even that the animal had to be lassoed and then killed, everything had to be taken packed on mules.   The caravan was nearly a hundred strong.   It comprised cattlemen, muleteers, a treasurer who had the care of the military chest full of silver dollars, the ponchos, gaudy handkerchiefs, and knives for presents to the country people, and a doctor. Young Ramon Páez was nominated secretary, his duties being to keep a record of the expedition and note down all that he saw about the flora, fauna and geology of the district they were about to visit.   This duty he performed most skilfully,* as anyone who reads his book can see.

Born at Achaguas in the Llanos, but brought up in New York, English was probably as familiar to him as his native tongue.   He had a practical acquaintanceship with botany and with geology, and had studied natural history sufficiently to classify the various animals that he encountered under their scientific names.   Not having seen much of his native land since childhood, his impressions of it are vivid in the extreme, and show that he was gifted with a most observant mind and a quick intellect.

* "Wild Scenes in South America," Ramon Páez. London, 1863. Ramon Páez wrote the book in English, having been brought up in New York.

Few sons could have passed their lives in such different surroundings to those in which their fathers lived, than the young scholar from a northern university, now for the first time to graduate upon the plains. The admiration that he bore for his celebrated father transcends in every line he writes about Our Leader, as he always calls his sire. Probably Páez felt an equal admiration for his son.

An English sportsman whom Páez had picked up, possibly in Caracas, also accompanied the expedition, an experienced mulatto cook, one Monico by name, and a negro called Gaspar, who was the washerman. Fifty cattle peons and a little horde of nondescripts, each of whom had some more or less illusory duty to perform, made up the personnel. Besides the pack mules, the expedition took a troop of about two hundred horses, on which to run the cattle, in addition to some twenty baggage mules.

This little army, so like an eastern caravan in its composition, save for the camels, set out from Maracay at daybreak. Everyone used the Llanero saddle, with its high cantle like the Mexican and its soft seat like the " recado " of the Argentine, its long triangular stirrups made for riders who ride barefooted or in sandals, and its gaudy " sobre-puesto," that is the piece of embroidered cloth over the soft " pellon," kept in its place by a broad surcingle.

Their hammocks and " cobijas," the Llanero poncho, rolled up tightly, were tied behind the saddles, with a mosquito net if the rider was a " blanco," that is a man belonging to the upper classes, but not necessarily white.

White is an elastic adjective in the Americas, comprehending those descended from old Spanish families, whose blood has never mingled either with Indians or negros, and men that in other countries would be called frankly " coloured," with a little dash of white. The

square " cobija," that corresponds to the poncho of the
pampas, and in both cases is a survival of the Spanish
cloak, is about six feet square. Made of two blankets,
one blue the other scarlet, with a hole in the middle
through which the Llanero puts his head, leaving the
ends to dangle on his horse's flanks, it is a most useful
garment, and may be said, as of the Spanish cloak,* to
cover everything. In cloudy weather it is worn with the
blue side outwards, as experience has shown the dwellers
on the plains that blue absorbs more heat. In the fierce
noonday sun the scarlet side is turned towards it, as the
Llanero, like the modern scientist, knows that red is
the colour that renders a strong light more tolerable
to bear.

As beds are scarcely ever to be found upon the Llanos,
the traveller slings his hammock between two trees upon
a journey, hanging his cobija on a rope he ties above the
hammock, to form a kind of tent.

Thus equipped, with a lazo neatly coiled in front of
his right knee and a cow's horn, carved in rude patterns,
with crocodiles, horses and bulls heads, or any device
that strikes the decorator's fancy, but filled invariably
either with Cocuy† or white rum from Carúpano, the
Llanero is ready for the road.

They set out from Maracay at daybreak, and by
what seems to have been an extraordinary long march
reached the town of Villa de Cura by the evening. Not
finding accommodation for so many animals in the stony
little plain, they pushed on to a place called El

---

* La capa todo lo tapa. The cobijas used to be dipped in a solution of
indiarubber to render them waterproof.

The writer's maternal grandfather, brought home several of these treated
Cobijas, presented to him by Páez. He showed them to the celebrated
Mackintosh, who, it is a family tradition, got the first idea of treating cloth
with indiarubber from these cobijas.

† Cocuy, a spirit made from the root of the Cocuiza plant. The spirit
resembles the Mescal of the Mexicans, which is also made from the root
of one of the Bromeliæ, or from a wild Aloe.

Rodeo, a few miles further on, and camped there for the night.

There they slept in the open on the slope of a hill upon their saddle gear. It was a rough initiation to Llanero life for a young man accustomed to New York. Next day they passed through San Juan de los Morros, with its fantastic peaks that seen from the Llanos appear to spring up like some island in the Pacific, or from a sea of dream. Passing Ortiz, they arrived at El Hato de San Pablo, a cattle farm belonging to " Our Leader."

A grave old negro overseer, kneeling on the ground, kissed Páez's hand as he dismounted, and led his horse away to bathe it at a pool, after the fashion of the plains, that know no curry-combs.

El Hato de San Pablo, though it belonged to Páez, who had been twice president of the republic, had a house little better than a barn. Comfort of any kind was contraband in the long, low, palm-thatched shanty, with its walls made of mud and reeds. The middle portion of the structure had no sides, but was a mere " Caney," that is a hut, built in the native style, copied from the dwellings of the native Indians.

The air blew freely through it, a desideratum in that climate as it was always cool, or at least as cool as it is possible to be upon the Llanos. On that account it was used as the dining-room. Windows were quite unknown, and only two of the rooms had doors. When it rained, in the dining-room, dry bullocks' hides were stretched between the posts on which the roof was laid, to keep the weather out. The furniture was to the full as primitive as was the house, and consisted of a rough table, balanced against the wall to keep it steady, two or three home-made chairs seated with bullocks' hide from which the hair had never been removed, except by usage, which left bare patches on the untanned skin, as if they had the mange. Grass hammocks swinging from the walls were used either as beds at night or rocking chairs by day, the sitter with one leg dangling keeping them in perpetual motion with his foot.

All round the walls, on antlers and bullocks' horns, was hung the saddle gear, the bridles, spurs and lazos of the occupants.

A German lithograph of La Santissima seated upon a throne, surrounded by several chubby angels, and crowned with glory, was the one concession to art or to religion, according to the taste of the beholder.

Though on the estate grazed many thousand head of cattle, milk was almost unprocurable, just as it used to be on the " Estancias " of the Argentine, for all the animals were wild and required the efforts of two or three vaqueros to lazo and to tie them up in the corral. As a concession to the status of the owner, two or three tame, or rather " tamed." cows had been imported from a neighbouring establishment. These answered to the names of Maravilla, Clavellina and Flor del Campo, and allowed themselves to be milked, half under protest, after their calves had sucked a little of their milk.

Each morning, as in the Argentine, a bullock was run up from the " rodeo " as near as possible to the dwelling house, lassoed and slaughtered. The offal, left where the animal had been butchered, was soon devoured by the troop of half wild dogs that on most ranches in South America get their own living like a pack of wolves.

Páez, who had had but little rest from war or state-craft for many years, must have been happy in his old surroundings, mustering his cattle in the early morning, then swinging in a hammock, thrumming a guitar, smoking eternally and listening to the gossip of the plains, of horses, cattle and their brands, the depredations made by the tigers, subjects quite as congenial to those who care for them, as the important matters of what the dwellers in it style the great world, losing their personal littleness in its immensity. In the midst of his retirement, occupied alone with plans to mark and sell his cattle, Páez was surprised with the news that a famous robber, José Urbano, had committed several murders close to San Pablo, where he was in residence. He instantly sent out a dozen of his men with peremptory orders not to return without the body of the robber, either alive or dead.

They left at nightfall and in the darkness crossed a trail that showed them ten or a dozen men had passed. Not doubting that they had got upon the track of the banditti, they followed it by moonlight until it led them to a lonely hut, in which a company of men were sleeping peacefully. Without a word the pursuers burst into the house firing a volley as they ran. Three were killed at the first fire, and it was not till then that Páez's men found they had shot innocent cattlemen, who had been sleeping in the hut after a hunt for their strayed animals.

Ashamed of their unfortunate mistake, they set out till they came on the right trail, and followed it to a ranch where Urbano was sleeping with one of his numerous mistresses.

Although taken by surprise, at bay and against overwhelming odds, he held out desperately, his mistress handing him a loaded gun as fast as he had fired. When he fell at last, at the feet of the sable Amazon, an amulet was found between his teeth, so firmly held in his death agony that it required the efforts of two men to open them.

It proved to be what is known on the Llanos as " the prayer of the Just* Judge," a curious amulet for a bandit to have worn. Tied on a horse's back, the robber's body was brought to Páez, who caused it to be exposed for four and twenty hours on the high road, as

* La oracion del Justo Juez.

farmers hang dead crows in a potato field to scare away the rest.

The cattle duly branded at San Pablo, Páez moved on to another property, La Yeguera, where the company included chickens, dogs, and a game-cock that crowed at intervals all through the night.

For several months Páez pursued the life that he loved best, and perhaps understood the best, riding all day after the cattle, hunting, and at night dancing with all and sundry, the Llanero dances of those days, La Maricola, El Raspon and La Zapa, now all merged in El Joropo, for to the last day of his life he was indefatigable in the dance.

Camped on the banks of a lagoon called Los Borales, seated on a pack saddle, Páez dictated to his son his refusal of the offer of a third term of the presidency.

He probably was right, for it was certainly undesirable that the presidency should drift into a dictatorship, as it had almost done under the Liberator.

He advocated the candidature of General Monagas, who had been for a long time his enemy, or at the best a jealous rival for the post. Páez did not forsee that his generous advocacy of Monagas' claim would prove his ruin, and shut him out forever from the free, wild life he was enjoying, when he wrote his refusal of the first place in the republic, seated on such a rustic chair of state.

In the midst of these rural occupations Páez was surprised by the visit of a tall, red-faced Englishman, Lord James Butler, who had come to redeem a promise he had made a year ago, when he had first met Páez in the capital.

Páez who always had a special corner in his heart for Englishmen, after the gallant conduct of the British Legion in the war of independence, welcomed him heartily.

The son of Albion* had brought an English speaking negro from Barbadoes with him. Nothing was more astonishing to the Llaneros than what appeared to them the negro's linguistic ability, and all day long they thronged to see him, asking him to speak English to them.

Lord James had taken a whole month to make the journey from Ciudad Bolivar to San Fernando de Apure in a clumsy country boat. From San Fernando he set out alone to search for Páez who was camped close to Achaguas, fifteen leagues away. It was an act almost of madness, for a man unaccustomed to the plains, and very nearly cost Lord James his life. Just as night fell a prairie owl sprang up under the feet of the mule that he was riding. It wheeled round rapidly and dismounted him. Left alone on the plains at nightfall, on foot, with his direction lost, his case was desperate had he been aware of it.

Even by day men born upon the plains frequently lose their way in that vast ocean of green grass. The clumps of palm trees, although most of them are known and have their own particular names, are so bewilderingly alike that few can steer by them.

Lord James knew nothing of all this or of his danger, and was proceeding onwards cheerfully, on foot. To be on foot upon the Llanos, even for a Llanero is nearly as forlorn a position as to be clinging to a plank, tossing amongst the waves. Luckily a Llanero who was looking for strayed animals saw the saddled animal, lassoed it at once and going back upon the trail came on Lord James, cheerily tramping on, quite in the wrong direction and unconscious of his plight.

During the time he stayed with Páez they got up a rodeo for his amusement and initiated him into Llanero ways. After a week they parted, as sworn brothers promising to meet again.

* El hijo de Albion.

Páez having collected several thousand head of cattle set off for Calabozo, leaving the cattle under his major-domo, to come on slowly to his estate in the interior.

Arrived at Calabozo, Páez was received with great rejoicing by the inhabitants, with whom he had always been a favourite. Banquets and balls succeeded one another, and the sudden change to luxury after two or three months of spartan living on the plains set up a fever that brought him almost to the grave. As soon as he could mount a horse he set out for the capital, where the new president Monagas had showed his hand, removing all the officers of the army whom Páez had appointed and replacing them by creatures of his own. Many of these had served with him in the revolutions of the years 1831 and 1835. Some of his ministers resigned in consequence, and the whole country was in a state of tension, waiting on events.

At that moment an old patriot General Juan José Flores arrived in Venezuela, after an absence of five and twenty years. Being much respected by all parties, many of the leading citizens sought his counsel and advice. He implored Páez to see Monagas personally, and find out what he had in mind. Páez agreed and set out for a place called Las Cocuizas, that Monagas had fixed on as the meeting place.

Upon the way a courier from Monagas overtook him, bearing a letter saying he had changed his mind and was not coming to the tryst. Then came news that Monagas had occupied the capital with an armed force and that the congress was overawed.

Páez was just setting out for the neighbouring re-public of Colombia, disgusted at the state of national affairs, when he received news that roused all the demo-cratic spirit by which he was possessed.

Congress finding itself thwarted at every turn, its decrees flouted and the approaches to the building held

by troops, was occupied upon a motion to transfer their
meeting place to Puerto Cabello, where they could de-
liberate with greater safety. At the height of the
debate a band of soldiers rushed into the house and
opened fire upon the members as they sat deliberating.

Five were killed outright and many wounded.
Amongst the slain was Santos Michelena, a man respected on all sides for his long services to the republic
and for his upright life. With him fell Guillerno
Smith, an English hero of the independence wars,
married to a Venezuelan lady.

A wave of indignation swept over the whole country,
and the deputies who had escaped the murderous fusillade took refuge in the various legations of the foreign
powers.

The people turned to Páez as their saviour, as they
always did in any difficulty.

He at once responded and took up arms against the
tyrant, but the justness of his cause did not provide him
with the necessary big battalions, without whose aid
justice and truth cannot prevail, or in this vale of tears,
prevail, when no one cares if they prevail.

Monagas controlled the army and the treasury, was
well established in the capital, and though not loved was
feared, and fear in South America in those days was a
more potent force than love.

Hurriedly levying some raw Llanero troops, Páez
met the forces of the government under the old chief of
his Guard of Honour, Cornelio Muñoz, at a place called
Los Araguatos and was defeated instantly, his raw levies
not being able to face the seasoned forces of the government.

He owed his life, as he had done many times before
during his adventurous career, to the swiftness of his
horse. Embarking hurriedly at Puerto Cabello, he
reached Jamaica, suffering acutely from malarial fever,

and almost penniless. All his estates were confiscated by the Monagists and all his followers bitterly persecuted. Páez removed from Jamaica to Saint Thomas, in which place he remained till 1849.

Then, most ill advisedly, he returned to Venezuela at the instigation of his friends, and putting himself at the head of a band of partisans endeavoured to reach the Llanos, where without doubt he could have maintained himself almost indefinitely.

Overtaken by the Monagists, he was obliged to capitulate at a place called Macapo, in the State of Guarico. Carried to Caracas, he was imprisoned in the Castle of San Antonio de Cumaná.

Situated in the eastern province, Cumaná a town upon the coast, is as hot as La Guaira or as Maracaibo, the thermometer rarely falling below ninety degrees of Fahrenheit. Heavily ironed and confined in a close cell, in such a temperature, Páez accustomed for the most part of his life to the free atmosphere of the Llanos, suffered severely. At times, so stifling was the cell that he had to lie flat upon the floor to breathe the little air there was under the bottom of the door, for both the window and the door were closed and bolted. Monagas without doubt hoped he would not survive such treatment.

The Lion of Payara was not easy to be made away with, and still had a long lease of life before him, though nearly sixty years of age.

His wife, whom he had long deserted for the more attractive Barbara* Nieves, a Valencian, with whom he generally lived when in Valencia, appeared at Cumaná and did all in her power to relieve his wants. It does not seem that the gay Barbara, the partner of his happy days did anything, or that she even visited him in prison. Páez who was never profoundly influenced by women

---

* Barbara Nieves is described as " bullanguera, amiga de fiestas y bailes," *i.e.* very gay and fond of feasts and dances.

at any period of his life, does not appear to have concerned himself about either* the wife or her coadjutress during his long exile in the United States, for neither of them is mentioned either in his Memoirs or in the reports of the newspapers of New York.

" At length," as his son Ramon says, " his powerful constitution gave way under this iniquitous treatment, and a rush of blood to the head occurred which would doubtless have terminated fatally but for the prompt assistance of two skilful physicians of the place."

As it was public property that Páez by the terms of his capitulation at Macapo was to be allowed to quit the country, the people of Cumaná, indignant at his treatment, rose as one man to demand he should be released. The Congress in Caracas, though filled with the creatures of Monagas, could not regard with equanimity the persecution of a man to whom the country owed so much. Monagas, forced by public indignation, was obliged to let him go, and sent the steamer El Libertador to Cumaná to carry him to the United States. One tribute indeed he paid to him. Being reminded that on a previous occasion when he was taken prisoner he had been received by Páez and treated more as a guest than as a captive, and urged to mete out the same treatment that he had received, he answered, " The idea‡ is very generous, but I fear that if I bring General Páez to my house, not only will he start a revolution, but make me a revolutionist." This was indeed a tribute to his personal magnetism.

When the Libertador arrived at Cumaná there was

---

* Possibly Páez held with the motive of a French musical hall song, " Quand je vois une tête de veau ça me rappelle ma legitime," for he was not one to be bound easily, even in bonds, forged duly in the Latin of the Church.

† " Wild Scenes in South America," Ramon Páez.

‡ La idea es muy generosa, pero temo que si traigo á mi casa al General Páez, el llevará á cabo la revolucion, hasta conmigo mismo.

U

no coal for her in the port.   The inhabitants, fearing a plot to make away with Páez at the last moment, flew to the timber yard and piled the wood upon the steamer's deck.   Then, finding it was insufficient, tore down the doors and windows of their houses, adding them to the pile.

Followed by an enormous concourse of the citizens, showering flowers on his head, they accompanied him in triumph to the ship.

Upon the 26th of July, 1850, he reached New York, where he received a public welcome from the authorities.

CHAPTER XXII

PAEZ seems to have been popular from the first in the United States. His career had been followed with interest and in those days high-handed aggression, disguised under the name of progress and regard for liberty, had not created the suspicion and distrust of the powerful neighbour, now prevalent, from Mexico to Cape Horn.

In fact, the Northern Eagle had not shown that eagles and vultures have many traits that both of them enjoy.

When all is said and done, Páez at the time he landed in the United States, was but the defeated leader of a party. He had been, of course, twice president of Venezuela, and his career as a patriotic leader in the war of independence had been heroic. For all that public opinion must have been very different at that time in the United States from what it is to-day. To fancy any ex-president of a South American republic, whose star had set, no matter how high his personal character, being received to-day with public honours in New York passes the power of ordinary man's imagination, however powerful it may be.

In 1850, when he landed in New York, he was just sixty* years of age, though he looked scarcely fifty, as he was described by two fellow countrymen.

" General Páez is of middle height. His countenance is cheerful, his eyes bright, his forehead high, and his hair turning grey. His manners are easy, simple

---

* Pamphlet entitled " El General Páez en los Estados Unidos," signed " Dos Venezolanos," New York, 1850.

and dignified, they are those of a perfect gentleman. His air of frankness and cordiality makes him most agreeable. He has been represented to the public as a mulatto.* On the contrary, he is as white as any man north of the Mason† and Dixon line.

"He dresses elegantly, a black coat and a white waist-coat with gold buttons, black trousers and patent leather boots. His feet are small. No one could imagine on seeing the General that he had just emerged from rigorous imprisonment, and from persecution of all kinds. . . . He told us that it was the case, as stated in the New York Press, that his cell was so small and the atmosphere in it so suffocating that sometimes he was obliged to lie down and place his mouth against the opening between the floor and the bottom of the door to get a little air. He attributes the good state of his health to the exercise he took during his imprisonment. When asked how he could do so in such a little space, he answered that the soldiers of the guard were always singing insulting songs to annoy him. When they struck up he always danced to their music till he broke out into a profuse perspiration, and then lay down to sleep.

"General Páez is evidently a man of indomitable spirit and an iron constitution, able to bear all the reverses of fortune with equanimity."

His son Ramon, who was imprisoned with him, says that throughout their imprisonment his father was the most cheerful and least cast down of the two. This speaks eloquently in favour of the strength of mind of a man suddenly dispossessed of all his fortune and his power, and then confined in a dark and dirty prison,

---

* Someone, perhaps a slave holder, had written to the press protesting against giving Páez a public reception, on the grounds that he had black blood.

† This was an arbitrary division drawn between the Northern and Southern States in those days.

where every moment he was expecting death. In one word, his manners are those of a distinguished gentleman and his carriage that of a valiant and a worthy soldier.

Time had indeed wrought a wondrous change upon the barefooted Llanero boy, who had washed the negro Manuelote's feet. Páez had now become an educated man, speaking both French and English, and with a bowing knowledge of Italian. He, who in his boyhood must have seen the Spanish gentlemen who then ruled Venezuela dressed in knee-breeches and silk stockings, with swords by their sides, was now arrayed in what in those days were known as citizen's clothes, in the United States. The change of costume was not an advance, æsthetically considered, although it may have typified the advance of what is styled the progress of the world, perhaps for euphony.

Though Páez had lost everything, fate still had in store for him, in years to come, one of the most astounding changes of fortune that has befallen anyone in history. In the meantime, the North Americans evidently took him to their hearts.

His martial bearing, frank manners and air of geniality evidently appealed, perhaps insensibly, to a population whose hearts no doubt were golden, but their exterior rough.

In 1851, Páez was received by the municipality of Baltimore with public honours.

In Washington the enthusiasm when he appeared was indescribable, the citizens of every class and age thronging the streets to see him pass.

Páez who had scarcely left his native land till he was sixty years of age, now set out like the young Anarcharsis* to see the world.

* " Voyage du Jeune Anarcharsis en Gréce," Jean Jaques Barthéolemy, Paris, 1788.

For the next ten years he seems to have travelled extensively, but making his headquarters in New York, where in his leisure hours he wrote his memoirs.

In all the countries he visited honours were showered upon him, for in fact he was the one surviving representative of a heroic struggle and of an age long passed away. It was but natural that in Mexico, General Antonio de Santa Anna, the self-styled Napoleon of the West, should have received Páez with acclamation; but stranger that King Louis of Bavaria should have turned Munich upside down to welcome one who all his life had been the enemy of kings. Still, London in the days of the virtuous Victoria went out agog to welcome Garibaldi, although perhaps in this case they partly looked upon him as the standard bearer of the party whose slogan, "To Gehenna with the Pope," served as the acid test of their belief.

The memoirs Páez left behind him, though they deal at considerable length and in the main with impartiality with all his early years, and are continued to the time of his expulsion by Monagas, come to an end before his latter travels. Thus we know nothing of his impressions of the foreign countries that he visited, or how he felt when seated next to the Empress Eugenie at a grand banquet in the Tuilleries.

In Venezuela since the year 1848, things had been altering rapidly, as gradually the country became more accessible to foreign influences. Slavery had been abolished, a few roads had been commenced to the interior, and in 1855 the first line of telegraph was laid between La Guaira and the capital.

The Monagas faction, for the last ten years in power, had grown unpopular. Public opinion grew so strong that in the year 1858, by a decree of the National Convention, Páez was reinstated in his military rank and all his honours were returned to him. All the decrees that had been passed that the Monagists that branded Páez as a traitor, were reversed and he was invited home.

New York rose to the occasion, for it had not forgotten Páez in his poverty, and still reverenced the man that it had welcomed as an exile more than ten years ago. Once more the authorities and the citizens combined to honour him. General McLellan organized a military parade to bid him farewell at the place of embarkation, and placed a splendid charger at his disposition to ride down to the port.

Through the chief streets the cortège took its way, with music and girls showering flowers on the old warrior's head, as he passed underneath their balconies. All went well till at the middle of Broadway, just where the crowd was thickest, the horse that Páez rode took fright, slipped and fell down upon him, crushing and mangling his leg. It was the irony of fate that the old Llanero, accustomed from his youth to ride wild horses, should nearly lose his life by a fall from a military charger in a slippery street.

His injuries were so severe that his life was despaired of, but once again his vigorous constitution saved him, though he was nearly seventy years of age.

So anxious were the people in Caracas for his presence, that Páez had himself carried on board the ship when he was fit to leave his bed.

At Cumaná, the scene of his imprisonment and persecution by Monagas, the whole town was in the streets to welcome him, whom they styled the Lion of Payara. The lion had indeed come back to his den.

Again he took the well-remembered road to his old house in Valencia, that he was destined to visit for the last time.

The journey to Caracas was one long triumph, and on his arrival there the people went mad with joy. Old soldiers of the war of independence crowded to welcome him and shake his hand.

To the young generation it must have seemed a legendary hero had come to life again.

Next year, he was proclaimed dictator, and head both of the civil and military power.

The wheel of fortune had come round full centre, and in his old age Páez found himself again acclaimed and hailed the saviour of his native land. He bore his honours modestly, but he had been too long away and had got out of touch with Venezuelan politics.

Forced, partly by his age and partly by his long absence from the country, to place his trust in others, he fell unfortunately under the influence of one Rojas, an arbitrary man and a reactionary, whose evil counsels pushed Páez into actions that destroyed his prestige.

Once more the federal party reared its head and General Falcon hoisted the standard of revolt. The town of Maracaibo and the Eastern province joined in the revolt, and Generals Rubin and Michelena, sent by Páez to attack Kallon passed over to his side. Páez was forced to come to terms with the revolutionaries, and at the hacienda of Coche, a few miles from Caracas, signed what is known as the Treaty of Coche, Pedro José Rojas signing for him, and General Guzman Blanco for Falcon.

By this treaty Páez agreed to abdicate and General Falcon was renamed president.

On May the 22nd, 1863, Páez left Venezuela for the last time, returning to New York stripped of his property and with hardly any means of livelihood except a paltry ex gratiâ grant from General Falcon. His wonderful public career was ended, and it appears that although hospitable New York received the illustrious exile with respect, that Páez was too proud to apply for the assistance that he needed, and which assuredly New York would have accorded him.

There still remains an episode of his career to chronicle, and one that must have moved and gratified him in his old age.

Páez, though long past seventy was still physically strong and hale, haler by far than many men of half his years.

Pushed by his poverty, at the age of seventy-eight, he set out for Buenos Aires as the commission agent for a cattle company. He arrived there in the month of June of 1868, bringing with him as his sole companion a great white dog, that answered to the strange name of Pinken.

Buenos Aires, quick to respond to generous impulses, could not see without compassion the legendary hero of a hundred fights obliged to seek his livelihood in an employment so unworthy of his merits and his years. All the chief families welcomed him with enthusiasm, disputing who should receive him as an honoured guest. He took up his abode with the Carranzas, and attached himself especially to a little boy, Adolfo, who afterwards became Dr. Carranza, the founder and the first director of the Museum of History of the capital.

The strangely assorted friends, followed invariably by Pinken, were soon known to everyone as they walked about the streets.

Under the hospitable roof of the Carranzas a group of exiles, all distinguished men, mostly advanced in age, used to meet nightly, for what is styled in Spanish, "un rato de tertulia," that is they sat, smoking and taking maté, or drinking lemonade, fighting their battles over once again, far into the night.

There met together the Colombian, Florencio Gonzalez, who had translated Lieber and Grinke and at the time lectured on literature in the university. All his life he had been a liberal, but had been involved in the plot to kill Bolivar and had to leave his native land. The octogenarian, Don Manuel Olazabal, one of the heroes of the war of independence in the River Plate, and General Campero, poor and an exile, waiting for the turn of fortune that raised him to the highest office in Bolivia, with all the " flower and cream "* of the literary world of Buenos Aires, made up the tertulia.

Seated on the ground of the low-roofed colonial house, the windows with their iron gratings open to the sandy unpaved streets, in full view of the passers by, as was the custom in these days, they unpacked the budget of their reminiscences.

Most of the " tertulianos " had plenty to unpack. Their lives had been full of adventures and of hair-breadth escapes by flood and field. As they talked on about the famous passage of the Andes, by General San Martin, the fight at Ayacucho and the last stand the Spaniards made at El Callao, the negro girl, or Paraguayan Indian, in their white dresses, their bare feet making a slapping on the floor like indiarubber, went and came, serving maté, silently waiting till the guest had sucked the boiling liquid through the silver tube.

Outside, amongst the orange trees in the patio, the fireflies flitted to and fro, like stars that had got adrift from heaven, amongst the dark metallic leaves. Sometimes a visitor would ride up to the grated window, rein up his horse and greet the company. Without dismounting, he would take a maté passed to him through the bars, sit listening silently, perhaps for a full hour, with a leg resting on his horse's neck and his great silver spur hung loosely from his heel. Then when the watchman's voice resounded through the silent street, informing the good citizens that in the name of the most Holy† Virgin

* Flor y nata.

† Ave Maria Purisima, las doce han dado, y sereno.

it was twelve o'clock, and a serene night, the rider, shifting back into his seat, would salute the company and vanish noiselessly along the sandy street.

Seated at card tables, the other guests would play tresillo, and the ladies dance the pericon to a guitar and an accordion.

Páez, Carranza says, was the most notable of all the veterans. When, "in the simple language of a hero and with the sincerity of a man of honour, he told the company of his adventures, they listened in amazement," to the account of things and of events they had learned at college, in their histories. He loved to draw the pictures of the chief actors in the war of independence, dwelling upon their personal characteristics and their abilities, almost invariably with eulogy. Even his enemies he spoke of with respect, for bitterness was foreign to his nature, generous and genial, and eager to forgive. When he spoke of Bolivar, he professed the greatest admiration for him, and as he recollected scenes in which they both had figured, tears filled his eyes occasionally and he would break off suddenly to talk of other matters, his spirit wandering back to Apurito and the adventures of their youth.

The government, hearing of the circumstances in which the veteran was placed, to its eternal honour hastened to alleviate them. The president, the illustrious Sarmiento the historian, wrote to the Senate in the following terms:

"General Don José Antonio Páez has arrived in this country, in pursuit of a modest industry, to maintain himself in his old age. Considering that this illustrious warrior is the sole survivor of the glories of the days of the Independence, and that his exploits, that have now passed into the realms of history, helped in great measure to secure the freedom for America, the President of the Argentine Republic, in order to secure him comfort in his old age, in recompense of his great services, determines and decrees.

1. That Don José Antonio Páez shall be placed on the Argentine effective, with the rank of Brigadier General.

2. That this decree shall be submitted to the Senate of the Nation.

Buenos Aires,
December 3, 1859."

The Senate gave its assent, voting unanimously. Peru soon followed the generous lead of Buenos Aires, with a substantial pension. His declining days, secured from want, Páez passed the next two years peacefully in Buenos Aires, the city that had honoured him in old age and poverty, and where he hoped to finish his career, although to his intimates he expressed the wish that after death his bones should be conveyed to Venezuela, the ungrateful country that had cast him out, as she cast out the Liberator.

The fate of both these now belauded national heroes was singularly alike. They rose, flourished and over-topped the mass of " honourable citizens " that from the beginning of the world have looked on men, such as were Páez and Bolivar, as toadstools may regard an oak. When the occasion serves they take revenge on them, for to overtop is to be hated by those who feel that no manure of education or of wealth can increase their stature by the paring of a nail.

Modest to a fault, and simple in his desires, as befits one who had known the extremes of fortune, Páez made few friends. Those he did make appreciated him at his full worth. In the two years the veterans who had first assisted at the Carranzas' tertulia, slipped away to that heaven that we make for ourselves in dreams, for heaven ready made would be at best, but a mere furnished lodging for the soul.

Although he limped a little, the result of his accident when leading the military parade in New York, Páez was still extraordinary active for his years, in body and in mind.

At the reunions at the hospitable mansion of the Carranzas, in spite of the burden of his eight and seventy years, Páez danced like a young man, " with incredible agility," and used to sing Andalusian songs and the Miserere from Il Trovatore, with a voice that had lost little of its strength.*

Páez, who in the fine phrase of Gúiraldes,† all his life liked " to assimilate horizons," wished above all things to meet the sole remaining Gaucho Chieftain, who in his native province, Entre Rios, lived in patriarchal state.

General Justo José de Urquiza had not indeed fought for the independence of his country as had Páez. Still he had combated the tyrant Rosas‡ and defeated him.

Urquiza lived in San José, a palace that he had built, six leagues from the town of Concepcion del Uruguay, in Entre Rios.

The road from Concepcion to San José was planted like an avenue with Paraiso trees. Woe to the man who touched them, for General Urquiza was a man who did not understand a joke.

* " Tenia una voz poderosa, con la que cantaba el Misere del Trovador, y saltaba en la sala con una agilidad increible, tarareando canciones andaluzas." El General Páez, Adolfo P. Carranza, Buenos Aires, 1924.

† "Don Segundo Sombra " Ricardo Gúiraldes, Buenos Aires, 1927. This author, who died too young, having ridden the Pampa of his life but one and forty years, has left in his last work, Don Segundo Sombra, one of the best studies of the Gaucho that ever has been penned. In it he enters into the very marrow of their bones, as they themselves would say.

‡ Rosas, after a career of crime and bloodshed, finally took refuge in the British Legation, and came to England in a man-of-war. He died a country gentleman, near Southampton, more or less in the odour of sanctity, for he still was rich.

All the length of the eighteen* miles the deer and ostriches were as tame as barn door fowls. No one was allowed to harm or chase them, and if a Gaucho, coming out of town with half a bottle of Geneva (always the Anchor brand) beneath his belt, should have been impelled to raise his hand and touch his pingo† with the spurs, yell and throw his Boleadoras at any of them, and chance to be found out, he had to expiate his misdemeanour either by being staked out for a night, his hands and feet stretched to their utmost limit, or pass a year as a foot soldier. No punishment was more dreaded by the centaurs of the plains than to be sent into the infantry.

Urquiza's flocks and herds were on a patriarchal scale. His cattle numbered five hundred thousand head. His heads of horses and of mares some twenty thousand. For leagues, riding through Entre Rios, only one brand was to be seen upon the animals. It was the " Marca de la flor,"‡ simple and easy enough to alter or disfigure with a hot iron, but as the saying runs, " fear guards the vines, and not the fence."§

The palace was a long low building in the colonial style, with two tall towers, fifty or sixty feet in height, called Miradores. A sentinel kept guard on one of them, as they commanded a wide view across the country.

A line of hitching posts¶ stood under the shade of some Ombús, and fastened to them, nodding in the sun, the horses of the peons and the guards were tied. In

* Melio Azdarach.
† Gaucho slang for a good horse.
‡ ⑂
§ Miedo guarda viñas, y no vallado.
¶ Palenques.

those days every peon caught a horse at night and tied him out at " soga," that is to a picket rope, giving him length enough to eat the grass. At break of day he saddled up, went out to " campear," that is to look up the stock, and his work over left his horse ready saddled for whatever might occur, tied to the hitching post.

At the front door two jaguars in iron cages snarled at the visitors. In the Zaguan there was a guard room where Gaucho soldiers dressed in loose jackets, caps with peaks, such as old-fashioned sailors used to wear, and either Turkish trousers, known as bombachas, or the national chiripa,* lounged about idly. They either were barefooted or wore potro boots, made from the hock-skin of a colt and rendered pliable by frequent rubbing and by grease. These boots were open at the toes, in order that the wearer of them might catch the stirrup easily when he mounted a wild horse.

Their spurs were iron, hammered by a local black-smith; the rowels measured several inches long, and the whole spur was kept in place by thongs cut from a hide. These spurs, called Nazarenas, the wearers let hang loosely from the heel, and as they walked they clinked upon the stones.

The sergeant and the officer wore boots and uniforms generally made of cotton drill in summer, or in winter of blue cloth. They maintained discipline with their raw hide whips, the flat edge of their swords, and various punishments, such as the staking out between four pegs, or piling several rifles on the neck of a man trussed up like a fowl. Still all were equal in a way, and spoke to one another courteously, even with ceremony, exchanging cigarettes and matés without difference of rank.

The guard was usually asleep, lying upon their saddles

* The Chiripa was a square of woven fabric, that was brought up between the legs, and fastened with a sash. It made a sort of very loose trouser, and was worn over wide, white cotton drawers, sometimes ornamented with coarse lace.

wrapped in their ponchos, their rifles all stacked in a corner and their swords hanging on a nail. Well did they understand that the first duty of a guard is to sleep soundly, for sleep refreshes and makes everybody equal, and he who sleeps is not oppressed by any kind of care.

The Zaguan* opened to the patio, and the rooms of the house opened into the patio, after the colonial style. Lofty and with their ceilings crossed by beams of wood, the rooms were airy although dark, except the ball-room. Of good proportions its walls were panelled round with looking glass, the ceiling was divided into squares of looking glass. Huge crystal chandeliers were disposed at intervals, giving the room an air of Versailles, designed by an inferior artist, yet not unpleasing by its strange contrast to the wild surroundings.

Upon the walls of the vast corridors hung pictures of Don Justo, dressed in a uniform that would have been conspicuous on Le Champ de Mars during the Second Empire. Mounted on a white horse he sat directing hordes of his Entrerriano cavalry, sabring the Masorqueros† as a mower cuts down corn. Except a field or two of alfalfa for the general's horses, and one or two of maize, there was no cultivation, for meat was the chief article of food. Thick forest came up within a little distance of the house, chiefly composed of Nandubay,‡ Tala, and Espinillo de Olor.

The ground fell sharply down to the stream called the Gená, through which the trail ran to the interior of the province. Sandy and shallow, the pass of the Gená once seen was not to be forgotten. Its utter solitude,

---

* The Zaguan is a passage between the door and patio.

† Los Masorqueros was the name given by the Liberal Party to the followers of the tyrant Rosas. In point of savagery, there was but little choice between the soldiery of either side. Few prisoners were ever taken, for the practice was to cut their throats with the long knives that all the Gauchos carried at their backs. This was entitled to perform the Holy Work, La Obra Santa, and was practised conscientiously.

‡ Acacia cavemia. Celtis Tala.

although the house was less than half a mile away, the hot moist atmosphere, the flocks of chattering green parrots, and the carpinchos, those amphibious rodents, shy and illusive, that plunged into the stream at the first sight of danger, the sweet perfume of the Espinillo de Olor, with its fluffy, yellow balls of flower, made up a picture of an older world, such as the first Conquistadores might have beheld. Two or three clumps of cactus grew near the water's edge; on a dead tree, cormorants were always sitting motionless. Perhaps they sit there still and fabulate.

To this patriarchal mansion, half palace and half fortalice, Páez was welcomed by its owner with enthusiasm. From the first moment two such men must have understood each other. Both had passed adventurous lives, suffered the extremes of fortune, had lived on horseback, and both were children of the plains.

Unfortunately there is no record of their conversation, but it may be supposed they fought their battles over again, recounted their adventures, and in the patio sat far into the night, smoking and drinking maté, as the fire-flies flitted through the trees.

Three days the visit lasted, and upon going, Páez presented to his host a pair of pistols that had accompanied him in his campaigns. He left his host feared and respected by the whole province, the arbiter of life and death to thousands, wealthier in flocks and herds than the wealthiest patriarch of the Old Testament.

In the short space of eighteen months the dream had vanished, and the great house left desolate and void. During the siesta, when probably the sleepy guards were sleeping peacefully, a band of ruffians headed by a negro of the name of Luna burst upon the scene.

The general, with his sabre in his hand went out to meet them accompanied but by his daughter, armed with a brace of pistols.

W

She opened fire killing one of the assassins, but was soon overpowered, and stretched out senseless by a blow from an iron-loaded whip. The general, fighting like a lion to the last, fell pierced with a hundred wounds.

The whole affair lasted but a few minutes, and before the astonished guard had comprehended what was passing, the murderers had swung themselves upon their horses and were far out upon the plains.

Forced to leave Buenos Aires by an outbreak of yellow fever that took toll of thousands, Páez set sail for the United States, where his son Ramon awaited him. Even then, in his eightieth year, he made a journey to Peru and was received with acclamation by the inhabitants of Lima and Callao.

His life's long gallop now was drawing to a close. On the 18th of June, 1873, still strong and active, and interested in life, he passed away to the celestial Llanos, where horses tire not and where it may be hoped he rides in glory, on plains as like the Llanos de Apure, as an all-seeing Providence thinks fitting to permit.

APPENDIX

My maternal grandfather, Admiral the Honourable Charles Elphinstone Fleeming, was in command on the West Indian station in 1828. His flagship was H.M.S. *Barham*. In those days, before telegraphs were invented, and communications were difficult, an admiral on board his flagship was a little potentate.

The Admiralty could worry him but little, and at rare intervals.

On board the *Barham* were Doña Catalina, my grandmother, a Spanish lady, her maid, and a whole menagerie of pets.

Ordered to Caracas upon a semi-political mission, the ship anchored in the harbour of La Guaira, then an open roadstead, with a troubled sea.

The day they made the port, as it was fated, my mother happened to be born. As soon as my grandmother could sit a mule, they went up to Caracas and took an ancient Spanish house near the cathedral. There my grandmother remained three years with her little daughter. The admiral came and went at intervals, now sailing north as far as Halifax, then visiting the Bahamas and Port Royal, but I should fancy, spending a good deal of his time in Venezuela with his wife and child.

Páez and he seem to have taken to each other from the first. Both were imbued with Liberal ideas, my grandfather later on carrying his into effect by representing Stirlingshire in the Reform Parliament.

Both men were fond of horses, and good horsemen.

Páez was one of the best riders of the plains, breaking a wild horse, throwing a bull down by the tail, an expert lassoer, and the best man with the lance in South America. It is not to be supposed my grandfather, a Scottish laird, on shore, equalled him in these accomplishments. Although he had been at sea since the mature age of eleven, he always hunted when ashore, generally in Warwickshire. At times he took a favourite horse to sea with him, so as to be well mounted with the Gibraltar Hunt, a pack he himself founded, bringing out ten couple of hounds from his estate of Cumbernauld, in Dumbartonshire.

Two such men naturally had much in common, and when the dismemberment of La Gran Colombia palled on them, they could fall back upon the theme that never wearies horsemen, since the beginning of the world.

Páez at that time was occupied with the great movement, for the autonomy of Venezuela, and Admiral Fleeming seems to have backed him, half officially if we can trust the note below the following outpouring of a simple spirit, in uncertain prosody.

Cancion Compuesta Para el Obsequio que el Jefe Superior de Venezuela, Xeneral José Antonio Páez, Dio al Honorable Señor Carlos Elphisson Fleming, Vice-Almirante de la Escuadra Britanica, el 21 de Abril de 1829. *

> Venid hijos ilustres
> De Vespucio y Colón
> A conocer á Fleming
> Honor de su Nacion

* El 21 de abril de 1829 se dio en La Viñeta, historica morada del General José Antonio Páez, una suntuosa comida al Vice-Almirante Fleming, Comandante en Jefe de la Estacion Naval de las Indias Occidentales. Se dijo entonces que su mision era apoyar al Jefe Supremo de Venezuela en sus propositos separatistas. Lo cierto es que tanto el marino britanico como su mujer, y la comitiva que los acompañaba, fueron singularmente agasajados por el elemento oficial, que trabajaba por la desmembracion de la Gran Colombia.—" Centon Lirico," José E. Machado, Caracas, 1920.

Al llegar a las costas
De nuestro septentrion
Venezuela lo admite
Con justa admiracion:
I sabiendo que es Fleming
De libertad pendon
Mas se empeña en amarlo
El Jefe Superior

Oh Fleming valeroso!
De la Inglaterra honor!
Tu nombre en las naciones
Resuena con amor;
I orgullosa la Escocia
Que te dio educacion
Entre sus glorias, hace
Feliz ostentacion

Dichosos los Gobiernos
De Colombia y Albion
Fecundos en varones
De tanta admiracion.
Viva, viva Bolivar,
Viva el nuevo Nelson,
Recibiendo de Paéz
Esta demostracion

Inglaterra y Colombia
En su perpetua union
Forman en sus principios
Una misma Nacion;
La Gran Bretaña viva,
I el mundo de Colon,
Vivan los colombianos,
Viva todo breton.

The Quinta de la Viñeta was in those days a country house outside the city. Now it is turned into a school for girls and stands in a dull street, well in the city's bounds.

A shady " Nispero " overhangs one of the patios, and may have stood there on the day when the Supreme Chief gave the banquet to my ancestors, for it is of enormous size.

All Venezuelan children know the story called " The Gardener* of La Viñeta." A story quaint and moving in itself, that illustrates the character of Páez, better than all that has been written of him. The gardener was an old Spanish grenadier, who had served in the war of independence, in Los Granaderos del Infante, one of the picked corps of Spain. When he saw Páez was in a bad humour, he used to wait for him, and standing in his path, point the hose at him, saying in a loud voice, " Do not attack me, general, or I will fire." This saying had a deep significance for both of them.

During the war of independence, after a skirmish at La Mirrael, near Sombrero, a little town upon the Llanos, the regiment of Los Granaderos del Infante was retreating to a wood of palms, hotly pursued by Páez and his cavalry. They gained the shelter of the trees, but Páez young and well mounted observed a wounded man, who struggling along, a quarter of a mile behind the rest, was making for the wood. The man was tall and rendered taller looking, by the high shako that he wore. Páez galloped up to him, calling him to surrender and brandishing his lance.

The man who knew Páez from having seen him at the battle of Mucuritas, shook his head and covering Páez with his musket, said firmly, " No me atropelle

* El Jardinero de la Viñeta.

mi general, porque lo tiro " and as he spoke he hirpled on towards the wood, still covering Páez with his gun.

Páez reined back, and tried by threats and promises to make him change his mind. The grenadier gave the same answer both to threats and menaces and always edged a little nearer to the wood. Struck with his bravery Páez redoubled his entreaties and his threats, but the grenadier steadily refused.

At last when but a little distance from the wood, Páez who saw that he was going to escape, grasped his lance firmly, felt his horse's mouth, and shouting, " Shoot and go to Hell " prepared for the attack. The Spanish soldier, threw his gun at the horse saying, " Shoot! how can I shoot, my gun is empty." The two brave men stood looking at each other, and then Páez who was in doubt and feared a trap, told him to take his gun up, and let his ramrod fall into the barrel. He did so, and it rang on steel, a proof the gun was empty. Then handing up his cartridge bag and haversack, the stubborn soldier said, " See, my general, they both are empty, I have not eaten for two days."

Páez was moved to admiration and compassion, for the forlorn, heroic figure and giving him his life, pressed him to change sides and serve with his command. The man refused, and then Páez who was always impressed by courage, said, " What can I do for you? " The answer was, " only allow me to rejoin my regiment." Páez assented, and the man with a military salute, disappeared into the wood.

Those kind of men cannot be said to save their honour, for it can never be in peril with them.

A few hours later in another skirmish, Páez saw the soldier's body senseless on the ground beside a pile of dead. As Páez got off his horse, and told the surgeon to bind up his wounds, and take him to the rear, the man revived, and said in a faint voice, " If I am not going to another world, I will remain with you, as long as I have life." When he recovered Páez installed him as his gardener in La Viñeta, where he must often have given flowers to my grandmother, and perhaps to the child playing beside her in the garden.

Nothing reveals the man, brave, honourable and tender-hearted better than does this simple tale.

When the time came for parting, Páez gave my grandfather two horses, Toni, a cream colour, and Caballero, a dark chestnut. They both died full of years at Cumbernauld.

BIBLIOGRAPHY

" Autobiografia del General Páez." (New York, 1867-69.)

" Campaigns and Cruises in Venezuela and New Granada."
(London, 1831.)

" Centon Lirico." José E. Machado. (Caracas, 1920.)

" Documentos de la Vida Publica del Libertador, Los."

" Don Segundo Sombra." Ricardo Guiraldes. (Buenos
Aires, 1927.)

" Efemerides Columbianas." Luis Gonzaga.

" Estudios Historicos." Aristides Rojas. (Caracas, 1926.)

" Estudios sobre Personajes y Hechos de la Historia
Venezolana." Pedro M. Arcaya. (Caracas, 1911.)

" General Páez, El." Adolfo P. Carranza. (Buenos
Aires, 1924.)

" General Páez en los Estados Unidos." Por Dos Venezolanos. (New York, 1850.)

" Historia de la Revolucion de Colombia." José Manuel
Restrepo. (Paris, 1827.)

" Historia de Venezuela." Baralt.

" Historia de Venezuela " (H.N.M.). Escuelas Cristianas.
(Caracas, 1927.)

" History of the Revolution of Caracas." Major Flinters.
(London, 1819.)

" Llanero, El." Daniel Mendoza. (Caracas, 1922.)

" Los Idiomas de la America Latina. Felix y Toloron.
(Madrid, 1872.)

" Memoirs of Bolivar." Ducoudray Holstein. (London,
1830.)

" Memoirs of General Miller." (London, Longman, 1828.)

" Memorias del General José Antonio Páez." Biblioteca
Ayacucho. (Madrid, 1916.)

"Memorias del General O'Leary." (London, 1879-88.)

"Memorias del General Rafael Urdaneta." (Madrid, 1916.)

"Memorias del General Morillo. (Madrid, 1825.)

"Narrative of the Expedition to the Rivers Orinoco and Apure." G. Hippisley. (London, John Murray, 1819.)

"Naturaleza y Civilizacion de la Grandiosa Isla de Cuba." Por Miguel Fernandez Ferrer.

"El Orinoco Ilustrado." Por el Pr. Joseph Gumilla. (Madrid, 1741.)

"Peace, War and Adventure: An Autobiographical Memoir by George Laval Chesterton, Captain in the Army of Colombia." (London, 1828.)

"Recollections of a Service of Three Years During the War of Extermination in the Republics of Venezuela and Colombia." (London, 1828.)

"Francia's Reign of Terror." J. P. & W. Robertson. (London, John Murray, 1839.)

"Resumen de la Historia de Venezuela." R. M. Baralt y Diaz. (Paris, 1841 ; Curazao, 1887.)

"Simon Bolivar." E. Loraine Petrie. (London, 1910.)

"Tauromaquia ó arte de torear á caballo y a pié." Josef Delgado. (Pepe Hillo). (Madrid, 1804.)

"Vida de Bolivar." Felipe Larrazabal. (1865.)

"Wild Scenes in South America, or Life in the Llanos of Venezuela." Ramon Páez. (London, 1863.)

INDEX